STRATFORD-UPON-AVON STUDIES 4

General Editors

JOHN RUSSELL BROWN
& BERNARD HARRIS

Already published in this series:

STRATFORD-UPON-AVON STUDIES 4

CONTEMPORARY
THEATRE

EDWARD ARNOLD (PUBLISHERS) LTD

41 Maddox Street, London W.1

First published 1962

Reprinted with corrections 1968

SBN: 7131 5025 4

110132

Printed in Great Britain by
Butler & Tanner Ltd, Frome and London

Contents

Preface to Second Impression

THIS book has been planned, like its fellows in *Stratford-upon-Avon Studies*, to use a diversity of approach. Its contributors had freedom, within the general scheme, to consider the English *Contemporary Theatre* from their own points of view. Besides ensuring a full coverage of the subject, the editors encouraged several writers to deal with identical plays and authors, so that a double perspective could sometimes be established. Such diversity is particularly necessary for a contemporary subject, for critical judgements have not yet been sifted by time and no one can say for sure which plays will be remembered tomorrow.

The first edition of these studies was published in 1962 and now, in 1968, their subject has developed and modified. But, apart from bringing the prefatory notes for individual chapters up to date and adding a postscript to the first chapter on Pinter and Wesker, the volume has been reprinted as it was first published. There were two main reasons for this. First, the early nineteen-sixties seem to have been a watershed for English theatre: Osborne, Wesker, Pinter and Arden had each created a distinct voice and the second 'generation' (including Edward Bond, John Bowen, David Cregan, Henry Livings, Joe Orton, Tom Stoppard, Charles Wood) had not then been recognised. Secondly, the editors believe that if the later development of the new dramatists was to be properly considered, especially the more recent plays of John Osborne and Harold Pinter, and some writers newly arrived, a completely new book would be needed. Moreover, this present volume considers more than post-war theatre: its scope includes Bernard Shaw and the drama of the nineteen-twenties and thirties; for comparison and assessment this time-scheme is stimulating and helpful, and would have to be sacrificed in a volume dealing adequately with the whole of English theatre since the second world war. A future volume of *Stratford Studies* should be devoted to the English theatre of the nineteen-sixties.

Here, then, is a volume of related studies of the English theatre, giving a wide and varied view of its achievements from the vantage point of its first confident postwar years. Allardyce Nicoll, by comparing plays of the fifties and sixties with those of earlier decades of this century, reassesses their originality, while Clifford Leech compares, in the first chapter, the work of two young dramatists in a way suggested by two young poets of another century. Further chapters

6

analyse particular aspects of plays by considering a number of relevant examples written by different playwrights: G. W. Brandt examines several solutions to the problem of making the theatre a vehicle for ideas, and Kenneth Muir considers the more significant attempts to use verse in the theatre. A. R. Jones traces the development of Bernard Shaw whose writings span a long yesterday of our theatre and provide fine opportunities for our actors today. H. A. Smith considers the shaping influence of romantic and Existentialist ideas on some plays, particularly *Waiting for Godot*. His chapter refers to Ibsen, Anouilh and Sartre, as well as to English dramatists, and is one of several which acknowledge the widely European nature of our theatrical heritage: G. W. Brandt's chapter discusses the influence of one group of Brecht's plays, Kenneth Muir relates Ibsen's use of prose and verse to that of English playwrights, and R. D. Smith views Simpson, Whiting, Pinter and Beckett alongside Ionesco and Chekhov. The book is completed with a study by John Jordan of the Irish Theatre, which has been called, variously, the master, partner, competitor, follower or leader of English Theatre, and with J. L. Styan's account of the new extension of theatrical art in television drama.

Each chapter has been provided with a prefatory note which gives factual information concerning dates and texts, and up-to-date lists of relevant books and articles. We have not tried to be exhaustive: rather we have noted the most readily obtainable editions and the critical works which we and the various contributors consider to be most useful for further reading along the lines of enquiry pursued here. The most recent playwrights are generally given more extensive annotation than those who already figure in works of reference. The editions quoted in each chapter are specified in the prefatory notes, and the titles of critical works referred to later by their authors' names. Two periodicals which are frequently mentioned are referred to by abbreviations, *T.D.R.* for *The Tulane Drama Review* and *N.T.M.* for *New Theatre Magazine*.

Several general books have been published since the first edition of these *Studies*: Laurence Kitchin, *Drama in the Sixties: Form and Interpretation* (1966) which includes reviews of performances; John Russell Taylor, *The Rise and Fall of the Well-Made Play* (1967); and *John Whiting on Theatre* (1966). Three collections of essays should also be noticed: *Experimental Drama*, ed. W. A. Armstrong (1963); *Aspects of Drama* (Sydney University Press, 1965); and *Modern British Dramatists*, ed. J. R. Brown (1968).

JOHN RUSSELL BROWN
BERNARD HARRIS

Acknowledgements

The editors and publisher wish to express their thanks to the following for permission to reprint extracts from copyright works:

the author and Methuen & Co. Ltd., for extracts from *Sergeant Musgrave's Dance* by John Arden; the author, Curtis Brown Ltd., and Random House for extracts from *The Ascent of F 6* by Auden; the author and Mrs. Rosica Colin for extracts from *Waiting for Godot* by Samuel Beckett; the Clarendon Press for extracts from *Palicio* by Bridges; the author and Simon and Schuster Inc., for extracts from *Television Plays* by Paddy Chayevsky; Chatto and Windus Ltd., for extracts from *The Cherry Orchard* by Anton Chekhov, translated by Constance Garnett; the author and Faber & Faber Ltd., for extracts from *The Cocktail Party* and *The Family Reunion* by T. S. Eliot; the author, Eyre & Spottiswoode Ltd. and Doubleday & Co. Inc., for extracts from *The Theatre of the Absurd* by Martin Esslin; the author and Princeton University Press for extracts from *Idea of a Theatre* by Francis Fergusson; the author and Oxford University Press for extracts from *Curtmantle*, the author and Actac Ltd. for extracts from *The Lady's Not for Burning* by Christopher Fry; the author and Methuen & Co. Ltd., to quote from Christopher Fry's Introduction to *The Lizard on the Rock* by Hall; Gerald Duckworth & Co., for extracts from *The Fugitive*, *The Eldest Son*, *The Silver Box* and *A Family Man* by John Galsworthy; the author and Faber & Faber Ltd., for extracts from *Free Fall* by William Golding; the author and Samuel French Ltd., for extracts from *Passers-By* by C. Haddon Chambers; the Trustees of the Hardy Estate and Macmillan & Co. Ltd., for extracts from *The Dynasts* by Thomas Hardy; the author and Appleton-Century-Crofts Inc., for extracts from *G. B. Shaw: Man of the Century* by Henderson; the author and *The Sunday Times* for a quotation from an article by Harold Hobson; the author and *The Guardian* for a quotation from an article by Philip Hope-Wallace; the author and John Calder (Publishers) Ltd., for extracts from Volume I of *Plays* by Ionesco; the authors and Samuel French Ltd., for extracts from *The Pelican* by Jesse & Harwood; the translator and Faber & Faber Ltd., for extracts from the *Agamemnon*, translated by Louis MacNeice; the author and Macmillan & Co. Ltd., for extracts from *The Silver Tassie* and *Juno and the Paycock* by Sean O'Casey; the author and David Higham Associates Ltd., for extracts from *Epitaph for George Dillon*, and the author and *The Twentieth Century* for a quotation from an article by John Osborne; the author and Jonathan Cape Ltd., for extracts from *Three Television Plays* by Alun Owen; William Heinemann Ltd., for extracts from *Six Characters in Search of an Author* by Pirandello; the author and Methuen & Co. Ltd., for extracts from *The Birthday Party*, *The Dwarfs* and *The Caretaker* by Harold Pinter and the author for an extract from a programme note to *The Room* and *The Dumb Waiter* by Harold Pinter; the author, A. V. Moore, Esq., Princess

Mary de Rachewiltz and New Directions Publishers, for an extract from *The Women of Trachis* by Ezra Pound; A. D. Peters and William Heinemann Co. Ltd., for extracts from *An Inspector Calls* by J. B. Priestley; the author and *The Observer* for extracts from articles by Alan Pryce-Jones; the Public Trustee and The Society of Authors for extracts from *The Quintessence of Ibsenism, Heartbreak House, Back to Methuselah, Too True to be Good, The Devil's Disciple* and *Major Barbara* by George Bernard Shaw; the author, Curtis Brown and Grove Press, N.Y., for extracts from *The One Way Pendulum*, the author and Curtis Brown for extracts from *A Resounding Tinkle* and the author for extracts from *The Hole* by N. F. Simpson; the author and Jonathan Cape Ltd., for extracts from *Chicken Soup with Barley* and *The Kitchen* by Arnold Wesker; the author for extracts from *The Triple Thinkers* by Edmund Wilson.

Note

Arnold Wesker. Born in Stepney, London, 1932.

The trilogy, *Chicken Soup with Barley* (1958), *Roots* (1959) and *I'm Talking about Jerusalem* (1960), were all first produced at the Belgrade Theatre, Coventry, directed by John Dexter; later they were performed at the Royal Court, London. *The Kitchen* was first produced at the Royal Court in 1959, and revived in 1961.

Jonathan Cape published the *Trilogy* (1960), from which quotations in this chapter are taken, and a revised version of *The Kitchen* (1961); the original *Kitchen* was published in Penguin's *New English Dramatists, 2* (1960). Penguin Books have separately published the other plays.

Wesker has written or given an interview in *N.T.M.* (1960) and *The Twentieth Century* (1961). Studies of his plays include A. R. Jones' in *Critical Quarterly* (1960) and H. Goodman's in *Drama Survey* (1961). The 1961 production of *The Kitchen* provoked interesting articles by John Whiting in *London Magazine* (September) and V. S. Pritchett in *The New Statesman* (7 July).

Harold Pinter. Born in London in 1930, he became an actor in 1949.

The Birthday Party, The Room and *The Dumb Waiter* were written in 1957; the first was performed in 1957 at the Arts Theatre, Cambridge, and the Lyric, Hammersmith; the others formed a double bill at the Hampstead Theatre Club and the Royal Court in 1960. *The Caretaker* was written in 1959 and performed at the Arts Theatre Club and the Duchess, London, in 1960. *A Slight Ache* and *A Night Out* were first performed on the B.B.C. Third Programme in 1959 and 1960; the former was staged in 1961 in a triple bill at the Arts and the Criterion; the latter was televised in 1960. Pinter has written and published five revue sketches, performed in London in 1959.

Methuen published *The Birthday Party and Other Plays* (1960), *The Caretaker* (1960), *A Slight Ache and Other Plays* (1961); all quotations in this chapter are from these editions.

Pinter has given interviews to *N.T.M.* (1961) and *The Twentieth Century* (1961), in an issue which prints one of his poems.

Martin Esslin's *Theatre of the Absurd* (1962) has a full study of Pinter and he is interestingly considered by Irving Wardle in 'Comedy of Menace', *Encore* (1958); John Arden's review of *The Caretaker* in *N.T.M.* (1960) is brief but perceptive.

Since this book was published, two short introductions have appeared: Harold U. Ribalow's *Arnold Wesker* (Twayne's English Author's Series; New York, 1965) and Ronald Hayman's *Harold Pinter* (H.E.B. Contemporary Playwrights Series, 1968).

For *N. F. Simpson*, see prefatory note to Chapter VI.

I

Two Romantics: Arnold Wesker
and Harold Pinter

CLIFFORD LEECH

★

THE subject of this chapter is the work of two young dramatists who have been attracting attention in London and in England as a whole. They are contributing to the notable revival in the English theatre which even the most sceptical among us are having to recognise. Arnold Wesker was born in 1932, a member of a poor family in the East End of London. He worked as a plumber's assistant, as a kitchen porter, and as a pastry-cook. His earliest play, *The Kitchen*, first acted in 1959, is set wholly in the kitchen of a large restaurant: it catches the atmosphere of hurry and noise and heat and quarrelling that lies behind the dining-room which is all that most of us see. Here he wanted us to observe the ordinary things which we customarily fail to notice; and to do this he drew upon a segment of life that he had directly experienced. He is best known, however, for the group of three plays that have been published under the general title of *The Wesker Trilogy*, plays with a strong autobiographical element and with an action spread over the last twenty-five years. Harold Pinter is slightly older: born in 1930, he became a professional actor at nineteen, and remained an obscure practitioner of his craft until at the age of twenty-seven he wrote his first play. He is best known for *The Birthday Party*, first acted in 1957, and *The Caretaker*, which attracted and bewildered and yet curiously satisfied London audiences in 1960 and 1961.

One reason why we may be interested in these two playwrights is that they are new arrivals in the London theatre and have quickly become known as possessing talent and integrity and promise. Another reason is that they are complementary dramatists, different in technique, in the nature of their skills, in the attitudes towards humanity that their plays exhibit. Wesker, as I have indicated, tries to give us the atmosphere of actuality, filling his plays with simple details of ordinary life (such details as the food people eat, the plain and hesitant words they utter). Pinter takes us to strange and impossible settings: in *The Birthday Party* to a seaside boarding-house with a half-crazed proprietress and only one guest, a guest who hides there in a never-explained fear; in *The Caretaker* to a room in an otherwise empty house, a room filled with an accumulation of rubbish amassed over the years, whose ceiling leaks, whose ownership is claimed by each of two brothers—a room where we find love and pity, cruelty and a forlorn solitude. And in Pinter's settings the things that happen are not ordinary things: we are often puzzled by them, but we have a sense that they correspond to things that do happen in our world.

Here a comparison with the past suggests itself. In 1798 the two young poets William Wordsworth, aged twenty-eight, and Samuel Taylor Coleridge, aged twenty-six, planned a collection of poems, to be called *Lyrical Ballads*, as a joint work in which their respective shares should be complementary. This, we remember, is how Wordsworth two years later, in the Preface to the second edition, described his own purpose in the collection:

> The principal object, then, proposed in these Poems was to choose incidents and situations from common life, and to relate or describe them, throughout, as far as was possible, in a selection of language really used by men, and, at the same time, to throw over them a certain colouring of imagination, whereby ordinary things should be presented to the mind in an unusual aspect; and, further, and above all, to make these incidents and situations interesting by tracing in them, truly though not ostentatiously, the primary laws of our nature.[1]

His poems were, as he indicates, largely narratives concerned with events of common life; the language was to be formed from the language that ordinary men speak; but a 'colouring of the imagination' was to make us see the events 'in an unusual aspect', so that they were at once things we could see any day and yet things that appeared novel because we saw them in his poems from a fresh viewpoint; and 'the primary laws of our nature', the essential lines of human thought and feeling and conduct, should be exhibited in these poems, so that

[1] *Wordsworth's Literary Criticism*, ed. Nowell C. Smith (1905), pp. 13–14.

they were not mere narratives but were statements of the basic facts of human nature. Many of the poems that Wordsworth printed in the *Lyrical Ballads* were rough experiments: in their cultivation of simplicity they appeared naïve, they invited a mockery which some readers willingly gave them. But the poet believed that—in a time when industrialism was advancing, when war was numbing men's minds, when popular literature and drama cultivated the easy thrill —it was needful that men should be made to see, and enter into, simple human emotions, simple ties of family and affection, everyday fear, everyday grief.

Wordsworth, however, spoke only of his own purpose. His collaborator Coleridge was silent until 1817, when he published his *Biographia Literaria*. There he described the complementary purposes that he and Wordsworth had had in mind in their joint work:

> In this idea originated the plan of the 'Lyrical Ballads'; in which it was agreed, that my endeavours should be directed to persons and characters supernatural, or at least romantic; yet so as to transfer from our inward nature a human interest and a semblance of truth sufficient to procure for these shadows of imagination that willing suspension of disbelief for the moment, which constitutes poetic faith. Mr. Wordsworth, on the other hand, was to propose to himself as his object, to give the charm of novelty to things of every day, and to excite a feeling analogous to the supernatural, by awakening the mind's attention from the lethargy of custom, and directing it to the loveliness and the wonders of the world before us; an inexhaustible treasure, but for which, in consequence of the film of familiarity and selfish solicitude, we have eyes, yet see not, ears that hear not, and hearts that neither feel nor understand.[2]

Using more learned language than his fellow-poet, he yet gives an account of Wordsworth's aim not substantially different from that in the 1800 Preface to the *Lyrical Ballads*. That aim was to break through 'the lethargy of custom', that dulling of the faculties that comes so easily when a person or an object or an event is habitually presented to our eyes, and to dissipate 'the film of . . . selfish solicitude' which the relentless pursuit of self-interest imposes on our vision. But Coleridge's own purpose, manifested in *The Ancient Mariner*, his main contribution to the *Lyrical Ballads*, was to present characters and scenes and events altogether strange ('supernatural, or at least romantic') and

[2] *Biographia Literaria*, ed. J. Shawcross (1907), ii. 5–6.

yet to give them 'a semblance of truth', so that against commonsense we believe in them, and 'a human interest' in that we feel a hidden relationship to exist between the poet's world and the world we customarily know.

The two streams of writing represented in the *Lyrical Ballads* perhaps always run side by side in the history of literature. On the one hand there is the man who wishes us to see the things around us more sharply than we normally do, to sympathise with other men, however different from us in upbringing or habit of life, to observe both in them and in ourselves the ineluctable and irreducible facts of human existence. And on the other hand there is the man who wants to penetrate beneath the skin of observable fact, to explore a dream-world which has a valid relationship with the world of doing and conscious thought. The two aims may alternate in certain writers, and in the greater writers they may be fused. But both aims are necessary, both stand out in sharp distinction above the mass of merely popular and derivative writing that makes us see neither the ordinary as alive nor the extraordinary as basically human. There was no sense of an inherited literary formula in either Wordsworth or Coleridge when they worked together on the *Lyrical Ballads*: each had a vision to present; each recognised the validity of what the other was doing; each had a sense that their joint work was appropriate for their particular moment in history.

It is hardly prudent to suggest a likeness between Wordsworth and Coleridge on the one hand and the two young playwrights, Arnold Wesker and Harold Pinter, on the other. These contemporaries of ours may indeed become writers of distinction. They may be little remembered in a few years' time. Certainly Wesker is fumbling yet, and the freshness he now has may disappear without a compensating gain in understanding. Pinter's recent play, *The Caretaker*, seems now to be the most impressive dramatic writing in English since the war, but we cannot know if he will go beyond it, we cannot know how even this play will look if there is a future from which it may be regarded. What can be claimed with assurance is that, whether or not these dramatists fulfil their promise, their writings represent an encouraging sign in the English theatre today. Neither is content merely to imitate his many predecessors in the drama, but they are ready to profit from the example of others when that can help to clarify their own vision: Wesker owes something to the blend of rhetoric and naturalism in

John Osborne's *Look Back in Anger*; Pinter's dramatic world has been helped into existence through his knowledge of Samuel Beckett's *Waiting for Godot* and the savage farces of Eugène Ionesco. They are to be associated with these and other recent innovators, but for each the writing of a play and the response to actuality are things that a man must do in his own way.

Like Wordsworth and Coleridge in 1798, Wesker and Pinter today are keenly aware of the nature of their contemporary situation. The two poets at the end of the eighteenth century were conscious of social disturbance as men stumbled further into industrial development, as a war or the threat of war engaged England and the continental powers, as the minds of men grew dulled through these things.[3] Now the threat is graver, and we may find in Wesker and Pinter young writers who are principally concerned to look our world in the face, with its twin dangers of a universal destruction and a universal society of per-suaded consumers. There is indeed in other contemporary writers a feeling that, the time for perception being perhaps short, it is the more important to strain towards a sharpness of view. We may note a passage in William Golding's novel *Free Fall* (1959) where the narrator, a prisoner of war, has just been released from solitary confinement in the dark. The drab setting of the camp's huts, the first fellow-prisoner he meets, are seen as newly created, with the glory on them that Wordsworth knew he could no longer perceive when he wrote the *Immortality Ode*. The passage may be compared with the dramatic presentation of the 'Look I'm alive' game in *I'm Talking about Jeru-salem*. Golding's account of the matter is more direct (imagined through his narrator's eyes, not conveyed to us through the words of a child off-stage) and is at the same time more remote in its 'literary' finish, its considered elaboration. But in essentials Golding and Wesker are conveying the same Wordsworthian notion:

> I walked between the huts, a man resurrected . . . I saw the huts as one who had little to do with them, was indifferent to them and the temporal succession of days that they implied. So they shone with the innocent light of their own created nature. I understood them perfectly, boxes of thin wood as they were, and now transparent,

[3] See, in particular, Wordsworth's comment in his 1800 Preface that 'a multitude of causes, unknown to former times, are now acting with a combined force to blunt the discriminating powers of the mind' (*Wordsworth's Literary Criticism*, ed. cit., pp. 16–17).

letting be seen inside their quotas of sceptred kings. I lifted my arms, saw them too, and was overwhelmed by their unendurable richness as possessions, either arm ten thousand fortunes poured out for me. Huge tears were dropping from my face into dust; and this dust was a universe of brilliant and fantastic crystals, that miracles instantly supported in their being. I looked up beyond the huts and the wire, I raised my dead eyes, desiring nothing, accepting all things and giving all created things away. The paper wrappings of use and language dropped from me. Those crowded shapes extending up into the air and down into the rich earth, those deeds of far space and deep earth were aflame at the surface and daunting by right of their own natures though a day before I should have disguised them as trees. Beyond them the mountains were not only clear all through like purple glass, but living. They sang and were conjubilant . . .

And now came what is harder to confess than cruelty. It happened as the first of my fellows left our hut and moved along the path towards me. He was a being of great glory on whom a whole body had been lavished, a lieutenant, his wonderful brain floating in its own sea, the fuel of the world working down transmuted through his belly. I saw him coming, and the marvel of him and these un-disguised trees and mountains and this dust and music wrung a silent cry from me . . .

It seemed natural to me that this added perception in my dead eyes should flow over into work, into portraiture. That is why those secret, smuggled sketches of the haggard, unshaven kings of Egypt in their glory are the glory of my right hand and likely to remain so. My sketches of the transfigured camp, the prison which is no longer a prison are not so good, I think, but they have their merit. One or two of them see the place with the eye of innocence or death, see the dust and the wood and the concrete and the wire as though they had just been created. But the world of miracle I could not paint then or now.   (Chapter X.)

The last words here are characteristic of the writer recognising his in-adequate communicating of his special vision (as Coleridge may have felt that even *Kubla Khan* was insufficient, something to be offered to the public only as a 'psychological curiosity'). But, despite the barrier erected by the over-evident striving with words, Golding has conveyed the look of things when, a condition of acute shock having passed, they are made to seem new. This is remote, however, from Pinter's way of seeing. For him the world is always old, shabby, sick, as it is for Beckett. What is urgent for them is to analyse the patient's symptoms, the motives that prolong existence, the principles that inhabit and shape even a dying organism. Yet, different as they are in the nature of their enquiry, as well as in their technique, Wesker and Pinter share an urge to look intently at what is around and within.

They share too a strong sense of a human being's responsibility for other human beings. Wesker's plays are, apart from *The Kitchen*, plays of family life, in which there is a special feeling for the ties which link men and women together both within a small group and on the world's stage. And in his very different way Pinter can convey the sense that no man can, untroubled, turn his back on another. At the end of *The Birthday Party*, we see Stanley, the man who has long been in hiding, being taken away by Goldberg and McCann, the grotesque emissaries of an obscure and relentless force or organisation or principle whose enmity Stanley has brought upon himself. Stanley's mind has been so ingeniously treated by these men that he has now lost the power of articulate speech, any power indeed of volition. As they are about to take him into the street to the waiting car, the owner of the boarding-house, Petey, tries to prevent what he knows is the abduction and the annihilation of a human being. He fails, and must carry the guilt of his failure. It is characteristic of Pinter that such a figure as Petey can only hint at this, can only for a moment attempt to reach Stanley with an appeal that he should help himself out of the situation. It is also charac-teristic of Pinter to make us feel that Petey's guilt is our own. Here we have the attempt at rescue, its quick failure, and the brief hint that the knowledge of failure is painful:

> STANLEY's *body shudders, relaxes, his head drops, he becomes still again, stooped.* PETEY *enters from door, downstage, left.*
>
> GOLDBERG: Still the same old Stan. Come with us. Come on, boy.
> McCANN: Come along with us.
> PETEY: Where are you taking him?
>
> *They turn. Silence.*
>
> GOLDBERG: We're taking him to Monty.
> PETEY: He can stay here.
> GOLDBERG: Don't be silly.
> PETEY: We can look after him here.
> GOLDBERG: Why do you want to look after him?
> PETEY: He's my guest.
> GOLDBERG: He needs special treatment.
> PETEY: We'll find someone.

B

GOLDBERG: No. Monty's the best there is. Bring him, McCann.

They help STANLEY *out of the chair.* GOLDBERG *puts the bowler hat on* STANLEY'S *head. They all three move towards the door, left.*

PETEY: Leave him alone!

They stop. GOLDBERG *studies him.*

GOLDBERG (*insidiously*): Why don't you come with us, Mr. Boles?

MCCANN: Yes, why don't you come with us?

GOLDBERG: Come with us to Monty. There's plenty of room in the car.

PETEY *makes no move. They pass him and reach the door.* MCCANN *opens the door and picks up the suitcases.*

PETEY (*broken*): Stan, don't let them tell you what to do!

They exit.

Silence. PETEY *stands. The front door slams. Sound of a car starting. Sound of a car going away. Silence.* PETEY *slowly goes to the table. He sits on a chair, left. He picks up the paper and opens it. The strips fall to the floor. He looks down at them.* MEG *comes past the window and enters by the back door.* PETEY *studies the front page of the paper.*

MEG (*coming downstage*): The car's gone.

PETEY: Yes.

MEG: Have they gone?

PETEY: Yes.

MEG: Won't they be in for lunch?

PETEY: No.

MEG: Oh, what a shame. (*She puts her bag on the table.*) It's hot out. (*She hangs her coat on a hook.*) What are you doing?

PETEY: Reading.

MEG: Is it good?

PETEY: All right.

She sits by the table.

Is Stan down yet, Petey?

PETEY: No . . . he's . . .

MEG: Is he still in bed?

PETEY: Yes, he's . . . still asleep.

MEG: Still? He'll be late for his breakfast.

PETEY: Let him . . . sleep.

Pinter's plays, for all their strangeness, have at their best a tautness of construction in which event follows event by strict necessity. Wesker's trilogy, on the other hand, is made up of plays that ramble over the years from the 1930s to the present day. It consists of *Chicken Soup with Barley*, first acted in 1958, *Roots*, first acted in 1959, and *I'm Talking about Jerusalem*, first acted in 1960. Although they form a single composite work, no one character appears in all of them. Ronnie Kahn, one of the central figures in *Chicken Soup with Barley*, is continually mentioned in *Roots* but never comes on to the stage; in *I'm Talking about Jerusalem* he is a minor commentator on the action. Other characters of the first play reappear in the third. Beatie Bryant, the central figure of *Roots*, is referred to several times in the last play, but we learn no more of her story than the second play told us. In their time-schemes, moreover, the three plays run into one another. *Chicken Soup with Barley* begins in 1936 and ends in 1956. The action of *Roots* is post-war and covers only a fortnight in the life of Beatie Bryant and her family. *I'm Talking about Jerusalem* begins in 1946 and ends in 1959. We thus seem to catch a series of random glimpses of Ronnie Kahn and his family, concentrating on him and his mother Sarah in the first play; on the girl who was his mistress, whom he tried to educate, whom he deserted, whom he finally and unknowingly brought alive, in the second play; on his sister Ada and her husband Dave in the third play. *Chicken Soup with Barley* is set in the East End which Wesker has known from his childhood; *Roots* and *I'm Talking about Jerusalem* in the English countryside not far from Norwich, where for a time he worked. He is a Londoner fascinated by the country and simultaneously repelled by the narrowness of thought and feeling that he finds there. For him the city is a place of physical constriction but with a readier contact with the totality of the present. In *Roots* Beatie, who has known the city, can never again be on terms of a genuine relationship with the world of her family and her childhood. In *I'm Talking about Jerusalem* Ada and Dave try to make for themselves a life in the country, independent of the crowd and the complicated apparatus of modern society: they fail, despite an attempt lasting thirteen years, to learn the country's ways: they return to the city, ready to make the best they can of living close to the corrupt heart of things. The play's title is an obvious echo of that song of William Blake in the 'Preface' to his poem *Milton*, where the poet's speaker assures us that he will not cease from fight

> Till we have built Jerusalem
> In England's green and pleasant land.

But no Jerusalem is built in Wesker's play: only the aspiration, though defeated, remains.

Wesker, it is evident, tries to get free from illusions: the illusion of a simple life in the countryside, the illusion of political hope, the illusion of permanence in any human situation. His plays tell us frankly of the squalid conditions under which people may live. They emphasise the sickness of old age, the pity (hard to tolerate) given to a weakness that grows with the years, the sudden swings between possessiveness and repudiation within a human tie. But against this background of mutability and precariousness, there is in Wesker's writing a recurrent insistence on the need, in the teeth of the evidence, to affirm the notion of human brotherhood and the demand for affection that humanity makes upon us. This is strikingly conveyed in *The Kitchen*, a short play which is at first view the purest documentary. It is indeed a picture of a quite possible world that is given to us, doubtless a near-replica of what could be found behind the scenes in many a popular restaurant. The play has the strength that comes from being rooted in the actual. But it is soon obvious that Wesker's kitchen and his workers are intended to have a symbolic function. Realistically enough, they represent different groups of the world's people: they are Italian, German, Irish, Cypriot, Jewish, as well as gentile English. Their problem of living together is the world's problem: this becomes for a moment explicit when the Cypriot porter Dimitrios calls the crowd in the kitchen 'the United Nations'.[4] But the basis of the play is not political. It is concerned with the human being's need for comfort and relaxation with others, a mode of existence that the sweat and bustle, the noise and elbowing of the kitchen will not allow. Peter goes berserk as an instinctive protest against the impossibility of coming near his inexpressible dream. The play has more sustained force than Wesker has since achieved. Its general avoidance of the explicit statement preserves it from the danger of seeming to offer a commonplace 'message'. Its speed and the apparent casualness of its incidents save us from demanding a stronger individuality in the characters. The people of the kitchen remain people we have glimpsed: they keep the secrets that each individual always partially hides beneath the uniform of his type.

But Wesker has not been content with this restricted view. In his trilogy he has tried to make us live with a family of our time, and respond to his chief figures with sympathy and intimate understanding.

[4] V. S. Pritchett comments on this: 'It is annoying when an artist explains.'

And, defiantly, he aims at an explicit statement of what he feels necessary for satisfactory living. *Chicken Soup with Barley* ends in wretchedness: Harry the father is ill and senile; his family is scattered; his wife Sarah is lonely and sick at heart because she sees the world's condition. Yet in the play's last words she urges on her son Ronnie the imperative need to care about what happens, to himself and to others, the need not only to face disillusion but to see it as irrelevant if one is to go on as a human being. Sarah is coming to the end of a long talk with her son

> SARAH: . . . You hear me, Ronnie? (*she clasps him and moans*) You've got to care, you've got to care or you'll die.
>
> RONNIE *unclasps her and moves away. He tries to say something—to explain. He raises his arms and some jumbled words come from his lips.*
>
> RONNIE: I—I can't, not now, it's too big, not yet—it's too big to care for it, I—I . . .
>
> RONNIE *picks up his case and brokenly moves to his room mumbling:*
>
> Too big, Sarah—too big, too big.
>
> SARAH (*shouting after him*): You'll die, you'll die—if you don't care you'll die. (*He pauses at door*) Ronnie, if you don't care you'll die. (*He turns slowly to face her.*)

We do not know if Ronnie will respond to her words. Wesker is aware that there is no logic in them, but they form an affirmation that, he suggests, we dare not abandon.

This has naïveté, and the simple strength of a naïveté recognised as such. There are, however, more dramatically effective moments in his other plays where he shows us what it means, for a moment, to be fully alive. One of these moments is Beatie's dance at the end of the second act of *Roots*. Beatie, a girl brought up in the countryside, has been away from home for some time. In London she has met Ronnie Kahn, has become his mistress, has learned from him something of the world of art and literature and politics: she has even tried to paint 'abstract pictures' of her own. When she returns to her family in the country, it is to tell them that she and Ronnie are engaged to be married, and that he is coming to meet them within a few days. Meanwhile she talks, most fluently and parrot-like, telling them of all Ronnie's ideas in Ronnie's own words. Her painting, it is evident, is a sham, an amateur's imitation of paintings she has seen, embodying no more of

her own experience than the words she takes over from Ronnie. Yet
something has happened to her, though it is nothing she can speak of.
She tries to tell her mother of the effect that music has on her, and,
though she cannot find words for this, she plays a gramophone record
of Bizet's *L'Arlésienne* suite and, as she listens and tries to convey her
response, she begins to dance. It is fierce, uncontrolled, ungainly
dancing ('*a mixture of a cossack dance and a sailor's hornpipe*'), but it has
its own rough ecstasy. The curtain comes down on her abandonment
to the rhythm. We are embarrassed by the roughness, but embarrassed
too because she has become so awkwardly alive. This living of hers
advances further at the play's ending. Her family are gathered together,
waiting for Ronnie to come and meet them on the day appointed.
They are hostile to Beatie, who has grown away from them, and ready
to be hostile to Ronnie, the stranger from the town who has infected
Beatie with his ideas. He is, it appears, late, and Beatie indulges herself
in quoting Ronnie more freely than ever, mocking at her family as
Ronnie might mock at them when talking to her. As the hostility rises,
Beatie shrinks in stature, becoming more and more a mere parrot for
Ronnie's words. And then a letter comes: Ronnie has decided that his
relationship with Beatie should end: he sends his awkward apologies.
Beatie's mother gets her revenge for the urging to come alive that has
made her uneasy since her daughter came home. 'The apple don't fall
far from the tree—that it don't,' she says. Beatie plunges this way and
that as she tries to find herself in her new situation, but now she begins
to speak in her own person, as she upbraids the family for its disregard
of past and future. She has an eloquence natural to herself, an eloquence
without fine phrasing or ordered thought, and the tide of life in the
play runs at its highest. Then, suddenly, she realises what has happened.
She breaks off and, in astonished heartbreak, she addresses the absent
Ronnie:

> God in heaven, RONNIE! It does work, it's happening to me, I can
> feel it's happened, I'm beginning, on my own two feet—I'm
> beginning . . .

In his letter, Ronnie had said 'It wouldn't really work' to try to hand
on 'a new kind of life to people'. Beatie has now discovered that it can
work. There is irony in that Ronnie will never know that his attempt
to make Beatie grow has suddenly borne fruit, irony too in that we
shall never know if Beatie continues to live in her new fashion:

Wesker leaves it indeterminate with a bare, dubious reference to '*Whatever she will do*'. But for a moment she lived. For a moment she was fully herself, articulate, passionate, caring. That, according to Wesker, is something.

In the following play he has a similar moment more elaborately contrived. It comes not at the end of the play, which is indeed a moment for set teeth in the recognition of failure, but incidentally during the play's course. Dave and Ada have been living in the country for seven years, and their child Danny has been born there. They want him to grow up with a fuller sense of life than most children have, to feel the excitement of seeing and moving and speaking. And here Ada plays with her son a game that they call 'Look I'm alive!' On the stage are the mother and father: the child is heard speaking off-stage, and we can imagine his excitement, as he acts the idea of coming to life for the first time, more fully than if we could see him. It is as if this child is more conscious of the wonder and freshness of the world and of his own being than any child that belongs in our society. An ordinary child we might see: this one is about to run on to the stage as the lights go out and the curtain falls. It is the most deliberate piece of writing that Wesker has yet accomplished, and it belongs essentially to the theatre. Strangely it comes in what is, as a whole, his most unsatisfactory play. *I'm Talking about Jerusalem* is not compelling as a documentary of life in the English countryside or as an introduction to individual characters or even as a plausible narrative. Its action is casually put together, although the logic of the drama should make us see Ada and Dave as driven, slowly but evidently, to an abandonment of their Utopian dream. Nevertheless, the game of 'Look I'm alive' almost justifies the tedium of the rest. His parents teach Danny to sharpen his vision of the things around him, but he has the power of responding more fully than they can. With them the game is a valid contrivance, not merely an educational process but a striving after their own lost innocence; with him it is immediate. This is Wesker's Wordsworthian dream: not the country, which is tarnished enough, but the beloved child is his incarnation of an imagined mode of being. Certainly in the scene where the game is played there is 'common life', but there is no doubt too of the 'colouring of imagination', the 'unusual aspect', the 'primary laws of our nature'. The things that Wesker shows us we have spent our lives in forgetting.

There is also a sense of being reminded of something when we read

Pinter, though here we are not so easily sure what it is. He writes the dialogue of a more obviously mannered playwright than Wesker. At first sight indeed his language appears deliberately flat and everyday. The characters speak the phrases that come commonest in human speech; they speak for the most part in very short sentences. But as we listen two unusual characteristics begin to emerge. One is extreme economy. Ordinary speech seems to be cut down to the minimum: the people are uttering the small change of everyday conversation, and yet they have nothing of the false starts or the circumlocutions that we fill out our talk with. But, more remarkable than this, in the theatre the short sentences flow into one another with no sense of the staccato. The dialogue comes in waves, rising and falling with the dramatic tension. This is more evident in *The Caretaker* than in Pinter's earlier plays, but first his manner of writing may be illustrated by a quotation from the opening passage of dialogue in *The Birthday Party*. The economy is here grotesque, as the husband and wife unconsciously parody, through their very conciseness, the morning talk of married people. And the grotesque character of the dialogue, though comic, leaves us uneasy, feeling in it a withheld threat:

> PETEY *enters from the door on the left with a paper and sits at the table. He begins to read.* MEG'S *voice comes through the kitchen hatch.*
>
> MEG: Is that you, Petey?
>
> *Pause.*
>
> Petey, is that you?
>
> *Pause.*
>
> Petey?
>
> PETEY: What?
>
> MEG: Is that you?
>
> PETEY: Yes, it's me.
>
> MEG: What? (*Her face appears at the hatch.*) Are you back?
>
> PETEY: Yes.
>
> MEG: I've got your cornflakes ready. (*She disappears and reappears.*) Here's your cornflakes.
>
> *He rises and takes the plate from her, sits at the table, props up the paper and begins to eat.* MEG *enters by the kitchen door.*
>
> Are they nice?
>
> PETEY: Very nice.
>
> MEG: I thought they'd be nice. (*She sits at the table.*) You got your paper?
>
> PETEY: Yes.
>
> MEG: Is it good?

PETEY: Not bad.

MEG: What does it say?

PETEY: Nothing much.

MEG: You read me out some nice bits yesterday.

PETEY: Yes, well, I haven't finished this one yet.

MEG: Will you tell me when you come to something good?

PETEY: Yes.

Pause.

MEG: Have you been working hard this morning?

PETEY: No. Just stacked a few of the old chairs. Cleaned up a bit.

MEG: Is it nice out?

PETEY: Very nice.

Pause.

MEG: Is Stanley up yet?

PETEY: I don't know. Is he?

MEG: I don't know. I haven't seen him down yet.

PETEY: Well then, he can't be up.

MEG: Haven't you seen him down?

PETEY: I've only just come in.

MEG: He must be still asleep.

She looks round the room, stands, goes to the sideboard and takes a pair of socks from a drawer, collects wool and a needle and goes back to the table.

What time did you go out this morning, Petey?

PETEY: Same time as usual.

MEG: Was it dark?

PETEY: No, it was light.

MEG (*beginning to darn*): But sometimes you go out in the morning and it's dark.

PETEY: That's in the winter.

MEG: Oh, in winter.

PETEY: Yes, it gets light later in winter.

MEG: Oh.

Soon we meet Stanley, the boarder who has hidden himself in this seaside lodging-house, and we learn of his fear when he knows that two strange men are coming to stay there, the first guests—apart from himself—that the house has known. Meg never understands what is happening; Petey knows but turns his back until, as we have seen, he makes his despairing attempt to save Stanley at the end. Goldberg and McCann, squalid, uncertain, whimsical, cruel—agents of the power that Stanley has somehow disobeyed—are the more frightening because they themselves are ill at ease. We never know the identity of what they represent. Like the 'Life-in-Death' figure in *The Ancient Mariner*, it simply 'thicks men's blood with cold'. But men serve it, men disobey it, men submit to it. Like Blake's upas tree, it grows in the human brain.

The Birthday Party is arresting and haunting, but at times we are made to feel that the line of composition is blurred. This is particularly so at the end of the second act, where Stanley is reduced to a passive sub-normality during the savage birthday party that Goldberg and McCann organise for him. The breaking-point comes in the act's final moments, in darkness, and there is confusion in the action. This may be intentional, to suggest that we do not know how or why a breaking-point comes in a man's mind. But on the stage it leaves the audience with a feeling that the acting or production has misfired. Pinter has not fully managed to convey his idea in theatrical terms.

This, or something like it, is to be found in *The Room* and *The Dumb Waiter* (both first acted in 1960 but, along with *The Birthday Party*, written in 1957[5]). These two short plays have theatrical life in them and intermittently give an edge to perception. But, in *The Room* especially, we are conscious of being invited to look for allegory and yet not sufficiently impelled to conduct the search. We can, by an effort of analysis, see why the blind negro who enters near the end of the play should call Rose 'Sal', should be her father, and should transmit his blindness to her when her hitherto passive husband has killed him. But the result of our analysis is not one that wholly convinces or that remains in the mind after the play has been read or seen. In *The Dwarfs* (broadcast 1960) the communication is much more uncertain. That the unseen, unheard dwarfs are the small compelled masters of the world in which live the three men whose voices we hear—Len, Mark, Pete—is evident enough. But they have not the authority of the equally invisible crabs of Sartre's *Les Séquestrés d'Altona*: Pinter has cramped himself too much in this composition to achieve the fluidity of experience, and the glimpses we get of the men and their masters seem arbitrary and fugitive. *A Slight Ache* (first acted 1959), though sharing the fertility of image that characterises *The Birthday Party*, seems commonplace in its mystery: the figure of the Matchseller (Death or Chaos or the Annihilation of Degree: anyway, an ending of

[5] Information from the dust-jacket of *The Birthday Party and Other Plays* (1960).

what has been known) is not made interesting in its own right; as a symbol it consequently remains inert. *A Night Out* (broadcast 1960) is less ambitious, remaining content with easily graspable satire: it may be the beginning of a less close-textured phase in Pinter's writing. Its dialogue is as disturbing a re-creation (not a replica) of common speech as we can find in *The Birthday Party*, but its subject-matter is of a typical kind, remote from the elemental world of both *The Birthday Party* and *The Caretaker*. It is these plays that, so far, constitute the dramatist's chief claim on our attention.

All of his writings have kept an audience wondering or baffled or fascinated. But only with *The Caretaker* has there been the experience of compelled, undeviating attention. The setting throughout is a shabby room at the top of an otherwise empty house. The room is full of rubbish—beds, old newspapers, old shoes, broken electric fittings, a gas-stove, a statue of the Buddha, a bucket suspended from the ceiling to catch the rain from a leak. There are only three characters. There is Davies, a tramp, old, repellent, brutally selfish, in turn cringing and boastful. There is Mick, who claims to own the room and whom we see silently in possession when the curtain first goes up. There is Aston, Mick's brother, who lets Davies share the room with him. At the end of the play Davies has been ordered to leave, and he pleads with Aston to let him stay. Where else, he asks, can he go? But Aston has turned away towards the dim light of the window, and Davies goes on pleading, falling away into silence before the curtain comes down:

ASTON (*rising and going to the window*): Anyway, I'm going to be busy. I've got that shed to get up. If I don't get it up now it'll never go up. Until it's up I can't get started.

DAVIES: I'll give you a hand to put up your shed, that's what I'll do!
Pause.
Can't you see what I'm getting at? I'll give you a hand! We'll both put up that shed together! See? Get it done in next to no time! Do you see what I'm saying?
Pause.

ASTON: No. I can get it up myself.

DAVIES: But listen. I'm with you, I'll be here, I'll do it for you, we'll do it together, and I'll take care of the place for you, I'll keep an eye on the place for you, at the same time, I'll caretake for you.
Pause.

ASTON: No.

DAVIES: Why not?

ASTON: I don't sleep well at night.

DAVIES: But damn it I've told you we'll change beds! Christ! We'll change beds! That'll do it. Can't you see the sense in what I'm saying?

ASTON *remains with his back to* DAVIES, *at the window.*

You mean you're throwing me out? You can't do that. Listen man, listen man, I don't mind, you see, I don't mind, I'll stay, I don't mind, I'll tell you what, if you don't want to change beds, we'll keep it as it is, I'll stay in the same bed, maybe if I can get a stronger piece of sacking, like, to go over the window, keep out the draught, that'll do it, what do you say, we'll keep it as it is?

Pause.

ASTON: No.

DAVIES: Why . . . not?

ASTON *turns to look at him.*

ASTON: You make too much noise.

DAVIES: But . . . but . . . look . . . listen . . . listen here . . . I mean . . .

ASTON *turns back to the window.*

What am I going to do?

Pause.

What shall I do?

Pause.

Where am I going to go?

Pause.

I could stay here. We could put up your shed.

Pause.

If you want me to go . . . I'll go. You just say the word.

Pause.

I'll tell you what though . . . them shoes . . . them shoes you give me . . . they're working out all right . . . they're all right. Maybe I could . . . get down . . .

ASTON *remains still, his back to him, at the window.*

Listen . . . if I . . . got down . . . if I was to . . . get my papers . . . would you . . . would you let . . . would you . . . if I got down . . . and got my . . .

Long silence.

Curtain.

The tramp Davies is an Everyman figure, looking for food and shelter at the least cost to himself, finding himself in a world where two brothers, strangely different, equally strange, both claim possession. One brother is good to him; the other makes half-promises, mingled with threats; both reject him. Mick is self-confident, always in control. Aston is one who has suffered; he has been judged mad, he tells Davies, and the prescribed treatment has freed him from hallucinations but made his brain lethargic; his words come slowly, and he is no longer clever with his hands. Aston and Mick are given thoroughly human backgrounds, but they are characters of a different kind from Davies. We are invited, however repellent the prospect, to identify ourselves with Davies: he is our representative as the central character in a morality play is. Aston and Mick are individualisations of forces, warring principles, dark angel and bright angel. They are brothers, and as they are together for a moment, in silence, near the end of the play, they smile faintly at one another. Between them there is understanding and affection, for they are of the same order, aristocrats in the universe: the principle of assertion, ruthlessness, mockery; the principle of suffering, love, compassion. The world can let Mick have his way, it yields itself to him. But the world torments Aston, declaring him mad, practising its science upon him to make him normal. Yet both possess the world, both ultimately are one, and Davies is far astray in trying to side with one of them against the other. If Mick is akin to Mephistophelis, Aston is an echo of Dostoievsky's holy fools. Yet in the end the play is the tragedy of Aston rather than the tragedy of Davies. When Love must deny its nature, when humanity must be turned away from, it is Love which receives the greater hurt. When the curtain comes down, Aston has turned away from us as well as from Davies: he suffers more than we or Davies can.

This is a sketch of an interpretation. Its probable inadequacy is not due to the play leaving gaps which we must fill in for ourselves. Rather, the material of the play is so complex that an interpretation can fail to take into account every detail of the pattern. It is a play to go back to, with the anticipation that its statement will not be easily exhausted.

In one respect at least the account of this play that I have given must be misleading. It is an intensely serious and moving play, yet at the same time it is shot through with comedy. During the London run there was every evening a great deal of laughter, at the grotesque words and actions of Davies, at his pretences, his illusions, his ludicrous appearance. And this did not at all get in the way of a deep and troubled response to the treatment of the human situation. Pinter, indeed, has both a remarkable sensitivity to man's plight, a power of embodying his vision in terms that are at once abstract and intensely humanised, and a command of theatrical resource. The comedy is not the audience's sop: being of the uncomfortable kind, it forces a challenge. The characters are, in Coleridge's words, 'shadows of imagination', but they are made to live as we watch the play: they have the 'semblance of truth' that Coleridge wanted, and they compel from us the 'poetic faith' that we are willing to give when the acknowledged fiction embodies a truth of a deeper sort.

But, if the point needed making before, *The Caretaker* has put it beyond question that Pinter is a dramatist of a different kind from N. F. Simpson, whose highly personal writing in *A Resounding Tinkle* and *One-Way Pendulum* has rightly won a degree of attention not far short of that recently given to Pinter. Simpson works tangentially in the relation of incident with incident, and often of speech with speech. He has a splendid facility in the straightforward reduction to absurdity of common human behaviour (as in the cross-examination of the witness in *One-Way Pendulum*), and in the more fanciful presentation of misapplied human effort (as in the training in choral singing given in the same play to a collection of speak-your-weight machines). He can imply a moral idea: if one's hobby is the constructing of a court of justice in one's dining-room, one may find oneself subject to the rigour of an intrusive lawyers' world: playing with serious matters may suddenly cease to be play. But such allegorising notions are incidental in Simpson. His plays are wholes because of a uniformity of style and spirit: the same kind of fancy operates throughout. But Pinter's most successful work is held together through a dominant idea, given consistent embodiment in the structural relationships of events and characters. Pinter, in fact, like Beckett, remains Aristotelian in his conception of drama. Simpson belongs with Ionesco in showing a limited regard for even the Stagirite.

The theatre has many forms of drama, to which we customarily give our preferences in turn. One kind of comedy or tragedy acquires a prestige or a modishness, and we are then often inclined to look with impatience on other kinds. But in our day there are many fields in which we should not be doctrinaire, but should be ready to find things of value in diverse shapes, including some shapes manifestly rough and mingled. It should cause us some pleasure that men as different as Arnold Wesker and Harold Pinter have become prominent in the same theatre at the same time. And we have noticed that some recent approaches to drama are different from either of theirs. Although, of the plays discussed here, only *The Caretaker* has a special degree of authority, Wesker and Pinter are among a group of young dramatists whose diverse writings have helped us to see more clearly both what lies around and what is commonly hidden.

Postscript (1968)

This article was written in 1961 as a salute to two young dramatists. After seven years it is of course a far from adequate assessment of their work. Wesker has since written *Chips with Everything* (published 1962), *The Four Seasons* (published 1966) and *Their Very Own and Golden City* (published 1966), and has given much time to his work with Centre 42. As with Ronnie in *Chicken Soup with Barley*, his later characters show assertiveness and independence yielding or half-yielding to the pressure of circumstance, the temptation to acquiescence and compromise. Technically he remains bold (mime and drill and song in *Chips*, the 'flash-forward' in *City*); his dialogue has not achieved the authority of a language one remembers; his characters are heart-felt but formula-driven. No dramatist of our time arouses more sympathy in readers and spectators; we honour the image of human nature that he centrally offers, and wish we could believe in it. What will happen, we may ask, when finally he loses heart?

Pinter's progress has been more diverse. Only one full-length play has come from him in the seven years: *The Homecoming* (published 1965), and that stands out among mid-century English plays. Different in style from *The Birthday Party* and *The Caretaker*, it has neither inconsequence nor allegory, but is a taut study of pauperism and impotence with sharply drawn and sharp-set characters. It is the least amusing of comedies, but made its London audience laugh feverishly. He has brought out several short plays, for theatre, radio and television: *The Collection* and *the Lover* (published 1963), *Tea Party* and *Other Plays* (published 1967). And some of his best work has been done as a writer of film scripts adapted from other writers' novels: *The Servant*, *The Pumpkin Eater*, *Accident*. He remains a master of dialogue, and his presentation of anguish is both fully serious and yet controlled by his power of comic perception. His stature is hardly to be questioned as that of England's major living writer of plays. Yet at times one may wonder if he has a strong impulsion to do more than solve technical problems. Solve them of course he does, and most often brilliantly.

Note

Bertolt Brecht (1898–1956). Born in Augsburg, Brecht lived in Germany and in exile in Scandinavia, the United States and Switzerland. His first play to reach the stage, *Trommeln in der Nacht* (Munich, 1922) won the Kleist Prize. As well as being a prolific playwright, he produced libretti, a ballet, radio plays, poems, stories and theoretical works on the theatre and opera; he directed many plays including his own, and founded, with others, the Berliner Ensemble in 1949. Methuen have published two volumes of translations of selected plays. The best English introductions are J. Willett's *The Theatre of Bertolt Brecht* and M. Esslin's *Brecht: A Choice of Evils* (both 1959). *Brecht on Theatre* (1964) and *The Messingkauf Dialogues* (1965), both translated by J. Willett, give a comprehensive view of Brecht's theoretical ideas.

W. H. Auden. Born in London in 1907, he published his first volume of poems in 1930. He went to the United States in 1939 and is now a U.S. citizen. His plays are *The Dance of Death* (1933) and, with Christopher Isherwood, *The Dog Beneath the Skin* (1935), *The Ascent of F6* (1936), *On the Frontier* (1938); these were produced by the Group Theatre, London. Faber publish all. R. Hoggart's *Auden, An Introductory Essay* (1951) has a section on the plays.

Clifford Odets. (1906–1963). The son of immigrant parents from Lithuania, Odets grew up in the Bronx, New York. His first play to be performed, *Waiting for Lefty*, was the greatest success of the American agitational theatre: this, as well as *Awake and Sing!* and *Till the Day I Die*, was staged by the New York Group Theatre in 1935. Odets then went to Hollywood as a script writer. He returned to social themes in *Golden Boy* (1937) and *The Big Knife* (1949). The Modern Library, *Six Plays of Clifford Odets* (1939) has useful introductions by Harold Clurman who directed Odets' early successes; quotations are from this edition.

J. B. Priestley. Born in Bradford in 1894, he has been actively associated with the theatre since the early thirties: he was a director of the Mask Theatre at the Westminster in 1938–9. His plays, often naturalistic in form, include *Laburnum Grove* (1933), *Eden End* (1934), the 'time plays', *Time and the Conways* and *I Have Been Here Before* (both 1937), the family comedy, *When We Are Married* (1938), *Johnson Over Jordan* (1939) and *An Inspector Calls* (1945). His views on the theatre are to be found in *Theatre Outlook* (1947) and *The Art of the Dramatist* (1957). Quotations in this chapter are from Heinemann's Collected Edition. A full-length study is *J. B. Priestley: the Dramatist* by Gareth Lloyd Evans (1964).

John Arden. Born at Barnsley in 1930 and trained as an architect, he wrote his first play for radio (1956). Four early plays were performed at the Royal Court Theatre. *The Waters of Babylon* (1957), *Live Like Pigs* (1958) and *The Happy Haven* (1960) have appeared in one volume of Penguin Plays. *Serjeant Musgrave's Dance* (1959), *The Business of Good Government* (1960), *The Workhouse Donkey* (1963), *Armstrong's Last Goodnight* (1964) and *Left-Handed Liberty* (1965) have been published separately by Methuen. Arden has also written television plays (*Soldier, Soldier*, 1960, *Wet Fish*, 1961) and a film script (*Top Deck*, 1961). *The Encore Reader*, ed. by C. Marowitz, T. Milne and O. Hale (1965) contains articles by and about Arden.

General. E. Bentley's *The Modern Theatre* (London, 1948) is highly recommended. F. Fergusson has an essay on 'Three Allegorists: Brecht, Wilder and Eliot' in his *The Human Image in Dramatic Literature* (1957).

II

Realism and Parables

(*from Brecht to Arden*)

G. W. BRANDT

★

We want a frankly doctrinal theatre. There is no more reason for making a doctrinal theatre inartistic than for putting a cathedral organ out of tune: indeed all experience shews that doctrine alone nerves us to the effort called for by the greatest art.[1]—GEORGE BERNARD SHAW (1891).

The theatre is still the theatre, even when it is didactic theatre, and in so far as it is good theatre it is entertaining. [2]—BERTOLT BRECHT (1936).

★   ★   ★

It is time someone reminded our advanced dramatists that the principal function of the theatre is to give pleasure. It is not the principal function of the theatre to strengthen peace, to improve morality, or to establish a good social system. Churches, international associations, and political parties already exist for those purposes. It is the duty of the theatre, not to make men better, but to render them harmlessly happy.[3]—HAROLD HOBSON (1959).

SINCE the visit of the Berliner Ensemble to London in 1956, Brecht's ideas have been in the English air. Not that his plays have been very conspicuous on the English stage: perhaps the ideas, only half digested, have kept out the plays. Audiences and producers alike may have been scared off by concentrating unduly on what they conceive to be the 'point' of Epic Drama: dropping in of symbols from the flies, alienation effect, projected captions, sudden irruption of songs, half-exposed stage mechanics, wholly exposed stage lighting, etc., etc. It is a pity.

'The satisfaction of Brecht's work,' John Willett rightly observes,

---

[1] *The Quintessence of Ibsenism* reprinted in *Major Critical Essays* (1932), p. 149.
[2] My translation from 'Vergnügungstheater oder Lehrtheater?', *Schriften zum Theater* (Suhrkamp), p. 66.
[3] *Sunday Times* (25 October, 1959).

'lies not in the form itself, but in that command of form which can shape it to fit a content that matters' (p. 225). With so varied a dramatic output as Brecht's it is not possible to reduce the content of all his plays to a common denominator: but we can say that the manner in which Brecht handled his plot was frequently, though not invariably, that of the parable. Brecht called *The Good Woman of Setzuan* a 'parable play'; the term has been given general currency in English by Eric Bentley who entitled his translation of this and *The Caucasian Chalk Circle* 'Parables for the Theatre'. It is a useful concept: I propose to develop it in this chapter and to look at some varied examples of the form.

Other Brecht plays, too (*St. Joan of the Stockyards, Mother Courage and her Children, Mr. Puntila and his Man Matti*), qualify as parables. Note that these are all negative parables: they illustrate a *wrong* state of affairs or *wrong* conduct.

Thus Mother Courage, small trader in war supplies, has to pay the price of her complicity in the general crime of war: she loses her three children who had been the motive for her way of life. And yet, we may well ask, could she have acted otherwise than she did in the circumstances in which she found herself? The answer is probably Yes. But she could not abolish the fact of war all by herself; individual rebellion would have cost her even more than complicity. What then should she have done?

Again, if Grusha, the Caucasian maidservant, receives justice at the hands of the honestly corrupt Azdak, such a happy outcome, we are told, could only take place in a 'brief golden age of near-justice'. It isn't likely to happen again in a hurry—at least, not unless we make it happen. Can we? Do we want to? How?

The three Chinese gods approve of the Good Woman Shen Teh's goodness; but solve her problems they cannot. Goodness, we may conclude—goodness that will not be mere exploitable weakness—is not practical as long as human nature is what it is, or more precisely as long as the society that shapes human nature continues to be what it is. The problem having been posed, the gods fly off in their cloud, and it is for the audience to supply the answer. The negative parable à la Brecht does not imply that there is no such thing as *right* conduct; but the audience are not spoon-fed with a readily digestible moral; they have to chew on the facts for themselves and come to their own conclusions.

Now let us attempt to fix some of the characteristics of the parable.

Both in narrative and in dramatic form it is obviously didactic, with a lesson stated or implied. It is perhaps *the* basic teaching method: 'And with many such parables spake he the word unto them, as they were able to hear it. But without a parable spake he not unto them: and when they were alone, he expounded all things to his disciples' (Mark, iv. 33–4).

The etymology of certain English words, derived from the Greek by way of the Romance languages, is evidence that the best way to reach the minds and hearts of people is by means of the parable: literally a placing side by side, a comparison. We may be engaged in a serious *parley*, or we may be merely *palavering*: we may be sitting in *parliament* or sprawling in the *parlour*: we may just be out on *parole*: but in many kinds of *parlance* we unconsciously attest to the fact that one of the surest means of human communication is the parabolical method.

Like allegory, the parable teaches by means of stories, images, conceits. But whereas allegory tends to be abstract and philosophical, the parable tends to be earthy, concrete and sensuous. It often comes in the guise of wit (not necessarily humour). The dramatic allegory puts onto the stage abstractions or generalisations in the place of autonomous characters: the World, Five-Wits, Lust, Science, Humanity, the King, Discretion. The dramatic parable employs more or less fully realised characters and hangs its generalisation, its lesson, on them.

On the other hand, the parable differs from the bald thesis play, though again both genres are didactic. The thesis play will be direct, specific, preaching an open message; the parable will be oblique and general—in short, poetic. Both may be ultimately realistic; but the forms of naturalism will not easily suit the parable.

A parable may occur in a play in narrative form: take Menenius Agrippa's 'pretty tale' of the belly and the rebellious members of the body in *Coriolanus*. Or it may be an extended incident within a play, like the choosing of the right casket at Belmont, whereby we may learn to choose not by the view. Or the parable may constitute the whole play: *Measure for Measure* is a parable on lust, continence, and right conduct in love.

Allegory—parable—thesis play: obviously the categories overlap. Nevertheless they are distinct, and the distinction seems to me a useful one. Frequently it is not observed. Thus—to take an example at random—Francis Fergusson blurs his categories when, in an otherwise admirable essay, he calls Brecht, Wilder and Eliot allegorists: they are clearly writers of parables. Observing these distinctions is not a mere matter of pedantry or verbal hygiene. It may materially affect the reading of a given text; in a play particularly, it may influence the concept, tone and style of a production.

Now we need not look exclusively to Brecht in examining the modern dramatic parable. There is a respectable home-grown English tradition in the field. If the English theatre was bogged down during the nineteenth century in social complacency and scenic realism, two trends unfavourable to parable-writing, it was 'the naughty life-forcer in the norfolk jacket' [4] who gave it a shot in the arm, some seventy years ago, once again injecting the health-giving serum of controversy. From *Widowers' Houses* onward, Shaw's method was usually that of the parable (excepting such purely disquisitional plays as *Getting Married* or *Geneva*). His moral parables held the distorting mirror up to society. He carved out a permanent niche for the bracing, sometimes infuriating play of social criticism. In the world of today, the dramatic parable is more likely to concern itself with social than with individual conduct. Shaw's success is history: but he did not overturn the supremacy of the play of 'pure entertainment'. The essentially complacent, intellectually untaxing, long-run or weekly-rep sort of play we have with us always, alas. The entertainment reassures, the parable disturbs. This is particularly so if it is a sermon preached from a critical posture—and why else preach? In practice such preachment is likely to come from the political Left.

Until recently, at any rate, the writer of parables with political overtones might easily find himself in trouble. This was certainly true of what I suggest (leaving *Troilus and Cressida* out of consideration for the moment) is the best anti-war play in the English language: Sean O'Casey's *The Silver Tassie*. It seems fitting that a study of certain trends in modern English-language drama should begin with an Irish play.

O'Casey's early successes had been associated with the Abbey Theatre in Dublin. *The Silver Tassie*, a 'hell of a play', as G.B.S. admiringly called it, brought him into conflict with his original sponsors. When he submitted the play script to Yeats in 1928, the apostle of the 'Theatre of Beauty' rejected it: obviously it was too socially involved, too political, too destructive of the heroic myth. Yeats was being blatantly unfair when he claimed in a letter to the

[4] W. H. Auden and C. Isherwood, *The Dog Beneath the Skin* (1935), p. 43.

author: 'The mere greatness of the World War has thwarted you' (quoted Krause, pp. 102–3). The exact opposite is true. Perhaps more than any other playwright, O'Casey has managed to cram the essence of modern war into the limits of one single play. But whereas Yeats cherished the notion of a drama 'remote, spiritual, and ideal', *The Silver Tassie* assailed the spectator with a long, silent scream of protest, like Helene Weigel's Mother Courage; it protested against man's inhumanity to man; more specifically and more dangerously, it protested against the remediable idiocy of war. A play so deeply committed, so irreverent, and reaching out so boldly from art into life, opinion and action, could not be fitted into Yeats's aloof and aristocratic concept. In the letter referred to above, Yeats declared his artistic credo that 'the whole history of the world must be reduced to wallpaper in front of which the characters must pose and speak'. *The Silver Tassie* boasts no such wallpaper or tapestry attitude. Far from being sublimated into cloudy and uncommitted myth, life is served up raw and palpitating in this parable on the nature of war. It was only natural, therefore, that the play should cause a breach between the Abbey and the inheritor of Synge's mantle, perhaps to the lasting detriment of both.

In fact, Yeats relented in the end, and the play *was* performed at the Abbey in 1935. Even then it ran into a volley of abuse from sections of the Irish press: a healthy sign that *The Silver Tassie* had kept its bite. It still has it today. Although it was a success on the London stage in 1929 and has been movingly done by the B.B.C. as a radio play, it has on the whole been conspicuously absent from British (or, as far as I know, any other) playbills. What is the reason for this? Political prejudice? A sheer oversight? The cost of mounting the play, with a cast of twenty-three, and four sets that had better be good? Or some of the structural and stylistic peculiarities of the play itself?

The only point that requires an answer is the aesthetic attack on the play, which has come under three headings. First, that Harry Heegan, the protagonist, is too feeble to carry the action. As Yeats put it: 'There is no dominating character, no dominating action, neither psychological unity nor unity of action . . .' Second, that Harry should not have been left out of the second act. Third, that the style of Act II clashes too sharply with that of the other acts of the play. Let us deal with these criticisms of what is, admittedly, a structurally unique play.

First: it is true that Harry is essentially passive; he does not carry the action, he is driven by it. Once he has been smashed and broken by war, he has no further dramatic function other than providing pathos. But then it would have been quite false to the theme of the play to raise him to tragic stature: the Moloch of war grinds up men regardless of personal qualities, of 'tragic guilt'. What interests us in Harry is not primarily his character but his fate; this is what makes him the representative of a whole generation. If at the end of the play we were given a tragic reconciliation, this would only serve to blunt our anger. There is no place here for any anodynes suggesting that, *malgré tout*, there is a higher harmony, that the spirit of man always triumphs in the end, that true happiness comes from within, etc., etc. This is a bloody story without any consolations. Harry was no great man, he was a footballer; and now he will never play again.

Second: it is precisely because Harry is no tragic hero that we get that 'remarkable second act', as Granville-Barker called it.[5] This is undoubtedly the finest bit of expressionist writing in the English language—more compassionate than those American parables on Industrial Man, *The Hairy Ape* and *The Adding Machine*. Its structural peculiarity is, of course, the omission of the hero. True, this is a dangerous procedure and one which does not lend itself to imitation; but its purpose here is plain enough. The action is generalised at this point: what is happening to Harry is as terrible as, but individually no more significant than, what is happening to any other front-line soldier. Harry is Everyman at war. The act shows his fate all right, but only by implication.

Third: this act does, of course, employ a wide range of expressionist devices in a quasi-symbolical representation of war. Soldiers, half turned into fighting machines, chant or speak in a stylised manner (note the ironical tension between the form and meaning of their speeches); a staff wallah and a front-line visitor mouth clipped platitudes; a deathlike soldier called the Croucher recites a topsy-turvy version of Ezekiel 37—not dry bones stirring into life, but the living turned into dry bones. The setting counterposes the ruins of religion (a smashed monastery, a crucifix with a broken arm) against the solid reality of a huge howitzer. Blasphemy, satire, mechanised speech and movement, an enemy attack shown largely in terms of stage lighting, all combine to lacerate the feelings of the audience. The soldiers perform an act of worship to the gun: 'We believe in God and we believe in thee.'

[5] In his Romanes lecture, *On Poetry and Drama* (1937).

But then, are the other three acts of the play naturalistic? Surely not. If Act II of *The Silver Tassie* is more highly stylised than the rest, this is only a matter of degree. Throughout the play, O'Casey employs a bold, very largely successful, mixture of rhythmical speech, a stylised Irish diction with frequent Biblical echoes, chanting, singing, music, rhyme, alliteration, evocative settings and theatrical business. The thrust of the play is such that all these disparate elements do in fact fuse together into a unity. Even out-and-out farce has its place in the persons of two characteristic O'Casey creations, old Simon and old Sylvester. Their set piece in Act IV, trying unsuccessfully to cope with that new-fangled monster the telephone, is one of the highlights of latter-day comic writing.

The moral of *The Silver Tassie* is no intellectual statement; it is an emotional appeal. O'Casey had sounded the same *cri du cœur* in more realistic terms in his earlier plays dealing with the Troubles. Thus, we recall Mrs. Tancred's words:

> O Blessed Virgin, where were you when me darlin' son was riddled with bullets, when me darlin' son was riddled with bullets! . . . Sacred Heart of the Crucified Jesus, take away our hearts o' stone . . . and give us hearts o' flesh! . . . Take away this murdherin' hate . . . an' give us Thine own eternal love!
>
> (*Juno and the Paycock*, Collected ed., i. 55)

We might, by a stretch of the imagination, conceive of an Irish mother rising to such eloquence under the pressure of personal tragedy. In *The Silver Tassie* we are shown not merely Ireland, but the whole world, at war. Stylisation has consequently gone further. No football player that ever was, in Dublin or anywhere else, would literally say as Harry says, now a cripple in a wheelchair, bringing in the football cup he had formerly helped to win for his club:

> Dear God, this crippled form is still your child. (*To* MRS. HEEGAN) Dear mother, this helpless thing is still your son. Harry Heegan, me, who, on the football field, could crash a twelve-stone flyer off his feet. For this dear Club three times I won the Cup, and grieve in reason I was just too weak this year to play again. And now, before I go, I give you all the Cup, the Silver Tassie, to have and to hold for ever, evermore. (*From his chair he takes the Cup with the two sides hammered close together, and holds it out to them.*) Mangled and bruised as I am bruised and mangled. (ii. 101)

Stylised the play may be; but no one could complain that it is obscure. It yields up its meaning at once. This must not be taken as an intellectual defect. On the contrary, it is a high virtue in a play with a message, a parable of elemental force.

This virtue is not conspicuously present in a product of the verse drama-cum-politics movement of the thirties: Auden and Isherwood's *The Ascent of F. 6*. This was first produced in 1937 for the (British) Group Theatre by Rupert Doone, with music by Benjamin Britten. Perhaps it is a little unfair first to class the play as a parable and then to fault it for not 'saying' enough, and saying it in a muffled fashion. But surely the joint authors (Isherwood was the one more responsible for the plotting[6]) were after bigger game than merely describing 'man's passion for mountaineering, and his fight to retain spiritual integrity'.[7] There is a parable buried somewhere under the scree of experimental playwriting. When brilliant young Michael Ransom climbs F 6, a mountain of importance in Imperial politics, with a devoted group of Alpinists, he and some of his companions perish in the attempt. The story is wreathed in mountain mists of symbolism. The very name of Ransom seems indicative: is his death not the price that power politics and suburban sensationalism are prepared to pay for their different gratifications? F 6 sticks out in the play as a symbol of lonely endeavour: we are reminded of Faust's ascent to salvation, of Peer Gynt's seeking his freedom on the heights.

But what precisely do these symbols say? The message of the parable is far from clear—in spite, or because, of the variety of techniques used: soliloquy, blank and rhyming verse, choric speech, radio announce-ments, pop songs. It is only fitfully illuminated by a long duologue between Ransom and the Abbot of a vaguely Buddhist mountain monastery. It seems that Ransom, the charismatic leader, wishes to escape from the temptations and corruptions of the power that all too easily could be his. This climb will somehow be wholly his own deed —or so he would like to think; in fact his very exploit is making him into a public figure. At the summit, in what I suppose we are to under-stand as his dying vision, he confronts the dreaded Demon of the mountain, who is none other than—his own mother. Like Oedipus, he can escape neither his fate nor his mother; perhaps the two are really the same thing. How are we to interpret this? That man is ultimately

---

[6] I am indebted for this information to John Moody.
[7] Audrey Williamson, *Theatre of Two Decades* (1951), p. 130.

not free? That we must gain insight into our secret motives? Or that self-knowledge is death?

The epilogue adds a sour note. The expedition has been a success politically, and Ransom, whose death has helped the Empire, has his praises sung in cliché'd terms by cliché'd ruling-class types. But the sting is in the tail. The anonymous suburbanite Mr. A., whose inane duologues with his equally faceless wife have accompanied the action all along, regards Ransom's monument and exclaims, 'He belongs to *us*, now!' Social satire has the last word: the road to F 6 is the road to suburbia.

Still, the message only comes through fuzzily. This demonstrates one thing, at any rate: the danger of formal playfulness standing between a parable and its audience. Auden and Isherwood's plot fails to provide (to use the concept popularised by T. S. Eliot) an objective correlative for their message. This failure is particularly damaging in what appears to be, on one level at least, a piece of social criticism.

The 'socially conscious' drama of New Deal America during the Thirties provides an interesting contrast. Much of this is strictly realistic in form. For example, Odets' *Waiting for Lefty* may use avant-garde gimmicks: dramatic spot-lighting, the audience addressed as a union meeting, swift blackouts; but basically it is a succession of pseudo-naturalistic scenes with a strong propagandist kick. The different episodes (cab-driver driven into militancy by desperate wife, young hack seeing his chances of marriage go on the rocks, etc.) make a direct, rather than a parabolical, impact. This is thesis writing with a vengeance, clear to the point of being agitational.

But the same author's *Golden Boy*, written in 1937 for the (American) Group Theatre, is not so much agitprop as a parable. Odets himself called an early draft of it 'a modern allegory'. (Here 'allegory' is to be understood in the sense I have tried to give to the word 'parable'.)

'The story of this play is not so much the story of a prize-fighter,' writes Harold Clurman, the first producer of *Golden Boy*, 'as the picture of a great fight—a fight in which we are all involved, whatever our profession or craft' (p. 430). This fight of Joe Bonaparte's (again, note the symbolical name) is the struggle for status, wealth and power. As in other American plays (O'Neill's *Marco Millions* comes to mind) the hero's upward climb of the ladder of success means a betrayal of his inner self, a corruption of the spirit. In *Golden Boy* this inner corruption is demonstrated by Joe's sacrificing his art to his success in the ring. In the Lombardo fight he breaks the hand with which he used to play the violin. (One cannot help wondering what sort of a musician he ever had it in him to be, on the showing of the play.) As he is cut off from the realm of the spirit, his personality coarsens and deteriorates. He drifts from the world of his 'lovable' father and his 'good' union-organising brother—a world seen through a haze of sentiment—to that of fight promoters and racketeers. His last exploit in the ring is a killing:

> In the interim, he has fallen in love, hoping, by a romantic attachment, to solve his inner dilemma. But he is a defeated man. He has nothing to live by now. Both worlds are closed to him, and he must die.   (Clurman, pp. 431-2)

Fast-moving, theatrically effective, *Golden Boy* still remains one of the best plays of its time and place. But doesn't its cinematic slice-of-life realism clash with its message function? Looked at more closely, the dialogue is not all that realistic: it has the wise-cracking texture of the Hollywood talk of the era, a stylistic device of heightened, rather than actual, realism. Or did nature imitate art, did people actually talk like that at the time? It is an exhausting thought.

A more pertinent question than that of surface realism is whether the prize-fighter really sums up the ethos of a whole competitive civilisation (as, for instance, Willy Loman does). The most naked form of the fight for power, boxing does seem a good image for Odets' parable. For all its modern trappings, the play at bottom poses the old question, 'For what shall it profit a man, if he shall gain the whole world, and lose his own soul?'

J. B. Priestley's *An Inspector Calls*, a British exercise in socially conscious drama, is far more direct in its message than *Golden Boy*. Although it was written only at the end of the last war, it is very much more old-fashioned in its technique. It is a parable that verges on the territory of the *pièce à thèse*. Maybe it is precisely its solid Pinero-like construction (justified perhaps by the time and place of its action: 1912 . . . Brumley, 'an industrial city in the North Midlands') that has made it popular in the Soviet Union, where it was first produced and where it has been performed more frequently than in Britain. Even so, its traditional realism is no out-and-out naturalism, either in structure or texture. Tape-recorder *verismo* is in fact a very rare thing on the English stage.

It has not perhaps been generally noticed (though Soviet critics must have observed) that *An Inspector Calls* is at bottom a variation on a well-known classical comedy. As its title would suggest, it bears a distant family resemblance to Gogol's *The Government Inspector*. In both plays a pretended inspector comes to investigate a milieu of seemingly rocklike respectability; in both, the pillars of society give way under the weight of their own guilt. After the final departure both of Khlestakov and of Goole, the real inspector is on his way, and we know that *his* investigations will be successful, because his examinees have already been stripped morally naked. I cannot say whether Priestley was conscious of this parallelism or not.

Gogol's comedy is realistic. The unmasking of the Birlings by Inspector Goole is a somewhat more schematic affair. Each member of the family proves to have some share in the death of one Eva Smith. Arthur Birling had her fired from his factory, his daughter Sheila had her dismissed from her next job in a dress-shop, Sheila's fiancé Gerald had a clandestine affair with Eva, Eric Birling had actually fathered her child and then stolen money to help her; and finally Mrs. Birling had turned down her request for aid from the local charity organisation. The plot, then, is clearly didactic and demonstrational.

Eva Smith, the victim of the Birlings' collective callousness, evidently stands for Everywoman. This is bluntly pointed out by the Inspector:

> One Eva Smith has gone—but there are millions and millions and millions of Eva Smiths and John Smiths still left with us, with their lives, their hopes and fears, their suffering, and chance of happiness, all intertwined with our lives, with what we think and say and do. We don't live alone. We are members of one body.   (iii. 311)

The main departure from realism is, of course, the enigmatic figure of the Inspector himself. The very name of Goole does not so much suggest an Irish origin as carry an ominous overtone. What indeed is he? A cruel hoaxer, as Gerald and the elder Birlings, still morally unpurged after their grilling, are only too ready to believe? An objectification of the family's guilty conscience? Or, more objective still, some kind of heavenly messenger? The question is deliberately left open. Goole moves about the stage, trailing clouds of supernatural mystery. This is theatrically effective. Perhaps it is also intended as a compensation of sorts for the play's lack of poetry: characterisation and diction are more than a little flat.

What the Inspector seeks to uncover is sin rather than crime, which is the more normal concern of the police. But the author seems to see sin not primarily as individual man's falling foul of his Maker, but rather in terms of what sociologists like to call interpersonal relationships. Sin then is wrong conduct, especially in the social sense of wrong conduct between the classes. The Birlings may be portrayed rather patronisingly: living in the age of complacency just before the First World War, they do not see the precariousness of their little world as we do, wiser by a generation: but clearly Priestley's parable is intended for us just the same. We, the people of today, may be morally as blind as the Birlings. We have to learn yet once again, as they must, that no man is an island entire of itself.

On its own level *An Inspector Calls* works well enough. If it is not a text to cherish in the closet, it is certainly a viable piece of theatre. It has not perhaps had quite the success it deserves in Britain although it has been popular enough elsewhere. Priestley notes in an Introduction that at one time 'in Germany, for example, at least 1,600 performances of it were given within about eighteen months' (iii. xiii).

Another post-war play that combines the telling of a parable with surface realism and at the same time employs a vaguely supernatural apparatus is T. S. Eliot's *The Cocktail Party*. To use slightly inappropriate political terminology, Priestley's play stands on the left, whereas Eliot might be said to be taking a right-wing position. More specifically: Priestley is concerned with right or wrong conduct primarily in its social implications, Eliot with conduct in the light of personal salvation.

The Cocktail Party is perhaps the best of Eliot's drawing-room plays, all of which can be regarded as parables. We are not here concerned with problems of versification; whether Eliot's dialogue is poetry or not, it is eminently speakable theatrical language which makes its points with great precision though rarely with any great quickening of the pulse.

Why is the play called a comedy, when its climactic event is the death of Celia Coplestone? There is of course a certain lightness of tone, a comic note in many parts of *The Cocktail Party*: this is established at once by Julia's twitterings about whether there was, or was not, a tiger mentioned in Alex's story, and about Lady Klootz and the wedding cake. A good many lines that may look a little tame on the printed page are cunningly placed theatrical laugh-lines. The very title of the play is really a joke. Like that of *Murder in the Cathedral*, it holds out the promise of a frivolous, mentally relaxing evening in the theatre—an expectation which the author then deliberately frustrates. What is more, the cocktail party announced in the title is never actually shown on the stage. The first party (for there are two) is merely the fag-ends of a cancelled party, a social evening that never materialised; the second is about to start just as the final curtain comes down. In purely theatrical terms, there is a good deal of comedy business, all of it of course in an appropriately quiet key: Julia's well-timed irruptions and interruptions; Harcourt-Reilly's bursting into song; Alex's unsuccessful culinary efforts on Edward's behalf.

The play contains shrewd digs at matters marginally related to its theme—psychiatry, for instance. When Edward volunteers his child-hood memories so as to supply material for what he takes to be an orthodox analysis, Sir Henry Harcourt-Reilly, the mystical consultant, replies:

> I always begin from the immediate situation
> And then go back as far as I find necessary.
> You see, your memories of childhood—
> I mean, in your present state of mind—
> Would be largely fictitious; and as for your dreams,
> You would produce amazing dreams, to oblige me.
>
> (p. 98)

This essentially serious point, which ties in with the play's concept that conscience and conduct are spiritual rather than clinical matters, is phrased in the manner of a dry joke. Similarly, a glancing blow is struck at that rather facile target, the film industry. Peter Quilpe, the second-rate novelist who has gone off to Hollywood to become a script writer, has returned to do the spade-work on a film dealing with English life. He is about to visit the Duke of Boltwell's place for purposes of research. On being told that it is sadly dilapidated, he explains:

> Exactly. It is. And that's why we're interested.
> The most decayed noble mansion in England!
> At least, of any that are still inhabited.
> We've got a team of experts over
> To study the decay, so as to reproduce it.
> Then we build another Boltwell in California.
>
> (p. 149)

Perhaps even the Alcestis myth which underlies the plot, or rather serves as a starting-point for it, might be regarded as a *jeu d'esprit*, a private joke of the author's. Most of the Euripidean material has been absorbed into the plot of *The Cocktail Party*: Lavinia (Alcestis) has 'died' to, rather than died for, Edward (Admetus); she has gone to Dedham (which we may take to be the underworld as much as a place in Essex); she is brought back from there by Harcourt-Reilly (Heracles). However, Harcourt-Reilly's tipsy singing seems an unresolved particle left over from the underlying plot: it harks back to Heracles' drunkenness in the house of Admetus but has no organic justification in *The Cocktail Party*. It is, of course, possible in a play so mined with booby-traps that I have missed yet another esoteric significance here. At the same time, a play is not a crossword puzzle; however many secondary meanings it may conceal, it should speak directly on the primary level: and this incident does not.

Yet none of this—neither the concealed nor the overt humour, which is in any case counterbalanced by passages of great seriousness— is sufficient to mark the play a comedy. It is a comedy because of its total vision. For Celia's death is to be regarded not so much as a horrible event (as do Edward, Lavinia and Peter, the spiritually myopic characters) but rather as a spiritual triumph. Harcourt-Reilly says of Celia:

> That way, which she accepted, led to this death.
> And if that is not a happy death, what death is happy?
>
> (p. 163)

This is the real point: the comedy is not primarily a comedy of laughter but that of a 'happy' view of the universe, in which even tragedy falls into place in a higher conciliation of opposites.

'There is a certain mellowness about *The Cocktail Party*,' writes D. E. Jones: 'Eliot has moved beyond the necessity for tragedy into the realm of eternal comedy. Under the Christian dispensation, all endings can be happy. Eliot has devised a kind of comedy generically like Dante's *Divine Comedy* . . . ' (p. 154).

Like *An Inspector Calls*, this play employs basically simple schematic arrangement of relationships in order to tell its parable. The four people who start out in what we may call, according to vocabulary and conviction, false relationships or spiritual error, are involved in all the mathematically possible permutations of the triangle situation. These triangles are: (1) Celia–Edward–Lavinia; (2) Edward–Lavinia–Peter;

(3) Lavinia–Peter–Celia; and (4) Peter–Celia–Edward. Grouped around these people 'in darkness' are the three helpers or 'guardians'. Like Priestley, though not necessarily with the same intentions, Eliot uses hints of the supernatural in order to reinforce the impact of his parable.

How are we to understand these guardians? Mysterious beings, in the world and yet not of the world, they work like spiritual freemasons for the ultimate good of their friends and acquaintances whom they fit into a grand pattern, a presumably God-inspired 'design'. There seems to be a hint here of the Community of Christians Eliot has written about in *The Idea of a Christian Society*. True, he has declared, '. . . I should not like the "Community of Christians" of which I have spoken, to be thought of as merely the nicest, most intelligent and public-spirited of the upper middle class—it is not to be conceived on that analogy' (pp. 60–1). But the guardians in *The Cocktail Party* are conceived precisely along those lines. Though delightfully eccentric at times, they are impeccably U: one feels that it is only their good breeding that makes them conceal their wings of righteousness under perfectly tailored clothes. Members of a 'Christian conspiracy',[8] they work in secret without always being fully aware of the pattern they are helping to weave. Thus, Harcourt-Reilly admits that when he despatched Celia on the mission that was to end in her death, he did not fully understand the words with which he dismissed her. But in his work he is guided by more than reason, for he says:

> When I first met Miss Coplestone, in this room,
> I saw the image, standing behind her chair,
> Of a Celia Coplestone whose face showed the astonishment
> Of the first five minutes after a violent death.
>
> (p. 162)

The pouring of the libation by the guardians, at the end of the second act, a point at which the rhythm of poetry becomes more audible in the play, also stands out as a moment when the secular spectator's credulity is stretched to breaking-point. Disbelief, willingly suspended so far, comes flooding back. The scene resembles the circumambulation of Amy's birthday cake in *The Family Reunion*, in that here, too, incantation and ritual combine to build up an atmosphere of

[8] The phrase is borrowed from W. Arrowsmith, 'English Verse Drama (II): *The Cocktail Party*', *Hudson Review* (1950).

oracular solemnity greater than the dramatic situation will bear. It is a short step from the sublime to the ridiculous.

We need not agree with one critic who declared the play to be 'nothing but a finely acted piece of flapdoodle' [9] if we suspect that a problem of human relationships and right conduct has been overlaid with needless mystery. Does this argue a coldly secular viewpoint in the observer? 'Literary criticism', Eliot has written, 'should be completed by criticism from a definite ethical and theological standpoint.'[10] It seems to me, not looking on the world through religious eyes, that *The Cocktail Party's* problems can be solved in secular terms. This is not necessarily to reject Eliot's solutions; but neither are they immune to criticism.

The Chamberlaynes' restored marriage is shown somewhat palely, in Act III, by small mutual courtesies and by the provision of sufficient eood for the second cocktail party, in contrast to the shortage on an farlier occasion. It may be unfair to take exception to this rather unexciting portrayal: simple domestic bliss is apt to be a low-temperature affair to the onlooker, especially when it is a patched-up *modus vivendi* between an unlovable woman and a man incapable of loving. Celia's death is a moving event *per se*, although it may be remarked that self-sacrifice is not confined to the religious. But it is somewhat chilling to find it surrounded with the trappings of Victorian missionary martyrdom, complete with 'foreign agitators' and heathen atrocities in a distant Imperial outpost. This relies too much on a ready-made push-button reaction in the spectator. Finally, it is not made clear how Peter is directed into the right path, which is one of the main dramatic functions of the last act. Perhaps his calm acceptance of his own mediocrity, now that his illusions about Celia have been dispelled, is in fact the fulfilment of his vocation. The play has already shown that it is Edward's role in life to accept

> The dull, the implacable,
> The indomitable spirit of mediocrity—

and this may also be Peter's role.

The parable, then, that Eliot sets before us in *The Cocktail Party* shows two ways of right conduct: the way of the world (the Chamberlaynes

[9] A. Dent, of the first production at the 1949 Edinburgh Festival (*News Chronicle*, 27 August, 1949).

[10] 'Religion and Literature', *Essays Ancient and Modern* (1936), p. 93.

and Peter) and the way of sainthood (Celia). The right decision for each person must be based on a recognition of one's *true self*—not mere desire and volition but 'the obstinate, the tougher self' that lies at a deeper level. Failure to live up to the imperatives of this deeper self is hell.

> What is hell? Hell is oneself,
> Hell is alone, the other figures in it
> Merely projections.   (p. 87)

According to E. Martin Browne, the first producer of *The Cocktail Party*, this was deliberately intended as a counterstatement[11] to Garcin's exclamation, 'Hell is . . . other people!' at the end of Sartre's *In Camera* (*Huis Clos*).

A total contrast in tone, language and intention is provided by John Arden's *Serjeant Musgrave's Dance*. This parable by one of the most controversial of the *nouvelle vague* playwrights who are making their presence felt in the British theatre, had rather a brief run at the Royal Court Theatre towards the end of 1959. Although its theatrical success was limited, it had the great virtue of crystallising and sharply dividing critical opinions; the one thing with which it did not meet was indifference. Some of the reactions to the play make an interesting study. They were, incidentally, comments on the parable as a dramatic form.

In the review from which one of the epigraphs heading this chapter was taken, Harold Hobson wrote:

> Another frightful ordeal . . . It is . . . simply no good at all for John Arden to come along to the Court Theatre, and employ actors, and a director, as skilled as Lindsay Anderson to tell us that war is wrong. We know that already. If we are told it again, we must be told entertainingly. For two long acts this play . . . may be said to be sinister, strange, even ominous: but entertaining it is not. The third act is a different matter . . .   (*Sunday Times*, 25 October, 1959)

Another critic was no friendlier:

> . . . our final impression is of an inordinately long-winded and rather foolish play.

Alan Pryce-Jones had this to say: 'This is a thoroughly honourable

[11] Introduction *Three European Plays* (Penguin Plays, 1958), p. 10.
D

evening, but at the end of it we are left to bode, and I boded' (*Observer*, 25 October, 1959). When Lindsay Anderson wrote him a private letter, stating that he detected 'in the notices of *Serjeant Musgrave* a kind of impatience—a fury at not being relaxed and entertained— which has led to grave injustice being done to a work of (I'm convinced) extraordinary talent and originality . . .' Pryce-Jones replied:

> . . . I am glad to return to a play which has received opinions so strongly divided: some hating it outright, others (like myself) having strong reserves about it, and a few delighting in it wholeheartedly . . .
>
> I called the evening an honourable one, not in a spirit of patronage, but because it is refreshing to find a playwright who makes his audience use their minds . . . Inevitably, this play recalls Brecht's *Mother Courage*, even to the extent of arousing similar misunderstandings between author and audience about the meaning of the central character. But John Arden has not, as yet, got anywhere near the technical mastery in centring his parable on a negative. The ideas are there all right, and at times the language leaps finely to meet them, but the parable itself shows a lack of authority. Having been put in a mood to accept it, we are never compelled thereafter to do so. We are still searching for a positive somewhere . . .
>
> To such technical problems Ibsen, perhaps, rather than Brecht holds the answer . . .   (*Observer*, 1 November, 1959)

Philip Hope-Wallace saw the play quite differently.

> *Serjeant Musgrave's Dance* by John Arden . . . is a long and challenging play. Even now, at curtain-fall, some of its import escapes me, but for the best part of three hours it has worked on my curiosity and often put that ill-definable theatrical spell on my imagination. I think it is something short of a great play. But wild horses wouldn't have dragged me from my seat before the end.
>
> . . . Pacificism, the author seems to say, which is only militarism written backwards, is futile. Better and safer the human anarchy of a strike-bound colliery township in all its hypocrisy and rancour.
>   (*Guardian*, 24 October, 1959)

Here we have three distinct attitudes: hostile, mixed, and friendly. Not surprisingly, it is the friendly critic who understands the message of the play. As Hope-Wallace suggests, the play asserts that somewhere, some time, the circle of violence engendered by war must be broken. Pitting force against force will always be self-defeating. We may feel

that the argument is loaded: Musgrave is too peculiar, indeed patho-
logical, a character to give any general validity to the parable. What
cannot be said is that the play is impenetrably obscure. Could it be that
some of the hostile critics found the message not so much obscure as
unpalatable?

Pryce-Jones was right in seeing *Serjeant Musgrave* as a negative
parable, Brechtian at least in this respect. We are only shown a *wrong*
reaction to an iniquitous state of affairs. But why should a playwright
dot all his I's and cross all his T's?

He must of course expect to run into trouble if he demands of the
spectator that he do his own brainwork in the theatre. A well-told
parable stirs up questions and then refuses to give all the answers. This
is hardly the proverbial tired businessman's idea of after-dinner fun,
and somebody has to give in—the would-be passive spectator or the
thrustful playwright. In the case of *Serjeant Musgrave's Dance* the anti-
parable faction won the day. The play has, however, been revived by
provincial theatres and university dramatic societies, and it was given
a successful TV production by Granada in 1961.

We recall that Brecht, who also insisted on the intellectual co-
operation of his audiences, frequently met with blank incomprehension
or subtle misunderstanding. We have seen before that Mother Courage,
for instance, cannot be conveniently labelled either all black or all
white; as in real life her character traits, or rather her actions, are
morally complex, and it is up to the spectator to do the sorting out.
She is in turn humorous, resourceful, crafty, loyal, irreverent, heroic,
hard-hearted, time-serving, compassionate, stupid, money-grubbing.
A lazy producer can save himself and his audience a good deal of
mental strain by ironing out the contradictions.

Thus, a common error is to give an heroic reading to her final
determination to get back into the business of war through which she
has lost all her children. Does she not—this is the easy sentimental
approach—symbolise the indestructible vitality of the common
people? She does not—or at least not in the first place. (Well-balanced
ambiguities are permissible.) The real point to be made is that she has
learnt nothing from her experiences. This is a less comforting doctrine
to the audience than the 'nobler' interpretation; but it will send them
out of the theatre (one hopes) checking the validity of some of their
own reflexes, and not merely happy in the thought that all's well with
a world where even war cannot kill off man's business instincts.

Similarly, it would make for an easier acceptance of *Serjeant Musgrave's Dance* if the fanatical sergeant were to be either wholly condemned or wholly approved of. But is it not disturbing to see a morally sensitive man trying to start a public massacre? It is. Does his fanaticism invalidate his moral protest as such? It does not. The contradiction between laudable indignation and reprehensible conclusions drawn from it may either alienate the spectators out of all sympathy with the play (as happened to some critics), or else it may jolt them into stirring moral speculations (as was the experience of some other critics).

It is only fair to say that Arden does not guide the spectators' response with any regimental firmness. The play is diffident in putting forward its moral—a diffidence in curious contrast with the violence of its action. Arden has explained this as follows:

> Complete pacificism is a very hard doctrine: and if this play appears to advocate it with perhaps some timidity, it is probably because I am naturally a timid man—and also because I know that if I am hit I very easily hit back: and I do not care to preach too confidently what I am not sure I can practise.   (Introduction, p. 7)

Perhaps a structural flaw in the play is the division in its dramatic purpose between the demands of suspense and surprise. Musgrave and the three Soldiers under his command are under great mental pressure, thinking about the impending day of reckoning, the recruiting-meeting in the town square. The study of this strain builds up suspense and constitutes the main psychological interest of the first two acts. Then, in Act III, the surprise is sprung: the hoisting up of the skeleton, and the training of the Gatling gun on the crowd. As a surprise it works powerfully. But the more genuine the surprise, the less the audience were in a position to understand the causes and the significance of the strain under which the Soldiers had been labouring before.

Arden's language in *Serjeant Musgrave's Dance* is earthy, with a rich north-country flavour; but it is not naturalistic for all that. It is a highly charged prose that at times abruptly rises into verse. There is no need to seek for the roots of Arden's dramatic poetry in Brecht, although the analogy is obvious enough.

> One does not have to work the characters up to a pitch of emotion . . . [writes Arden] in order for them to spring spontaneously into verse . . . There is no reason, it seems to me, why the transition

should be made at all, why the actor should not just come forward and say his verse bit, with everybody else talking prose . . . I personally believe that the traditional English ballads, even in their poorer forms such as the nineteenth-century street ballads, are a type of basic poetry which we despise at our peril. (N.T.M., 1961)

The essentially poetic conception of *Serjeant Musgrave's Dance* is reinforced by recurrent colour imagery—particularly black (the blackness of the night, of the coal-fields, of the haunted mind of Black Jack Musgrave himself); white (the snow of the winter scene, the white skeleton of Billy Hicks); and red (the colour of blood, of the Mayor's gown and the Soldiers' coats). Visually as well as verbally, these colours are firmly established in the very first scene, with references to the darkness of the night, the snow, the red and black of the Soldiers' pack of cards, and the Bargee's taunting of the Soldiers as 'blood-red roses'. Arden has suggested the paintings of L. S. Lowry, in all their starkness, as a good starting-point for visualising the play (Introduction, p. 5). In the Royal Court production, several other clear, hard colours supported the basic scheme we have just noted. 'The opening of the Second Act in the public house is set in brown and blue, against a pale blue winter curtain; it has the strict severity of a Dutch painting, and takes up exactly the moral precision of Musgrave himself'.[12] Indeed, Arden's chief reason for setting the play, with deliberate vagueness, between 1860 and 1880 was not that he wanted to evoke the past as such but rather that the period gave him the clear theatrical and poetic image of the redcoats, the blood-red roses.[13]

This colour image takes on its full meaning in the song Attercliffe sings in the prison scene:

> I plucked a blood-red rose-flower down
> And gave it to my dear.
> I set my foot out across the sea
> And she never wept a tear.
>
> I came back home as gay as a bird
> I sought her out and in:
> And I found her at last in a little attic room
> With a napkin round her chin.

---

[12] S. Hall, *New Left Review* (1959), p. 51.
[13] I am indebted for this information to John Arden.

> Oh are you eating meat, I said,
> Or are you eating fish?
> I'm eating an apple was given me today,
> The sweetest I could wish.
>
> Your blood-red rose is withered and gone
> And fallen on the floor:
> And he who brought the apple down
> Shall be my darling dear.
>
> For the apple holds a seed will grow
> In live and lengthy joy
> To raise a flourishing tree of fruit
> For ever and a day.
> With fal-la-la-the-dee, toor-a-ley,
> For ever and a day.   (pp. 103-4)

On the surface this song, an authentic echo of the traditional ballad, only tells the story, in veiled poetical form, of Attercliffe's unfaithful wife who was seduced by the grocer. But the imagery is switched and extended when Attercliffe adds in the final words of the play:

> They're going to hang us up a length higher nor most apple-trees grow, Serjeant. D'you reckon we can start an orchard?

And now the rose stands not only for Attercliffe and his fellow-soldiers: it stands for violence as such and, more specifically, the impending death of Musgrave and his men. The apple becomes a complementary image symbolising the ways of peace. Obliquely the question has been put to the audience: Will the Soldiers' death have been in vain? Can it be given any posthumous meaning? Can the circle of violence be broken?

In its protest against the folly and beastliness of war, *Serjeant Musgrave's Dance* does not use the all-out expressionism of *The Silver Tassie*. But like O'Casey's play it uses elements of realism in order to build up an image going beyond realism. The parable has been made to yield poetry-of-the-theatre.

Indeed some such poetry-of-the-theatre is common to all the parable plays discussed above, however much they may differ in dramatic technique or poetic intensity. And here we come to the feature that gives the parable such a powerful effect on the stage, over and above the intellectual and moral quality of its message. Although it clearly must appeal to the spectator's reason, it has a quality beyond mere rationality, an aesthetic appeal that teases and haunts the mind. If we regard the parable as a mathematical demonstration, the equation never quite works out, without for that reason being wrong. An incommensurable element remains; the message gains by being more than a message. Apart from what they may teach us about how to order our lives, the Wise and the Foolish Virgins stay with us as an image.

*   *   *

Even if in audience appeal it has not been able to rival *Chu Chin Chow*, *Salad Days* or *Dry Rot*, the dramatic parable has for a long time been a fruitful aspect of drama in the English language. Now that new voices are coming to be heard in the theatre of this country (Behan, Jellicoe, Bolt, Pinter, Wesker, Osborne and others, writers more sharply aware of the new realities of the world of today) we may expect the parable, with or without social and political commitment, to have a new lease of life. There is no reason to think that it will occupy the centre of the stage. Nor is there any reason to think that any one theatrical style—illusionism or symbolism, revue-fashion or ballad-fashion—will come to embody it exclusively.

But a doctrinal theatre is needed today as much as ever it was, seventy years or seven hundred years ago: a theatre which will do more than render men harmlessly happy, although incidentally it will render them (purposefully, rather than harmlessly) happy as well: a theatre once again become a *speculum vitae*, a lens for focusing the mind and energy of the nation, a forum, a temple and a song.

Notes

George Bernard Shaw (1856–1950) was born in Dublin, and came to London in 1876. From January 1895 to May 1898 Shaw wrote theatre criticism for *The Saturday Review*, under Frank Harris's editorship: these important statements are in *Our Theatre in the Nineties*, 3 vols. (1931). Shaw had to wait for the Vedrenne–Barker era at the Court Theatre (1904–7) for the artistic understanding he required. Shaw produced his own plays there, and Granville–Barker the rest of the repertory. The success of *John Bull's Other Island*, which ran for 121 performances, did much to establish Shaw's audience: other Court successes were *You Never Can Tell* (149 performances) and *Man and Superman* (176 performances). From 1901 to 1913 Shaw wrote a play a year, and the following chapter is principally concerned with this central period of Shaw's career. *Heartbreak House*, begun in 1913, was produced in 1921, and *St. Joan* in 1924. Shaw was awarded the Nobel Prize for Literature in 1925.

Editions. Constable publish the Collected Editions of Shaw's works (1930 onward). There is a *Complete Plays* (Odhams, 1934) containing all the major works, and these are also available in Penguin editions. *Complete Prefaces* (1934) is a necessary addition to the *Complete Plays*, to which page references are given in this chapter.

Criticism. Substantial criticism of Shaw is found in A. Henderson's *George Bernard Shaw: Man of the Century* (1956), and Eric Bentley's *Bernard Shaw* (1957; revised edition). Among early lives are those by Holbrook Jackson (1907), Frank Harris (1931), G. K. Chesterton (1909), and P. P. Howe (1915). There are important collections of Shaw's correspondence: Alan Dent edited *Bernard Shaw and Mrs Patrick Campbell: Their Correspondence* (1952); Christopher St. John edited *Ellen Terry and Bernard Shaw* (1949); and C. B. Purdom *Bernard Shaw's Letters to Granville Barker* (1956). Further studies are by St. John Ervine (1956) and Alick West (1950). A comprehensive study is Hesketh Pearson's *G.B.S. A Full-Length Portrait* (1951); A. C. Ward's *Bernard Shaw* (1951) has a bibliography. Among special studies are E. Strauss's *Bernard Shaw, Art and Socialism* (1942), and Christopher Caudwell's 'George Bernard Shaw: a study of the bourgeois superman', in *Studies in a Dying Culture* (1938). Of theatrical interest are Desmond MacCarthy's *Shaw's Plays in Review* (1951), and Eric Bentley's *The Modern Theatre* (1948) and Francis Fergusson's *The Idea of a Theatre* (1949). F. P. W. McDowell in *Drama Survey 1* (1961) takes 'Another Look at Bernard Shaw' and lists recent books and articles. In their *Theatrical Companion to Shaw* (1954), R. Mander and J. Mitchenson provide a pictorial record of first performances of his plays from 1892 to 1950.

Since this chapter was written, Dan Lawrence has edited Shaw's *Collected Letters* (1965) and Martin Meisel written an illuminating study of *Shaw and the Nineteenth Century Theater* (1963).

III

George Bernard Shaw

A. R. JONES

★

SINCE the recent revival of interest in dramatic art, Shaw has dropped out of the centre of serious critical discussion. English critics and dramatists look to Europe for their models and stimulus, to Brecht and Ionesco as they once did to Ibsen and Chekhov. It is ironical that just as Shaw once rejected the work of his contemporaries and dismissed the theatre of his time as moribund, so, in turn, Shaw himself appears to have been repudiated. In a recent issue of the *Twentieth Century*[1] devoted to contemporary theatre, the contributors to which were largely playwrights, actors and directors, Shaw is not mentioned at all. Shaw's struggle to revive the moribund late-Victorian stage is closely parallelled by the contemporary attempt to revitalise the popular theatre. Indeed, had Shaw not already done a good deal of the work, we probably would not now be talking in terms of a theatrical revival at all. Whatever vitality has remained in the theatre during the first half of the century is largely attributable to his efforts. Shaw succeeded in relating the world of the theatre more closely to the intellectual and social life of his time and his success or failure may surely have some relevance to the recent attempt to do just that. Yet the younger dramatists have failed to capitalise on his achievement. One wonders why those playwrights, such as Osborne, Wesker or Arden, who are themselves interested in once again using the theatre as a vehicle for social and political ideas reject the example of Shaw.

Shaw carried through his fight virtually single-handed although he had an ally in Ibsen, or at least in Ibsen as he chose to see him. The forces ranged against him were considerably more confident, more formidable and more commercialised than those that face the present-day dramatist. The Establishment was much more firmly entrenched;

---

[1] February, 1961.

the theatre largely in the hands of actor managers, and our contemporary public sapped by mass media might be considered vital compared
with the late-Victorian Philistinism fed by material complacency.
Technically his point of attack was 'what was called a well made play' [2]
and 'plays written round popular performers who give value to otherwise useless plays by investing them with their own attractiveness'. His
aim was to dramatise 'not only ourselves, but ourselves in our own
situations' and thus to bring drama more closely into line with the
social realities of his time. Indeed, Shaw's diagnosis of the decadent state
of the theatre has a very familiar ring, and his proposals for the reform
of drama have a modernity which his plays appear to lack. He was
unashamedly asking for naturalism in the theatre and for plays which
were primarily concerned with the discussion of moral problems:

> Now an interesting play cannot in the nature of things mean any-
> thing but a play in which problems of conduct and character of
> personal importance to the audience are raised and suggestively
> discussed . . . the drama arises through a conflict of unsettled ideals
> rather than through vulgar attachments, rapacities, generosities,
> resentments, ambitions, misunderstandings, oddities and so forth as
> to which moral question is raised. The conflict is not between clear
> right and wrong: the villain is as conscientious as the hero, if not
> more so; in fact, the question which makes the play interesting (when
> it is interesting) is which is the villain and which the hero. Or, to put
> it another way, there are no villains and no heroes.

Discussion was to be the centre of the new drama; the 'well made
play' that was constructed with 'an exposition in the first act, a situation in the second, and unravelling in the third' was to be replaced by
plays in which the exposition is followed by 'situation, and discussion'
or which begin with discussion and end with action or in which discussion interpenetrates the action from beginning to end. His objective
was to ally theatrical spectacle with the discussion of problematic
moral ideas so that drama became an efficient vehicle for carrying
ideas into the audience. In formulating his conception of the way in
which he saw drama developing, Shaw always kept distinct in his
mind the sense of theatrical invention, on the one hand, and moral
didacticism on the other—in other words, form and content were seen
by him as separate entities. 'Rhetoric, irony, argument, paradox,
epigram, parable, the rearrangement of haphazard facts into orderly

[2] *The Quintessence of Ibsenism*, 'The Technical Novelty in Ibsen's Plays'.

and intelligent situations: these are both the oldest and the newest arts of the drama; and your plot construction and art of preparation are only the tricks of theatrical talent and the shifts of moral sterility, not the weapons of dramatic genius.'

The 'weapons of dramatic genius' were the ability to manipulate the discussion of interesting moral problems within the framework of a naturalistic drama so as to involve the audience, so that the audience 'are not flattered spectators killing an idle hour' but 'guilty creatures sitting at a play.' They are involved not in the enjoyment of a pastime or entertainment but are involved as if watching a murder trial—and a murder trial, in fact, in which they themselves are seated in the dock. Shaw conveniently summarises for us what he calls 'the technical novelties' of the new drama:

> first, the introduction of the discussion and its development until it so overspreads and interpenetrates the action that it finally assimilates it, making play and discussion practically identical; and, second, as a consequence of making the spectators themselves the persons of the drama and the incidents of their own lives its incidents, the disuse of the old stage tricks by which audiences had to be induced to take an interest in unreal people and improbable circumstances, and the substitution of a forensic technique of recrimination, disillusion, and penetration through ideals to the truth, with a free use of all the rhetorical and lyrical arts of the orator, the preacher, the pleader, and the rhapsodist.

Although he suggests that the discussion and the play should be 'practically identical', he nevertheless sees them as two separate entities. Also he is interested in involving the audience, not in the action of the play, but through the action in the discussion which arises more or less naturally out of the immediate dramatic situation. He associates this technique with Ibsen—or rather with the quintessence of Ibsen— though it has never been in doubt that Shaw is speaking not of Ibsen's, but of his own dramatic theory and practice.

Shaw was not originally associated with the theatre, except in his capacity as a dramatic critic, but came to the theatre from the outside. Had he started his career as an actor, he would not, one suspects, have talked so slightingly about plot construction and theatrical inventive- ness. Shaw's first attempt to write a play was in collaboration with William Archer. Archer considered that he could construct a play but could not write dialogue; Shaw, on the other hand, felt that he could

write dialogue, but had little patience with construction and it was on
this basis that the collaboration began. 'Archer, with an encyclopaedic
knowledge of the world's drama, a naïve love for it, unbounded
admiration for the "well-made piece" in the Scribe-Dumas *fils* manner,
and an inventive faculty of the feeblest; Shaw, with a genius for clever
and witty sayings, which he had developed by years of platform
speaking, and with the utmost scorn for plays with plots, which he
lumped with artificial flowers and clockwork mice.' [3]

The collaboration was hardly successful; Shaw wrote the first act
without using Archer's plot at all, and having then used up all the plot
at the beginning of the second act, went back to Archer and demanded
some more. The partnership collapsed before it had begun, but it
stimulated Shaw to write his first play, *Widowers' Houses*, which was
quickly followed by *The Philanderer* and *Mrs. Warren's Profession*. In
these *Plays Unpleasant*, Shaw circumvents his inability to construct
plot and incident largely by using the plot of the despised 'well-made'
play and parodying it. The discussion is loosely fitted into the plot and
arises, though somewhat awkwardly, out of the dramatic situation. The
characters are unnaturally self-conscious about themselves and their
motives and Shaw's adaptation of Ibsen's retrospective method—that
is the method by which the main action out of which the play arises is
completed before the curtain goes up—allows scope for a good deal of
analysis and diagnosis. Shaw set so much store by the discussion that
he was annoyed with de Lange, the first producer of *Widowers'
Houses*, for not allowing a blackboard on the stage so that the value
theory of Stanley Jevons could be explained to the audience.[4] Yet,
whatever the dramatic inadequacies of these *Plays Unpleasant*, Shaw's
anger with society is never in doubt. He attacks poverty and slums,
sexual morals, and hypocrisy, and the three plays are sustained by the
force of his moral indignation and by the way in which he balances and
dramatises the debate between the various attitudes. If the plots and
characters are themselves flat and uninteresting, the discussion is kept
suspenseful and alive. The interest of the plays resides chiefly in the
animation of the dispute, the conflict is between ideas which are given
a general validity, carried by characters and situations which are not
entirely credible. Shaw partially succeeded in the attempt to dramatise
ideas and ideological conflict, but it is the characters who are moved

[3] A. Henderson, *George Bernard Shaw: Man of the Century* (1956), p. 523.
[4] *ibid.*, pp. 539–540.

about by the ideas and not the ideas which arise out of the dramatic conflict between characters. Yet Shaw in these plays is attempting to affirm individual human vitality and to expose the illusions with which society surrounds itself in order to hide its own self-interest. His debt to Ibsen is clearly stated; *The Philanderer* revolves around the Ibsen Club and the idea of the New Woman, and in the famous last scene of *Mrs. Warren's Profession*, Vivie leaves her mother in a way recalling Nora leaving his husband and family in *The Doll's House*. But Shaw has captured little of the dramatic inevitability of Ibsen's plays and substitutes ironic comedy for pitiless tragedy. Moreover, in spite of their assumed naturalism, these plays have an artificial and contrived quality which is not wholly compensated for by the sharp, witty exchanges between characters. All three are anti-romantic comedies, but none of them entirely carries dramatic conviction. While Shaw shows some affection towards his characters, he does not allow them to take on a dramatic existence of their own and while his sense of the ironic and comic possibilities of his plot are fully exploited, he lacks all sense of pathos. His characters and plots move towards discovery, but he does not convince us that they move also towards self-awareness. Clearly, Shaw was misled by his belief that in writing plays, the plot was unimportant and that if he could re-vitalise the content of drama, the form would look after itself. As a result his plays leave the audience with an unsatisfactory impression of the tension existing between content and form. Moreover, Shaw's interest in his characters as representative of certain economic and social features of the contemporary scene, overlays the audience's interest in them as dramatic characters in their own right.

Eric Bentley considers that Vivie's scenes with her mother in *Mrs. Warren's Profession*, are 'first-rate', 'presented with a poignant irony only equalled in modern drama by certain scenes in Ibsen and Strindberg' [5] yet in these scenes, although the audience is aware of the conflict of moral and economic attitudes represented by the daughter and her mother, the emotional relationship between the two is not developed dramatically so as to be emotionally convincing. We, as audience, are expected to assume that a 'strong emotional nexus . . . ties Vivie to her mother' merely because they are stated as being daughter and mother although the play depends for its effect on the fact that they are otherwise strangers. It is undoubtedly ironic that Vivie

[5] *Bernard Shaw* (revised edition, 1957), pp. 105–6.

should first accept her mother as 'a wonderful woman . . . stronger than all England' when she learns of her profession and her motives in joining it, and then reject her when she realises that in spite of everything her mother too is 'a conventional woman at heart'. But the irony can carry only intellectual assent, not dramatic conviction, and is hardly poignant.

In the *Plays Pleasant* and in *Three Plays for Puritans*, Shaw continues to use the plots of romantic comedy and to adapt them to his purposes, but the dramatic conflicts are more sharply defined and, for the most part, the discussion interpenetrates the action. *Arms and the Man*, *The Man of Destiny* and *You Never Can Tell* are light-hearted compared with *Plays Unpleasant*. *Arms and the Man* parodies the traditional romantic play in which the ideals of love and war are first satirised by the presence of the realist Bluntschli and then confirmed when he falls a victim to love and idealism. Shaw clearly associated his play with Ibsen:

> My Bulgarian hero, quite as much as Helmer in *A Doll's House*, was a hero shown from the modern woman's point of view. I complicated the psychology by making him catch glimpse after glimpse of his own aspect and conduct from this point of view himself, as all men are beginning to do more or less now, the result, of course, being the most horrible dubiety on his part as to whether he is really a brave and chivalrous gentleman, or a humbug and a moral coward. His actions, equally of course, are hopelessly irreconcilable with either theory. Need I add that if the straightforward Helmer, a very honest and ordinary middle-class man misled by false ideals of womanhood, bewildered the public and was finally let down as a selfish cad by all the Helmers in the audience, *a fortiori* my introspective Bulgarian never had a chance.[6]

Moreover, he told his biographer that '*Arms and the Man* was an attempt at Hamlet in the comic spirit: Shakespeare, modified by Ibsen, and comically transfigured by Shaw'.[7] The play itself hardly seems durable enough to sustain the weight of such comparisons. Illusion and reality are contrasted and illusion—modified by contact with reality—prevails. The play is lively, the action moves quickly towards sudden reversals and discoveries, and the wit is confident. In fact, in these plays Shaw is learning just how to construct a 'well-made play' or, at least, how best to adapt the theatrical stock-in-trade to serve his own purposes. In *Arms and the Man* he rings the changes on romantic comedy, in

[6] Henderson, *op. cit.*, pp. 539-40.   [7] *ibid.*, p. 584.

Man of Destiny, as in *Caesar and Cleopatra*, on heroic drama, and in *You Never Can Tell* on the drawing-room farce. It is true that, as he says in the Preface to the play, 'the much criticised Swiss Officer in *Arms and the Man* is not a conventional stage soldier', nor is his Napoleon the conventional Bonaparte, nor Caesar the conventional Roman emperor, but all these exist, dramatically, in so far as they off-set their conventional stage counterparts, just as the plays in which they appear are off-set against the plots of their conventional *genre*.

Yet clearly Shaw was, consciously or otherwise, trying to find a new dramatic form in which discussion and drama would coalesce and he tried to construct such a formula from the elements of the conventional theatrical tradition. He attempted to reform the theatre by leading it from the inside, rather than by revolutionary onslaught. From *Widowers' Houses* to *Captain Brassbound's Conversion*, ten plays in less than ten years, he produced an amazing variety of plays, but although he had already done much to rehabilitate wit, intelligence and social comment in the theatre, he had not achieved a completely individual voice. By parodying the plays of his immediate predecessors, he had produced plays superior to anything they had managed but he had not produced anything different in kind. What he was clearly looking for was a way to present the interplay of ideas in the theatre within a form tight enough to give the ideas drama and direction but flexible enough to ensure that the ideas themselves do not become distorted or falsified through the exigencies of plot or character. In *Candida*, and *The Devil's Disciple*, for instance, though the plots are close to Victorian melodrama, the interest remains centred on the dialectic maintained by the three characters caught in a traditional eternal triangle situation. As Shaw explained, *The Devil's Disciple* is 'stuffed with everything from the ragbag of melodrama; reading of a will, heroic sacrifice, courtmartial, gallows, eleventh-hour reprieve, all complete with—as Ellen Terry used to say of her acting—just that little bit of my own that makes all the difference'.[8] The vitality of Dick Dudgeon is matched only by the intelligence and aristocracy of General Burgoyne; the inhumanity and hypocrisy of the family and townsfolk, represents the system supported by organised religion and the stupidity of General Swindon, the stupidity of authoritarian government. Both Anderson, the preacher, and Judith, his wife, undergo a conversion towards self-awareness and away from the conventional patterns of

[8] *ibid.*, p. 549.

behaviour in which society has cast them. Both are affected by Dick
Dudgeon's vitality and both, like him, learn to stand by 'the laws of
their own natures'. The improbable melodrama of the dramatic situation is overlooked because Shaw himself refuses to take the plot
seriously and because interest is kept alive by sparkling dialogue, quick
reverses, and an interest in the resolution of the situation between
Judith, her husband, and Dick Dudgeon. Shaw is so successful in keeping our minds on the discussion, and eyes averted from the plot, that
when Dick casually mentions the death of his mother the remark goes
almost unnoticed. In *Candida* the traditional eternal triangle is similarly
played out as a domestic comedy between a parson, his wife, and a
poet—also of the devil's party—and again they learn to stand by 'the
laws of their natures'. The reversal of roles in which Dick becomes the
puritan and Anderson the rather romantic man of action, is paralleled
when Marchbanks finds a strength of character he had not thought he
possessed and Morell comes to recognise his own weakness and
dependence. In *Caesar and Cleopatra*, the sense of fantasy that Shaw
developed later emerged for the first time. The interest is again dialectic,
not really in the dramatic history of the relationship between Cleopatra
and Caesar but in two spheres of intellectual and artistic interests which
meet, discuss and define their differences, and separate. Both in the
process define 'the laws of their own natures', and, thus, in the typical
Shaw manner, are educated through conflict when their way of life is
challenged and they are faced with the realities of choice and the
realities of their own situation. The life of a Shaw character begins
where the play ends, and the play is in itself a testing and a discarding
of illusion. The characters like Vivie, Judith or Morell are dispossessed
of their illusions, others like Anderson, Marchbanks, Cleopatra are
converted from illusion to reality. At odds with the tenets of naturalism
—for which he professed to stand—Shaw is never in doubt that drama
is a matter of illusion and that, far from mirroring nature, reality and
life were outside the theatre, with the audience and not on the stage.
Yet he was always careful to define his characters' social, economic
background, the context in which their role is rooted. His sharp sense
of the contemporary scene and of contemporary habits of thought, link
the plays to the wider issues from which the discussion springs and in
which it has a reality altogether larger than the purely theatrical.
Widowers' Houses and *Mrs. Warren's Profession* are frankly doctrinaire
but from then on the social implications of the plays are less directly

concerned with inciting political action and turned more towards
revealing the morality or immorality in man's relations with man and
with society—the traditional concern of the comic dramatist.

★   ★   ★

In *Man of Destiny* and in *Caesar and Cleopatra* Shaw begins to take an
interest in the extraordinary man, an interest which overtakes to some
extent his professed interest in the ordinary man in ordinary situations.
This extraordinary man becomes the superman in *Man and Superman*:
embodiment of the Bergsonian life force. The war between the sexes
that Shaw carries on so brilliantly in his earlier plays, becomes the war
between the artist and the mother-woman. The woman-question,
which Shaw took over from J. S. Mill, is now not merely a social and
political concern, a matter of emancipation and social equality, but of
instinctual life itself. The extraordinary man is, in *Man and Superman*,
mated with the extraordinary woman; with anti-romantic reluctance
but with the feeling that he is serving the high destiny of life itself.
It may well be objected that the traditional romantic illusions that Shaw
discards so firmly are beginning to be replaced by illusions equally as
romantic. Shaw reverses the traditional roles by dramatising the pursuit of the man by the woman. John Tanner, in spite of the mytho-
logical aura Shaw's stage directions throw around him, evades Ann
Whitefield's assaults with the traditional flirtatious vocabulary of the
stage virgin, while Ann pursues him with purposeful single-minded-
ness. Shaw had reversed these roles before, in *Widowers' Houses* and
The Philanderer, but in *Man and Superman* he sees the pursuit of the
male by the female as a biological and metaphysical necessity. It
becomes not merely an occasion for comedy but, as the Don Juan
interlude makes clear, an opportunity to expound a Bergsonian idea of
godhead and human destiny. The capitulation of Tanner to Ann is due
to his realisation of what Don Juan calls 'life's incessant aspiration to
higher organization, wider, deeper, intenser self-consciousness, and
clearer self-understanding'. The Bergsonian conviction that life is
evolving towards the creation of higher and more complex forms of
life clearly appealed to Shaw's optimistic rationalism and fitted in well
with his Fabian belief in the inevitability of gradual social amelioration.
In Dick Dudgeon the vitality of the romantic hero is allied to a sensitive
Protestant conscience; in Ann Whitfield, impulsive, 'vital genius' is
associated with self-control and respectability.

E

In his ideas as in his conception of character and plot, Shaw is not challenging the conventions of his audience head-on but is rather attempting to extend the range of possibilities within what he knows to be restricting and hypocritical conventions. In social and political terms, as in terms of the drama, he is engaged, not in revolution but in reform. Ann is determined and self-willed but in her dedication to the higher purposes of the life force she carefully maintains the decorum of Victorian morality. Indeed, Shaw's social and artistic attitudes are closer to Dickens than to Ibsen and his Bergsonian Protestantism recalls Dickens' optimistic faith in the principle of Universal Benevolence. Shaw learnt how to turn the stock-in-trade of the Victorian theatre to his own advantage. By accepting the stage conventions as he found them, he translated the stage into a forum for intelligent, witty discussion of contemporary ideas. His intentions were frankly didactic and reformist but just as he never really challenged the basic conventions of the theatre as he inherited them, so he never really questions the assumptions of Victorian life. His socialism is balanced by his admiration for the Carlylean Superman; his rationalism by the mystique of Bergsonian metaphysics; and his realisation of social evils by his belief in the essential benevolence of humanity. He shared the Victorian's profound faith in the inevitability of progress and subscribed to their optimism about the future.

His more thorough-going analysis of society is contained in *Major Barbara*. Shaw's biographer, Archibald Henderson, voices the traditional view of the play in describing it as 'a powerful sermon, with the ironic ending: the unscrupulous use of wealth and power triumphing over the spirit of Christianity and benevolence because its adherents are too lazy and timid to "turn their oughts to shalls" . . . Shaw affirms that in the case of Undershaft as well as in that of Mrs. Warren, Capitalism forces an inescapable decision: between the "crime" of poverty and the social "virtue" of a lucrative profession'.[9] Yet, as Henderson reports Shaw as saying, it is not 'a choice between opulent villainy and humble virtue, but between energetic enterprise and cowardly infamy'. The play is, in fact, a study in the realities of power as opposed to the shams of false and hypocritical ideals and conventions. The greatest sin is poverty and the triumvirate of Undershaft, the realistic man of power, Cusins the civilised man of thought, and Barbara, the idealist, is one that may change the face of society.

[9] *op. cit.*, p. 584.

Barbara, disillusioned with the Salvation Army because it is maintained on the profits of making whisky and munitions, is converted
to her father's business when she learns the relation between money,
power and idealism. That Cusins, the professor of Greek, should be
chosen to inherit the business of munitions-making established a
realistic relation between power and thought, money and morality.
It is not a question of unscrupulous power triumphing over apathetic
Christianity, but an indictment of religious and political idealism for
neglecting the social realities of power. Poverty is the root of social
evil, and money the source of social power is the inevitable conclusion
towards which both Barbara and Cusins are forced. Morality is not a
matter merely of good and evil but is also a question of the weak and
the strong, and only when men are safe enough from poverty and
insecurity can they afford to consider questions of morality at all. This
is the lesson that Snobby Price has learnt through experience of
poverty: 'I'm fly enough to know wots inside the law and wots outside it; and inside it I do as the capitalists do: pinch wot I can lay me
ands on: In a proper state of society I am sober industrious and honest:
in Rome, so to speak, I do as the Romans do.' Undershaft knows that
he can convert a 'half-starved ruffian in West Ham' by a regular wage
and decent housing so that by the end of a year 'he will shake hands
with a duchess at a Primrose League meeting, and join the Conserva-
tive Party'. Shaw clearly realised what many Labour reformers never
have, that working-class prosperity leads to social snobbery and
political apathy. Idealism, he knew, must be well founded on an
analysis of power and power was an economic reality. Barbara's conversion from the Salvation Army to the world of Undershaft is the
transition from illusion to reality. The play is not so much an attack
by a Socialist on Capitalism, as a statement of a Fabian that healthy
Socialism could only grow gradually out of a healthy capitalism. Just
as in *Man and Superman* Shaw sees life evolving towards higher and
more complex beings, so in *Major Barbara* he sees the new society
evolving from the old; Barbara and Cusins are the natural inheritors of
social power, for, as Undershaft knows, the idealists must first capture
the source of power before attempting to transform society.

★   ★   ★

Between 1901 and 1913, that is between *Man and Superman* and
Heartbreak House, Shaw produced a play a year. It is the period of *The*

Doctor's Dilemma, Androcles and the Lion, Pygmalion, the two discussion plays, *Getting Married* and *Misalliance,* as well as, of course, *Major Barbara.* He learnt to move easily and with superb skill within the conventions of the comedy of manners. Indeed, Francis Fergusson criticises Shaw for adapting too readily to these conventions:

> If one thinks over these elements—the sentimental story, the farcical-profound paradoxical thesis, and the complacency of the audience—one may get spiritual indigestion. But if one sees a performance, one may understand how it all hangs together for those two quick hours: it is because its basis in the upholstered world of the carriage-trade is never violated. On this basis it is acceptable as a string of jokes which touch nothing. And Shavian comedy of this period still flatters and delights our prosperous suburbs.[10]

Clearly the 'upholstered world of the carriage-trade' is not dramatically violated, but we are also aware how successfully drawing-room comedy has been transformed into a vehicle for ideas and, moreover, for ideas not usually used as furnishings in upholstered Victorian drawing-rooms. The characters may not be life-like, nor the settings really convincing, but the vitality of the plays is in the argument, in the dialectic itself. He has mastered the theatrical conventions to such a degree that he seems able to interest an audience dramatically whatever the nature of the discussion. His control of dramatic techniques, his ability to hold an audience, cannot be lightly dismissed, and to capture an audience's attention while questions of morality, politics and metaphysics are endlessly debated, calls for a considerable dramatic talent. Moreover, the fact that this talent, as Francis Fergusson testifies, 'still flatters and delights' says something for the vitality and freshness of the plays. The same cannot be said for other Victorian drawing-room comedies. Indeed, Shaw exploits the full range of comic possibilities within the conventions of the comedy of manners while, at the same time, developing a robust and vigorous dialectic. *Getting Married,* for example, is plotted as a rough-and-tumble drawing-room farce, yet presents a wide variety of possible attitudes to marriage and exposes the hypocrisies of the existing laws governing marriage. Also, *Misalliance,* though less controlled and less inventive as farce, explores the relations between the sexes and between parents and children. The most obvious feature of Shaw's mature drama is its theatrical effectiveness *in spite* of the limitations of the conventions in which he worked.

[10] *The Idea of a Theatre* (1949), p. 194.

Edmund Wilson observes that, 'it always used to be said of Shaw that he was primarily not an artist, but a promulgator of certain ideas. The truth is, I think, that he is a considerable artist, but that his ideas—that is, his social philosophy proper—have always been confused and uncertain.' Wilson goes on to argue that Shaw's success as an artist is to a large extent attributable to the confusion and conflict of his own ideas. 'In the theatre', he says, 'Shaw's conflicts of impulse, his intellectual flexibility and his genius for legerdemain—all the qualities which have had the effect of weakening his world as a publicist—have contributed to his success as an artist.' [11] Seen in this light, the characteristic Shavian irony is the immediate dramatic result of the conflict in Shaw himself. Moreover, such a view has the advantage of freeing Shaw the propagandist from Shaw the dramatist and of enabling us to see him in the context of the theatre rather than in the context of the history of ideas.

As a dramatist who enlivened the theatrical scene of his time, Shaw is writing in the tradition of Goldsmith, Sheridan and Wilde. As a thinker, dramatising the conflict in his own mind, he faithfully reflected the intellectual scene of his time. Shaw belongs quite firmly to the world of the Edwardians and late Victorians. *Pygmalion* is the dramatic expression of the characteristic Victorian success story. Shaw called the play a romance because, he explained, 'it is a story of a poor girl who meets a gentleman at a church door, and is transformed by him, like Cinderella, into a beautiful lady'.[12] Eliza Doolittle escapes from her class through education in diction, manners and taste and, like Shaw's earlier heroes and heroines, achieves sufficient independence of mind and character to enable her to follow the laws of her own nature. She does not find her prince and marriage, but finds herself. Eric Bentley remarks that as a play 'it is a singularly elegant structure', but it is a 'personal play' without any wider implications other than the conflict between 'vitality and the system'.[13] Yet Shaw has in this play dramatised the liberal Victorian myth of personal independence through economic security and social salvation through education. In spite of his derisive attacks upon society, Shaw shared the optimistic faith of his contemporaries. Shaw, in fact, conferred religious status upon the Victorians' optimism by elevating the belief in progress to the principle of life itself. His belief in the superman and his faith in

[11] *The Triple Thinkers* (1939), p. 229.
[12] Henderson, *op. cit.*, p. 616.   [13] *op. cit.*, p. 124.

evolution came to dominate his writings and his drama. He saw his own positive contribution to drama in this light:

> . . . I tried slum-landlordism, doctrinaire Free Love (pseudo-Ibsenism), prostitution, militarism, marriage, history, current politics, natural Christianity, national and individual character, paradoxes of conventional society, husband-hunting, questions of conscience, professional delusions and impostures, all worked into a series of comedies of manners in the classic fashion . . . But this, though it occupied me and established me professionally, did not constitute me an iconographer of the religion of my time, and thus fulfil my natural function as an artist. I was quite conscious of this: for I had always known that civilization needs a religion as a matter of life and death; and as the conception of Creative Evolution developed, I saw that we were at last within reach of a faith . . . Accordingly, in 1901, I took the legend of Don Juan in its Mozartian form and made a dramatic parable of Creative Evolution.   [Preface to *Back to Methuselah*]

The 'cyclonic energy' which, Shaw thought, characterised the work of Michelangelo, Beethoven and Goethe was derived from a religion of life, a belief in the dynamism of the superman; the energy and vitality of his own heroes and heroines—particularly heroines—was derived directly from his religion of Creative Evolution, the irresistible surge of life upwards towards higher forms. This 'religion of life' whose primary article of faith is the assumption of the perfectibility of the individual, associates Shaw not only with his contemporaries but also with the romanticism of Rousseau, Godwin and Shelley. Bergson's metaphysics have their source in biological theory and depend on his interpretation of evolution; Shaw's adaption of Bergson brings together social, political, economic and literary romanticism, established, he thought, on the 'science of metabiology'. In fact, as in the dramatic field, Shaw breathed new life into the moribund conventions of the Victorian theatre, so in his thought and beliefs he resuscitated the dying impulse of nineteenth-century romanticism.

In *Pygmalion* the ascent of Eliza from flower-girl to duchess to self-sufficient womanhood is a fable that dramatically expresses Shaw's complex romanticism. In *Heartbreak House*, which is more allegory than fable, in criticising the direction in which he sees society to be evolving, he expresses his romantic dissatisfactions. *Pygmalion* is closer to fantasy than to social reality, but in *Heartbreak House* the idealists are all disenchanted and the realists overwhelmed. The mood of disillusionment and futility which is sustained throughout *Heartbreak House* owes something to Chekhov although the characters and ideas are clearly Shaw's. Towards the end of the play Shotover warns that society is in danger of foundering on the rocks for lack of navigation, but the central characters, disillusioned in their personal lives, do not abandon their dream of a regenerated society. Yet it is not only 'the cultivated, leisured Europe before the war' that is exposed and destroyed in this play. The catastrophe of the war finally and dramatically marked the end of an era and severed Shaw from the social and intellectual world in which his roots were so firmly embedded. He never completely regained contact with the political and ideological scene of post-war England and although he continued to write with the same theatrical vigour and control, his satire lost its edge and his comic gift began to desert him. His faith in the superman, in the individual, was strengthened, but his belief in the collective, political man was weakened. In *Back to Methuselah*, Lilith affirms her faith in the species and in the survival of man's genius but the emphasis is on the individual and not on man in society. In *The Apple Cart*, a characteristic play of his later period, Shaw attacks the basis of democracy itself. He shows how the democratic process may be exploited and perverted by big business and by petty, selfish men. He suggests the need for a strong, benevolent leadership and makes the monarch his hero. In *St. Joan*, his most successful later play, the lonely individual, alienated by her genius both from the Church and from the State, is martyred by the society she wished to save.

In his attitude towards society and, indeed, towards ideas, Shaw shows a typical, Victorian paternalism. He patronised and scolded society for more than twenty years as if it were a public school and he the headmaster. When society failed to realise the ambitions he had for it, he looked to individual men of intelligence and power as the source of regeneration. His admiration for Stalin, Mussolini and Hitler demonstrates the strength of his belief in the superman and the extent of his disillusion with society. He dogmatically asserted the validity of his own analysis of society and did not question the assumptions on which his own ideals rested. His self-confidence was enormous and his own vitality apparently inexhaustible. As a metaphysician, Shaw is an embodiment of the English spirit of amateurism. He was willing to pronounce on any subject and took all knowledge as his province. Yet, whatever the limitations and eccentricities of Shaw as a thinker, it is as a dramatist that his reputation must finally be assured. The difficulty is that he himself so confused his function as a playwright with his role as self-appointed prophet. Moreover, as so many of his plays are dramas of ideas, the temptation to reject his plays because history has already rejected so many of his ideas is hard to resist. His attempts to solve the major problems of man and of civilisation are inextricably bound up with his attempts to re-vitalise the English theatre, but his success as a dramatist does not depend on his success or failure as a thinker.

Shaw's passion was for thinking. He valued honesty, courage, integrity and intelligence in individuals, equality and order in society. He came to admire power however indiscriminately wielded. He was always more interested in man's moral character than in his psychological make-up and although not a Christian, Shaw uses religious concepts framed in religious terminology to express his morality. In his plays he constructs a moral profile of his characters in such a way that their public faces are clearly recognisable although they lack inner life or psychological depth. They become representative figures, typical of certain social attitudes. In the action of the plays these attitudes are brought into the open and judged. Shaw uses the stage as a court of morals in which the folly of his times is exposed. If we compare him as a satirist with Ben Jonson, for example, the limitations of his satire become clearer. Jonson's satire is incisive and assured, his moral indignation carries conviction and is firmly rooted in a comprehensive system of personal and religious values. His characters, like Shaw's, are representative figures, but his analysis of society is penetrating and inclusive. In many ways Jonson's attack upon the evils of capitalism is more thorough and profound and more closely linked with his awareness of the human condition. Shaw's satire is tentative and superficial in comparison. Nevertheless, Shaw's moral insecurity is turned to dramatic advantage in so far as he brings human behaviour into question and through discussion and debate of conflicting attitudes, involves the audience in the final judgement. Although the Prefaces are dogmatic, in the plays that follow them Shaw maintains an attitude of detached irony. He delighted in the free play of conflicting ideas which sometimes degenerates into a kind of Gilbertian buffoonery but more often helps to intensify interest in the seriousness of the conflict. Yet Shaw's dramatic world is narrow and enclosed compared with Jonson's open inclusiveness.

Dramatically, Shaw was only really comfortable among the cultivated, leisured middle-classes. Towards the working-class he extended
compassion without full understanding. He strenuously deplored the
poverty and ignorance that stood in the way of their joining these
middle-classes. Dramatically, Henry Straker, Snobby Price, Mr.
Doolittle and other representatives of their class, are little more than
stage Cockneys. Similarly, Shaw's aristocracy is equally unconvincing.
Indeed, his range of social types is strictly limited and they tend to
recur, thinly disguised, in play after play. They are nearer to 'humours'
than to characters and, for the most part, suffer from an emotional
anaemia which they attempt to remedy by their passionate devotion to
conversation. His artists are languid, romantic and ineffectual and his
business tycoons practical, single-minded and ruthless. His heroines are
striking without being glamorous, dominant without being over-
bearing, endowed with a severely practical intelligence. His heroes are,
for the most part, idealists who recognise the limitations of their
idealism particularly when confronted by the heroine. His characters
have little or no private life of their own, suffer few inner torments or
anxieties, are not driven relentlessly on by fate or by subconscious
forces over which they have little control. Everything is declared, open
and above board, everything is capable of a rational explanation and
there is a reasonable solution to every problem. In Ibsen, Chekhov and
Strindberg, life is seen as an iceberg nine-tenths submerged, but in
Shaw life has few mysteries. Even religion is a matter of applied
science. Shaw dismissed psychology because it re-introduced the
irrational as the basis of human behaviour and welcomed Marxian
economics because they seemed to put social and political action on a
sound, scientific footing. Shaw's dramatic range, like his dialectic, is
brilliant and intensely interesting but severely circumscribed. His plays
throw a penetrating light on the folly, vanity and greed of man, but
the area illuminated is not large.

★   ★   ★

Shaw's prose style has long been considered a model. It is lively
without being colloquial, balanced without being artificial. Above all,
it is lucid, direct, precise and persuasive. It is rhetorical style that
smoothly and easily follows the rhythms and intonations of speech and
is capable of considerable variation. Shaw's dialogue is polished,
confident and agile:

SWINDON: You are aware, I presume, Mr Anderson, of your obligations as a subject of His Majesty King George the Third.

RICHARD: I am aware, sir, that His Majesty King George the Third is about to hang me because I object to Lord North's robbing me.

SWINDON: That is a treasonable speech, sir.

RICHARD: Yes. I meant it to be.

BURGOYNE: Don't you think, Mr Anderson, that this is rather—if you will excuse the word—a vulgar line to take? Why should you cry out robbery because of a stamp duty and a tea duty and so forth? After all, it is the essence of your position as a gentleman that you pay with a good grace.

RICHARD: It is not the money, General. But to be swindled by a pig-headed lunatic like King George——

SWINDON: Chut, sir—silence!

BURGOYNE: Ah, that is another point of view. My position does not allow of my going into that, except in private . . .

[*The Devil's Disciple*, p. 242]

Dialogue as assured as this is rare in English drama in the period between Congreve and Shaw. The speed of the exchange is skilfully controlled, the three characters are concisely delineated. The direction of the argument is quickly changed and the alterations of tone are immediately conveyed. Moreover, Shaw's style enables him to move without apparent strain from dialogue of this kind to a more exalted rhetoric which stops just short of hysteria:

CUSINS: Then the way of life lies through the factory of death?

BARBARA: Yes, through the raising of hell to heaven and of man to God, through the unveiling of an eternal light in the Valley of The Shadow. Oh, did you think my courage would never come back? did you believe that I was a deserter? that I, who have stood in the streets, and taken my people to my heart, and talked of the holiest and greatest things with them, could ever turn back and chatter foolishly to fashionable people about nothing in a drawing room? Never, never, never, never: Major Barbara will die with the colours. Oh! and I have my dear little Dolly boy still; and he has found me my place and my work. Glory Hallelujah!

[*Major Barbara*, p. 503]

Clearly in writing this kind of exclamatory rhetoric Shaw is not entirely at his ease though it does indicate the range of his style. The limitations of his style are restricting and sometimes damaging. His is essentially a public voice and cannot capture intimacy, or tenderness, for example. At moments of emotional intensity the inadequacy of the style is clearly apparent:

> MORELL: It's all true, every word. What I am you have made me with the labour of your hands and the love of your heart. You are my wife, my mother, my sisters: you are the sun of all loving care to me.
> CANDIDA: Am I your mother and sisters to you, Eugene?
> MARCHBANKS: Ah, never. Out, then, into the night with me!
> CANDIDA: You are not going like that, Eugene?
> MARCHBANKS: I know the hour when it strikes. I am impatient to do what must be done.
> MORELL: Candida: don't let him do anything rash.
>
> [*Candida*, pp. 151-2]

What is crisp and precise in the exchange of ideas between Dick Dudgeon and Burgoyne, in the climax of *Candida* becomes soggy and vague. What ought to be the intimate intensity of the moment, is, in fact, a moment of rhetorical emptiness. Shaw's style is impersonal and incapable of conveying anything but generalised feelings. None the less, generally, Shaw is only concerned with broad effects in establishing moods and feelings and in the plays we are mainly aware of the vigour, wit and flexibility of his language. The limitations of his style faithfully reflect the limitations of his whole dramatic range.

Looking back on his achievement, we can see how Shaw, in spite of his own protestations to the contrary, is related to Goldsmith, Sheridan and Wilde as a dramatist who revived and extended the comedy of manners. He was willing, however, to introduce social and political ideas into his plays and to relate his drama closely to the intellectual life of his time. In a period in which the theatre had become marginal, a place for relaxation and fantasy, Shaw insisted on drama as a serious art form. The world in which he wrote and which his plays so sharply reflect seems remote from modern life. The modern dramatists' debt to him is considerable, but they are unlikely to acknowledge him, for the popular plays that hold the London audiences, the plays of Terence Rattigan or Peter Ustinov, for example, are derived directly from Shaw and it is this whole tradition that the contemporary dramatist has repudiated.

Note

John Osborne, born in 1929, worked as a journalist before making his debut as an actor at the Empire Theatre, Sheffield, in 1948. While working with the English Stage Company at the Royal Court Theatre in 1956 he came to immediate fame with his *Look Back in Anger* (1956). This was followed by *The Entertainer* (1957), in which Sir Laurence Olivier starred. Both plays have been filmed, and *Look Back in Anger* has been produced in many European cities. With Anthony Creighton, Osborne wrote *Epitaph for George Dillon* (published, 1958, Penguin; *New English Dramatists*, 2). *The World of Paul Slickey* appeared in 1959; *Luther* and a television drama, *A Subject of Scandal and Concern*, in 1960. Since this chapter was written, have come *Inadmissible Evidence*, *Plays for England*, *The Hotel in Amsterdam* and *Time Present*, the last two appearing together in 1968.

The principal intention of the following chapter is to set the work of Osborne and his close contempories into a relationship with the works of earlier dramatists of this century, in terms of their content and form. Since it was written, John Russell Taylor's *The Rise and Fall of the Well-Made Play* (1967) has provided detailed studies of individual dramas.

Some general works have examined this period from very different angles: Ernest Reynolds has a recent survey of the theatre from 1900 in *Modern English Drama* (1949, revised edition 1950); this is notable for its dealing with spectacle drama, light opera, melodrama, as well as the more usual dramatic literature of character and ideas. J. L. Styan's *The Elements of Drama* (1960) draws many of its detailed examinations of plays in production from the theatre of the present century. Richard Findlater's *The Unholy Trade* (1952) is a trenchant criticism of the place of the theatre in present-day society, and pays attention to its commercial as well as its artistic nature: the book was an interim study which deserves to be brought up to date. Laurence Kitchen's *Mid-Century Drama* is another interim study, and devotes much of its space to discussions and interviews with actors, actresses and producers. Two books of wider range relevant to the discussion are Ronald Peacock's *The Art of Drama* (1957) and Eric Bentley's *The Idea of a Theatre* (1949). J. Russell Taylor's *Anger and After*, B. Gascoigne's *Twentieth Century Drama* and M. Esslin's *The Theatre of the Absurd* were published after the present chapter was written.

Inevitably, much of the comparison of changing taste and form in the contemporary theatre is to be found in periodical and journalistic criticism and references to statements of particular importance are given in the course of this chapter. Stephen Potter made a brief comparison of 'London Theatre: 1918 and 1945' in *Penguin New Writing 27* (1946), 152–62. Robert Speaight wrote on drama in the collection entitled *Since 1939* (1949), and usefully set the contribution of dramatists since the beginning of the war into wider perspective. Of a similar scope is Peter Noble's *British Theatre* (1946). One of the best accounts of the repertory theatre movement during this century is Norman Marshall's *The Other Theatre* (1947).

IV

Somewhat in a New Dimension

ALLARDYCE NICOLL

★

'THE first night of John Osborne's *Look Back in Anger* at the Royal Court on May 8th, 1956, was a turning-point in the history of the modern British theatre.'

This statement, frequently repeated in diverse forms during recent years, has now become a truism: 'turning-point', 'break-through', 'upsurge', 'revolution' are all terms which seek to define the quality of the new movement. Concerning the positive value of its achievements there has been variety of opinion. Some critics have been inclined generally to condemn, although only a very few in the hostile camp fail to applaud certain particular plays inspired by the revolutionary objectives. Other critics are excitedly enthusiastic in general, although even the most zealous have been forced to express their doubts; Kenneth Tynan wonders whether the break-through has not broken down, and Peter Brook admits that

> even Noel Coward in making his attack on what we know to be an inadequate *new* theatre is really saying—despite himself—not that the old theatre was good—but that the new one is almost as bad—and in its own way, just as middle-class.[1]

Wherein lies the truth we, as contemporaries, cannot tell with assurance; only time's perspective can give us that answer; and accordingly little real profit can accrue from trying to estimate which of these plays will remain memorable and which will slip into oblivion. One thing, however, contemporaries may do is to set the plays of their age against the theatre's historical background, and perhaps there may be some virtue in an attempt briefly to view the products of this modern dramatic movement, not in isolation, but in association with the playhouse of the past.

[1] 'Search for a Hunger', *Encore*, viii (1961), 12.

For this there is ample justification. All the terms, from 'turning-point' to 'revolution', applied to these plays of the past five or six years stress their newness, emphasise that the younger playwrights have boldly made a complete cleavage between their efforts and the dramatic styles current in the years preceding 1956. We are, then, invited to make the comparison. But this comparison, if it is to be something more than a vague pitting of 'old' against 'new', demands that we should look, as objectively as possible, at the relationship between the 'new' endeavours and at the whole progress of the stage during our century.

Just as soon as we take this approach, casting our gaze backwards, we suddenly discover, to our surprise, that many of our younger playwrights have, in fact, leap-frogged back over the early fifties and the forties and landed in the Edwardian and Georgian eras. Outwardly, of course, they appear to inhabit a distinct world of their own, yet the number of earlier themes which they have chosen to re-exploit seems to demonstrate that in the period 1900–30 they have found metal which to them is attractive.

An immediate example presents itself. Basically, *Look Back in Anger* deals with the theme of a gently nurtured girl who is strangely magnet-ised by a lower-class intellectual; her mother, we are told, has been and remains vigorously opposed to the marriage, but the girl's retired-officer father, although puzzled, exhibits remarkable understanding; by the side of the ill-assorted pair stands, or lounges, an ineffective, faith-ful, devoted friend. Now, all the elements, or ingredients of this theme are exactly similar to those which were largely cultivated between 1900 and 1930. Again and again, as in *The Best People* (1926) by David Grey and Avery Hopwood, we find a gently nurtured Marion intent on marrying an 'intellectual' chauffeur Henry, while her father, a retired military man, stems the tide of rigid feminine opposition with perplexed understanding. *The Best People* does not exhibit a sentiment-ally devoted friend, but many other plays include him in the picture. Generally, the plots were worked round to a happy ending, but in some at least the atmosphere remained dark. The heroine of John Galsworthy's *The Fugitive* (1913), for instance, is a young wife, Clare Dedmond, who elects to run off with a writer Kenneth Malaise, described, in terms not unreminiscent of Jimmy Porter, as 'a tall man, about thirty-five, with a strongly-marked, dark, irregular, ironic face, and eyes which seemed to have needles in their pupils'—whose

vituperative comments on the world are often akin to those we listen
to in *Look Back in Anger*:

> Blessed be the respectable! May they dream of—me! And blessed be
> all men of the world! May they perish of a surfeit of—good form!
> . . . Not a word, not a whisper of liberty from all those excellent
> frock-coated gentlemen—not a sign, not a grimace. Only the
> monumental silence of their profound deference before triumphant
> Tyranny.

Clare and Malaise sink down in their attic, and eventually she commits
suicide.

Obviously, Osborne's play shows a vigorous drive which distinguishes it from most other preceding works of a like kind; obviously,
too, it strikes a new note in concentrating upon Jimmy Porter's un-
inhibited egoism. Whereas almost all the earlier plays had treated the
theme as a story, starting at the beginning and moving to a determined
close, *Look Back in Anger* omits the preliminaries, focuses attention
upon the life being led by the pair, and ends inconclusively, with the
abject degradation of the girl at Jimmy Porter's feet. Nevertheless,
despite the vast difference in atmosphere, the fact that this play deals
with a theme freely exploited during the first decades of the century
and only occasionally handled by dramatists of the forties and early
fifties deserves to be noted, particularly since *Look Back in Anger* does
not in this respect stand alone. Repeatedly we find that recent plays,
so far from introducing fresh subject-matter, elect to give new twists
to topics and styles current in the earlier period. In that connection
N. F. Simpson's description of his *One Way Pendulum* as 'A Farce in a
New Dimension' may seem symptomatic. A farce-comedy of which it
reminds us is Kaufman and Hart's *You Can't Take It With You* (1936):
even although no direct resemblance exists between the plot of this
piece and that of Simpson's, an undoubted general connection can be
traced between the two plays. Both contrast the eccentrically absurd
with the normally accepted patterns of law-abiding humanity. The
chief distinction rests in the fact that the one presents the absurdity
within a framework of eccentricity which at least partly may be
admitted to come within the sphere of the possible, whereas in the
other the frankly impossible is conjured up before us. There is, too, the
further distinction that, although of course the very title of *You Can't
Take It With You* advertises a point of view, a 'message', the action
develops without symbolic overtones and the emphasis is laid upon the

adroit exploitation of dramatically amusing situations for their own sake, while *One Way Pendulum* resembles dozens of modern plays in shifting attention to the symbolic and in refusing to rest content with the treatment of any action which does not offer the opportunity of proffering broad, generalised social comment.

★   ★   ★

The more closely we examine the dramatic themes characteristic of the century's early decades and those which have been treated on the stage during recent years, the more clearly do we discern the associations between them. One particular example may be taken as an illustration.

When the plays of 1900–30 are reviewed as a whole, we must be struck by the frequent occurrence of three special topics which sometimes appear separately, sometimes come in pairs, sometimes are intertwined. These may be described as the 'Artist' topic (particularly the artist as poet or playwright), the 'Passer-by' topic and the theme of the 'Famous Man'. In order to appreciate their force and significance, some explanatory comments are essential.

Let us take the 'Artist' first. Offhand, we might well be prepared to say that within the enormous range of drama from the sixteenth century on to the end of the nineteenth the whole world had been represented; from kings to beggars, from clerics to labourers, from merchants to thieves, everyone seems to be here. There is, however, one marked exception: in the plays produced during these three centuries and a half there are hardly any painters, sculptors, poets, novelists or dramatists in important roles. In Elizabethan and Jacobean times we can think only of one or two persons of this kind and even then they generally appear either as incidental figures or as satirical caricatures— the Poet and Painter in *Timon of Athens* or the skits presented during the 'War of the Theatres'. Bellamont, a portrait of Chapman, in *Northward Ho* is virtually unique, and even here Bellamont's profession, as such, has no particular significance. The Restoration period and the eighteenth century introduced more fully developed caricatures into burlesques, such as Buckingham's *The Rehearsal* and Sheridan's *The Critic*, while occasionally, as in Fielding's *The Author's Farce*, the profession of writing was treated satirically, but we have to wait until the appearance of Frederick Reynolds' engagingly comic *The Dramatist* in 1789 before meeting with anything more extended, and almost another century was to pass by before H. J. Byron, in *Cyril's Success* (1868), dealt with an author-character in a serious manner. Once more, there came a gap, and then, from the last years of the nineteenth century on through the early years of the twentieth artists of all kinds came swarming on the boards. In 1895 Shaw presented his young poet Marchbanks, followed on with his painter Dubedat in 1906, and in 1911 made Fanny produce her first play. After showing us the young playwright Arthur Gower in *Trelawny of the 'Wells'* in 1898, A. W. Pinero in *The Big Drum* (1915) introduced his Philip Mackworth, 'a novelist, a poet, a would-be playwright'. Kenneth Malaise in John Galsworthy's *The Fugitive* (1913) is a sardonic author, Geoffrey Marsh in *Windows* (1922) a novelist, Christopher Wellwyn in *The Pigeon* (1912) a painter. J. M. Barrie has his painter, Bodie, in *A Kiss for Cinderella* (1916); Jim Benziger is an author and Hilary Cutts a painter in B. Macdonald Hastings' *The New Sin* (1912); in G. D. Gribble's *The Masque of Venice* (1924) both Jonathan Mumford and Mrs Weir are novelists. How prevalent the type had become may be indicated by the number of plays which without any valid reason at all describe characters as painters or playwrights; thus A. A. Milne has no dramatic purpose in making young David Clifton (*Wurzel-Flummery*, 1917) a would-be dramatist, nor is any such purpose served when Miles Malleson, in *Love at Second Sight* (1927), describes John Nightingale as 'unmistakably a painter with a real studio of his own and proud of it'.

If artists had their run on the early twentieth-century stage, so did 'passers-by' of all kinds, and these too were characteristic figures. No doubt we might use the term 'passers-by' for Autolycus, Shepherd and Clown in *The Winter's Tale*, but fundamentally their dramatic position was completely distinct from that, say, of Nighty the cabby and Burns the tramp who enter into that play of C. Haddon Chambers which takes its title, *Passers-by* (1911), from their presence. Sometimes these persons were, like those of Haddon Chambers', waifs from the streets; many plays such as Galsworthy's *The Pigeon* (1912) brought in variants of a vagabond Ferrand, a flower-seller Mrs. Megan and a drunken cab-driver Timson. Sometimes they might be almost styled intruders like the Cheerful Knave who gives his name to Keble Howard's American play of 1910. Sometimes they come on to the stage and then disappear; often, after passing-by, they elect to settle down within the environment into which they have drifted.

The third dramatic topic, that of the 'Famous Man', is also characteristic of this period. Obviously, hundreds of older dramas, from *King Lear* onwards, had dealt with great men, chiefly monarchs, at the close of their careers, but the atmosphere of these plays remains quite distinct from the spirit of such a play as A. A. Milne's *The Truth about Blayds* (1921) wherein we are presented with a great Victorian poet celebrating his ninetieth birthday and being greeted by an emissary from the society of younger writers. This play of Milne's may in general stand as representative of numerous others which thus focused attention upon men (usually poets or painters) famous for their achievements; it may also stand, in particular, as representative of a constantly repeated dramatic situation which involves three main characters—a prominent octogenarian or nonagenarian, a devoted daughter and a visiting spokesman for the younger generation.

For our present enquiry the interesting thing is that these three topics, separately or interwoven, have been suddenly resuscitated in recent years. The title of Doris Lessing's *The Truth about Billy Newton*, for example, manifestly recalls that of *The Truth about Blayds*, produced forty years earlier. In this drama a great scientist-philosopher has been put in front of us; T. S. Eliot gives us *The Elder Statesman*; Angus Wilson offers us a distinguished liberal-historian in *The Mulberry Bush*. Here, however, we must once again observe the 'new dimension'. In a sense, Milne's play and Eliot's belong together in that they are both purely 'dramatic', their stories are told in human terms without any symbolic connotations. No general conclusions can be drawn from contemplation of Blayds, and the motto of Lord Claverton's fate may be found in the final comment of his daughter Monica:

> In becoming no one, he has become himself.
> He is only my father now, and Michael's,
> And I am happy.

Our younger writers, on the other hand, are mostly inclined towards avoidance of the purely human relationships; their emphasis is laid upon wider interpretations and symbolism tends to invest all their action. Thus the figure of Billy Newton has been set by Doris Lessing against the background of a teen-age gang and the preparations of an anti-H Bomb demonstration; each of Newton's three former wives has a special significance—one representing the 'Establishment', a second typifying the spirit of individualistic liberalism and a third having, of course, to be a Russian komissar who has made the trip to England especially for the purpose of attending her ex-husband's celebration party. In exactly similar wise, John Whiting's *Saint's Day* shows us the grand old man, a poet named Paul Southman, within a symbolic framework not unreminiscent of the atmosphere in some of Nikolai Andreev's dramas.

Artists in general, and particularly poets and playwrights, fascinate this later age as much as they did the earlier, though, quite apart from the recurrent symbolism, we sense a shift in orientation. During the first years of the century, we receive the impression that, with a few exceptions, these characters were being observed objectively and that one reason for their popularity lay either in the glamour which surrounded them or in the opportunity they offered of presenting persons colourfully different in dress from men of the ordinary run and with manners less inhibited. When, however, we turn to the modern period we often suspect that the playwrights themselves are subjectively entering into their own creations, or at least that they are investing these creatures of their imagination with qualities subjectively conceived. And in somewhat similar manner we feel that the modern passers-by, of which there are many, have been tinted in shades more subjective and certainly more symbolic than had been given to their predecessors.

A convenient example for brief examination is the *Epitaph for George Dillon* (1958) by John Osborne and Anthony Creighton. This has as its central theme the story of how a middle-class and middle-aged Mrs. Elliot, much to the annoyance and disgust of her husband, brings into her home a young, penniless, lazy, impertinent and aggressive would-be dramatist named George Dillon. Replete with seduction, despair and anger, the scenes are serious, not amusing. Yet the basic situation, surprisingly enough, finds an almost exact parallel in a farce of 1910 which, by a peculiar coincidence, its author, R. S. Warren Bell, called *Company for George*. Here a middle-class and middle-aged Mrs. Birch, also much to the annoyance and disgust of her husband, brings into her home a young, penniless, lazy, impertinent and aggressive intellectual. Just the same kind of relationship between the old and the new may be discovered in many plays written since 1956. In *Billy Liar* (1960) by Keith Waterhouse and Willis Hall we have a play, set in the now familiar working-class environment, which presents as its chief character a youth who cannot stick to the truth, for whom prevarication is congenital. Some of the scenes are amusing, but the

general treatment is almost that of a serious 'documentary'. Nevertheless, the Billy Fisher of this drama stems from a tradition which the
early twentieth century inherited from Samuel Foote's *The Lyar* (1762)
and which goes back, through an anonymous *Mistaken Beauty, or The
Lyar* of 1682, to Pierre Corneille's *Le menteur* of 1644 and beyond. The
situation and character are the same even if the earlier works show
lovers whose propensity for lying leads them into ludicrous scrapes
while *Billy Liar* closes on a pathetically sentimental stage direction.

★   ★   ★

One might without difficulty adduce other themes and topics of this
kind, but those cited above may be taken as generally representative.
Brief attention, however, should be given to a separate although
intimately related subject, that of dramatic styles.

A prime feature of the present-day theatre is its lack of any prevailing characteristic form. Any young dramatist, Christopher Fry
points out,[2]

> sitting down to write a play two hundred or three hundred years ago
> would not have had to give very much thought to how he would
> approach the stage. The form and the manner were already there to
> be taken up and used. His whole attention could be given to letting
> his talent use them. But now he may set off in a dozen or more
> directions. The plays of Shaw, Brecht, Tennessee Williams, Eliot,
> Rattigan, Giraudoux, are unlike each other in a way that the plays
> of Congreve, Wycherley, Vanbrugh, and Farquhar, were not. A
> theatre may be the richer for many styles; at any rate more varied
> (though I doubt if it's an aid to intensity). But a playwright at the
> beginning of his task may find the lack of a universal manner a dis-
> advantage. For one thing, it is much more difficult to imagine his
> play in performance; and then, if he sees it in performance, the
> variety of criticism may be as great as the variety of prevailing styles,
> and this is unsettling, and no help to creative growth.

When we go to the theatre nowadays, we can have no idea what
shape a new play will assume. It may be rigidly naturalistic both in
dialogue and in setting; its setting may be non-realistic while its speech
remains faithful to common utterance; the whole performance may
aim at the inculcation of a rationally conceived message; there may be
presented to us a nonsense world as fantastic as that of *Alice in Wonder-*

[2] Introduction to John Hall, *The Lizard on the Rock* (1956).

land or of the universe created by Edward Lear. When the curtain rises we may have before us a play written by an author who regards direct address to the audience as degrading, on the other hand, the author may cultivate a form that 'cuts right across the restrictions of the so-called naturalistic stage'.[3]

In his comparison between the position of the young playwright today and his predecessor several hundred years ago Christopher Fry is entirely correct, but at the same time we must observe that many, indeed most, of the latest dramatic forms were being exploited during this century's first decades, a period when experimentalism was rife. Recently, a critic, speaking of Osborne, Wesker, Behan and Delaney, acclaims their detailed realism—'toast is burned, clothes are ironed, bobs have to be found for the gas meter';[4] yet this, of course, is only Daly naturalism, itself an 'improvement' upon the earlier innovations of Tom Robertson. The working-class themes were introduced to the theatre sixty years ago by Maxim Gorki and his lead was soon followed in this country by Stanley Houghton, Harold Brighouse and others. Reference has already been made to the relationship between Andreev's symbolic methods, also imitated by several early twentieth-century English dramatists, and those of John Whiting's *Saint's Day*. Before 1930 more than one author was seeking to shatter the 'well-made' play tradition by adopting cinematic devices—the short scenes, the flashbacks, the dream sequences. During the same years impressionistic 'psychological' dramas were being written, and expressionism temporarily gripped the avant-garde stage. The stamp of all these forms and of numerous others is clearly to be seen in the new drama of today.

There is, of course, no valid reason why modern playwrights should not thus borrow from and re-fashion themes and forms already established; after all, that is frequent theatrical practice. Yet the fact that the reaction against the themes and forms of the forties and early fifties has carried the modern dramatists back, not to the Greeks or the Elizabethans, but to the Edwardians and early Georgians, obviously deserves to be noted; and care has to be taken not to regard all the modern variations on past models as inventions of the present age. At the first performance of two Pinter plays at the Royal Court Theatre in 1960 the author provided a programme note which stressed the fact that

[3] John Osborne, *The Entertainer* (1957), preface.
[4] A. Alvarez, 'The Anti-Establishment Drama', *The Partisan Review*, (1959), p. 609.

> There are no hard distinctions between what is real and what is un-
> real, nor between what is true and what is false. The thing is not
> necessarily either true or false; it can be both true and false.

The statement may perhaps be accepted, but not the implication that
this is something fresh for the drama: Pirandello's whole creative life
was dominated by precisely that concept. So, too, Arnold Wesker,
commenting on a play which he was then engaged in writing, declares
that 'there is a whole scene in *Chips with Everything* in which absolutely
nothing is said';[5] and once again the implication is that here is a startling
novelty. What we have to remember is that the now unduly neglected
John Galsworthy excited London audiences with just such a wordless
scene when he produced his *Justice* in 1910.

Wesker's reference to a scene 'in which absolutely nothing is said'
reminds us that Fry, in speaking of the present age's dramatic diversity,
alluded not merely to form but also to manner, not merely to the
structural shape of the plays but also to their media.

Fundamentally, the younger group of theatre authors have followed
the stylistic patterns set in Edwardian times. During that period, except
for a few forlorn efforts by men such as Lascelles Abercrombie and
Gordon Bottomley, poetry was banished from the stage. Prose,
established firmly by Henry Arthur Jones and A. W. Pinero, became
the single acceptable form for dramatic dialogue. Towards the middle
of the century poetic drama once more began to attract attention, but
in rejecting so much of the work of their immediate predecessors,
most of the young playwrights of today have cast over the styles of
T. S. Eliot and Christopher Fry, thus reverting to the model set several
decades ago. For the most part, their allusions to Fry's brilliant language
are derogatory; they have tended to regard any attempt to write
dialogue in a poetic manner as anathema. True, a very few, such as
John Arden, make some experiments in the writing of verse dialogue,
and others, such as Bernard Kops in *The Hamlet of Stepney Green* and
The Dream of Peter Mann, seek to enrich the content of their work by
the introduction of song, sometimes not very felicitously; but, in
general, prose is the sole medium for their dialogue.

Prose, however, has obvious limitations, and the drama continually
strives for opportunities; prose is the language of reason and the stage is
the proper place for emotions; modern conversational utterance has

[5] 'Art is Not Enough', *The Twentieth Century* (1961), 192.

become stale, stilted and flat. Naturally, with the familiar establishment of the prose medium in Edwardian and early Georgian days
several of the playwrights started to search for ways of escape—or
rather for means whereby they might, while keeping to the realistic
form, allow their characters to speak more richly. One such triple
device they discovered—the introduction of hysterical types, the free
provision of liquor on the stage and the bringing-in of what might
be called professional orators. This triple formula, to take one example,
finds apt illustration in Harold Chapin's *The New Morality* (1921).
Here the heroine Betty is shown as almost out of her senses with jealous
rage; in the strained domestic circumstances both her husband, Colonel
Ivor Jones, and Wister, the husband of the lady at whom her hysterical
wrath is directed, find comfort in imbibing large quantities of drink,
thus loosening their tongues; while Betty's brother, Geoffrey Belasis,
called in to help disentangle the resultant confusion, is by profession a
barrister used to eloquence. Now, just this triple formula has become
common in modern plays: John Mortimer exploits the hysterical
woman in *The Wrong Side of the Park*; Ronnie in Arnold Wesker's
'*Trilogy*' is a native spouter, ever ready to spring up on a soap-box or a
chair: everyone knows that in these modern plays the consumption of
whisky and beer is prodigious and unremitting.

The triple device certainly has its advantages. Yet even the playwrights of 1900–30 soon came to realise that nerves and drink, when
overdone, are apt to become boring; they recognised, too, that many
tense dramatic situations exist in which neither an hysterical woman
nor a loquacious tippler may properly be introduced; and they saw
that not all plays could admit of the appropriate intrusion of a professional orator, whether legal or political. There was, then, the necessity
in the earlier dramas, as there is still in the modern, of developing a
form of speech, uttered not under the impulse of mental strain, not
induced by alcohol, not the result of training in professional eloquence,
which could, without breaking the realistic pattern, go beyond the
kind of speech proper in actual life to the particular situation. In the
search for such a kind of dialogue, however, as the Georgians and
Edwardians discovered, the difficulties and the pitfalls are numerous.
Clearly, much of the virtue of the early Irish dramatists, J. M. Synge in
particular, derived from the fact that they could exploit a vital form
of folk-speech, rich in simile and metaphor, invested with a native
delight in rhythmic design and melodic broidery. English playwrights

possessed no such model upon which to work: the material they commonly dealt with was of an entirely different sort. The expression of emotions in real life was inhibited, partly because social pressure had inclined men to conceal their passions, partly (and perhaps mainly) because the words and phrases which might have expressed the passions had become clichés and were thus rendered stale and flat.

In these circumstances, one immediately obvious dramatic device, consciously or unconsciously evoked, was to permit the language, at moments of tension, to depart from the sphere of actuality—but, as soon as that approach is taken, there is the immediate danger that the speeches will assume a 'literary' form. When we turn back now to the plays of 1900-30, maybe the quality that most impresses us is this 'literary' flavour in many of their scenes. In *The Pelican* (1924) by Tennyson Jesse and H. M. Harwood, for example, we get utterances like

> Morality depends on mechanics. It always has, especially when it is artificial, as in the case of women . . . Victorian morality began to wilt with the introduction of the safety bicycle, the motor-car was its death-blow, and there is still the aeroplane. St. Paul and John Knox have proved no match for Dunlop and Daimler——

or

> Yes, this having cut yourself off all these years as you have. You ought to have something that's for yourself, for *you*, not only just 'giving' all the time.

'Literary' dialogue, however, just as 'realistic' dialogue, changes from period to period; we recognise the 'literary' quality in many of the 1900-30 plays, but perhaps it is not so easy to detect its presence in those of 1956-61. Nevertheless, despite all our present fears of indulging in a 'literary' style and our belief that we are avoiding it, it seems almost certain that before many years have gone by many speeches in the plays of today will sound as stilted as the corresponding speeches in the earlier dramas. Here, for instance, is a passage from Arnold Wesker's *The Kitchen*:

> All we know is that they suddenly started shouting at each other. And you know Peter always shouts more than the other, and you can always hear Peter—well, so then it stopped, and then a few seconds later they were fighting, and I saw Gaston raise a pallet knife and Peter knock it out of his hand . . .
>
> (Penguin edition, p. 21)

In John Whiting's *Saint's Day* (1951) we get this:

> If the villagers could organize themselves, or could be moved by a moment's rage they would come here and kill us.
>
> (1957 edition, p. 33)

The stylistic patterns of 1924 and 1957–60 are not so very different in kind.

Along with this we observe in the earlier works a kindred device, which might be described as an attempt to stress and underline a concept of the author's own while striving to keep as much as possible to the realistic manner. This often resulted in a strained effect precisely because we feel that the ideas thus expressed were, as it were, forced in and often called for apology.

For an illustration we might take a short extract from C. Haddon Chambers' *Passers-By* (1911):

> NIGHTY: (*Draws chair close up to* WAVERTON) My views? That's easy, guv'nor. Every child born, boy, is entitled in abundance to the air, light and water that Nature provides. (*He taps* WAVERTON *familiarly on the knee.*) It's the duty of the State to see the children ain't done out of their rights. Then again, the State demands children in quantity—very well, it's the duty of the State to see that the quality's all right. Every child is entitled to 'ealthy parents. A 'uman incapable—— (WAVERTON *raises a warning finger.*) Yes, poor bloke! It ain't 'is fault. The thing is, don't breed 'em like that! The future of the race is with the children. Legislate for the children.
>
> WAVERTON: Bravo Nighty . . . You're a Statesman.

This nowadays sounds very artificial, and we might be prepared to cast it contemptuously aside until we turn, let us say, to this short extract from Arnold Wesker's *The Kitchen*:

> DIMITRI: Hey, Irishman, what you grumbling about this place for? Is different anywhere else! This stinking kitchen is like the world —you know what I mean? It's too fast to know what happens. People come and people go, big excitement, big noise. (*Makes noise, gesticulates and runs wildly about, and then stops.*) What for? In the end who do you know? You make a friend, you going to be all your life his friend, but when you go from here—pshtt! you forget! Why you grumble about this one kitchen?
>
> PETER: You're a very intelligent boy, Dimitri. (p. 42)

Two things require to be emphasised here. The first is that the impressions created by these two passages depend not upon the authors but upon the convention utilised by both. Indeed, it would have been an easy task to select scores of similar extracts, many of them even more emphatic, from plays both of the early period and of the later. Secondly, we must observe that the convention itself arises from the basic fact that the realistic type of drama does not offer to the writers an instrument fully adequate for meeting the deeper demands of the stage.

Moving on from this, we next discern the most common of all the pitfalls, that of declamation and ejaculatory utterance. We can hardly look at any single serious dramatic work of the earlier years of this century without encountering emotional scenes cast in such a form, with exclamation marks and dashes and italics and dots confessing the inability of the prose lines to measure up to the demands made by the situations:

> My family goes back to the thirteenth century. Nowadays they laugh at that! I don't! Nowadays they laugh at everything—they even laugh at the word lady—I married *you*, and I don't . . . Married his mother's maid! By George! Dorothy! I don't know what we've done to deserve this; it's a death blow! I'm not prepared to sit down and wait for it. By God! I am not.[6]

Exactly similar in method are dozens of speeches which may readily be culled from our modern plays:

> Oh, why am I here! You must all wish me a thousand miles away! . . .
> Oh, Hell! Now the bloody bells have started! . . . Wrap it up, will you? Stop ringing those bells! There's somebody going crazy in here! I don't want to hear them! . . .
> Have you looked at them? Have you listened to them? They don't merely act and talk like caricatures, they *are* caricatures! That's what's so terrifying. Put any one of them on a stage, and no one would take them seriously for one minute! They think in clichés, they talk in them, they even feel in them—and, brother, that's an achievement! Their existence is one great cliché that they carry about with them like a snail in his little house—and they live in it and die in it! [7]

Possibly because of a conscious or unconscious awareness of these pitfalls and because of a recognition of the fact that the prose medium,

[6] John Galsworthy, *The Eldest Son* (1912).

[7] John Osborne, *Look Back in Anger* (1957), pp. 88 and 25; *Epitaph for George Dillon* (1958; Penguin edition 1960), p. 188.

however brilliantly handled, cannot express all that should be expressed, a few of our playwrights of today have elected to pursue another path, one which ultimately must lead to the final exclusion of dialogue altogether. This path, in effect, is a double one. Attention has been drawn above to the final stage direction in which the action of *Billy Liar* closes wordlessly, and attention, too, has been drawn to the scene innocent of dialogue planned by Wesker for *Chips with Everything*. Once more it must be stressed that the device is of 1900–30 vintage. Reference has been made to the wordless scene in Galsworthy's *Justice* (1910) and to this it may be added that, even without going beyond that author's works, the presentation of such a scene either medially or to provide a curtain finale by no means stands alone. At the end of Act II, Scene ii of *The Silver Box* (1906) a child's cry can be heard beyond the open window:

> MRS BARTHWICK *turns her back to the window. There is an expression of distress on her face. She stands motionless, compressing her lips. The crying begins again.* BARTHWICK *covers his ears with his hands, and* MARLOW *shuts the window. The crying ceases.*

A lengthy stage-direction closes *The Mob* (1914). So also at the end of *A Family Man* (1921):

> BUILDER: (*To himself*) Pluck! Pluck! (*His lips quiver again. He presses them hard together, puts his pipe back into his mouth, and, taking the Will, thrusts it into the newly-lighted fire and holds it there with a poker.*
>
> *While he is doing this the door from the hall is opened quietly, and* MRS BUILDER *enters without his hearing her. She has a work-bag in her hand. She moves slowly to the table, and stands looking at him. Then going up to the curtains she mechanically adjusts them, and still keeping her eyes on* BUILDER, *comes down to the table and pours out his usual glass of whisky toddy.* BUILDER, *who has become conscious of her presence, turns in his chair as she hands it to him. He sits a moment motionless, then takes it from her, and squeezes her hand.* MRS BUILDER *goes silently to her usual chair below the fire, and taking out some knitting begins to knit.* BUILDER *makes an effort to speak, does not succeed, and sits drawing at his pipe.*

Clearly the operative words are 'makes an effort to speak, does not succeed'.

With Galsworthy, as with other playwrights of his generation, the introduction of these silent scenes was quite undeliberate in the sense that they were the mere result of the author's making a virtue out of necessity. In recent years, however, the device has been puffed up, like the frog of the fable, into an airy philosophy. Wesker's scene 'in which absolutely nothing is said' has been inspired by a deliberate intent: 'in fact,' he says, 'I am working very much towards a reduction not only of scenery, but of dialogue as well.' Nor is he alone. Recently, in 'Search for a Hunger', Peter Brook has presented his credo: 'I don't believe in the word much today because it has outlived its purpose. Words don't communicate, they don't express much, and most of the time they fail abysmally to define.' And in this intellectual atmosphere even the very term 'poetic' has been made to suffer a metempsychosis. Martin Esslin, in writing about Pinter's dramatic work, states that this 'is a return to the really basic elements of drama, the suspense created by the elementary ingredients of pure pre-literary theatre', and then from that proposition proceeds to argue that during the last ten years

> there has been another and in many ways more original approach to a poetic theatre: this is the type of play in which the language is deliberately flat and unpoetic and the poetic element is made to reside in the power of the action itself as a poetic image.[8]

The confusion in thought here reminds us of Wesker's remark that 'if I have any importance at all, it is not because of my style, but because of what I am saying'. Certainly it is true, as J. W. Lambert has indicated, that the dialogue in Pinter's plays shows 'the lowest common denominator of human speech';[9] typical is the sentimentally conceived Pied Piper of Doris Lessing's *The Truth about Billy Newton*, a character almost completely inarticulate who can communicate only through the notes of a flute. In a sense, we may almost discern here a nostalgic groping-back to the early twentieth-century's silent film.

Undoubtedly, lacking a characteristic medium apt to serve the requirements of drama, today's young playwrights are heavily handicapped, struggling against mighty odds; even a cursory glance at dramatic history should perhaps make us pause before we claim inadequacies as achievements or find in action alone the qualities of supreme 'poetic' creation. 'The appeal of the inarticulate', declares Fry elsewhere,

> and the pleasure of hearing the speech of the streets and the living-room, even brilliantly recorded, isn't the whole duty of man so far as

[8] 'Pinter and the Absurd', *The Twentieth Century*, clxix (1961), 176–85.
[9] Introduction to *New English Dramatists*, 3 (Penguin Books, 1960).

language is concerned. It is an instrument which reflects the full life of man, and if we let it dwindle we dwindle with it.[10]

★   ★   ★

This, however, raises a fundamental question, a question which takes shape clearly when we compare and contrast the work of this group of young dramatists with the work of their predecessors half a century ago. For the most part, the writers in the earlier period, even although they eagerly experimented in various forms, were fundamentally intent upon the theatre and tried to pursue that objectivity which the theatre demands. Since that time the world has changed mightily and as a result many young authors are obsessed by the idea that we inhabit an absurd universe, so that, as Martin Esslin declares, 'it is enough to transcribe reality with meticulous care to create the impression of extravagant irrationality' (*loc. cit.*, p. 137).

Maybe the young authors are philosophically right, although the proposition may well be challenged; but here we are concerned, not with philosophy, but with the fate of the theatre. In place of the interest and belief in the stage which animated the first decades of this century we have an uneasy feeling that some of our playwrights doubt the value of the very medium in which they work. Friedrich Dürrenmatt in 1955 asked whether the present-day world could possibly be reflected on the stage and others have whispered similar doubts. There is some truth in Oscar Budel's statement that many a modern playwright

> himself assumes his audience will no longer accept theater as theater, that it is too aware of the theatre as being a 'swindle', not real . . . Therefore, the playwright too wishes to make known his awareness of the unrealness of theater by analytically dissecting it, by playing with it, or making fun of it.[11]

Such a statement, even while it is fully justified, again reminds us paradoxically of the dependence of supposedly 'modern' approaches upon Edwardian and Georgian methods and of the difference between them. Many, many years ago the attitude expressed here formed the basis of Italy's 'Teatro del Grottesco', and we do not even have to cross the Channel in order to see it exemplified on the stage. J. M. Barrie

[10] Christopher Fry, 'Talking of Henry', *The Twentieth Century*, clxix (1961), 190.
[11] 'Contemporary Theater and Aesthetic Distance', *PMLA*, lxxvi (1961), 291.

was only one dramatist in the period 1900–30 who constantly exhibits an 'awareness of the unrealness of theater by analytically dissecting it, by playing with it, or making fun of it'. One example will serve. In *Alice Sit-by-the Fire* (1905), two girls Amy and Ginevra have a bout of theatre-going, and then proceed to misinterpret their parents' lives in accordance with the stage patterns they have seen. 'Amy', cries Ginevra, after returning from the playhouse, 'how I love that bit where she says so unexpectedly, with noble self-renunciation, "He is my affianced husband." 'Isn't it glorious!' replies her companion. 'Strange, Ginevra, that it happened in each play.' Barrie, and his audience, saw the 'swindle' as clearly as our present-day playwrights and critics, who seem to imagine that only to them the light has been vouchsafed.

Three things, however, even although adumbrated in the past, are new. The first is the mighty bandying-about of dramatic philosophies. 'Realism', 'naturalism', 'distancing', 'epic', 'method', 'involvement', 'alienation'—the concepts batter upon us like a nightmare's phantasmagoria. The second is the trend towards self-centredness on the part of the playwrights, sometimes assuming form simply as an anxious passion for expressing their own views, sometimes taking shape in private myths. In speaking of his *Saint's Day*, John Whiting has told us that 'the so-called symbolism' of this piece 'is no more than the use of people, places, things, even ideas and quotations from literature, which have a personal significance'.[12] When we consider the earlier works of 1900–30, we get a general impression of carefully weighed reflection, even among those playwrights with a 'message' to convey, and we likewise feel that the subject matter has been thought-out in terms proper to each particular drama; when we consider the modern only too often there is an impression of egocentric sentiment to the neglect of dramatic values. Even John Arden has declared that

> you could take whole chunks out of *One Way Pendulum* and put them in *A Resounding Tinkle*, or vice-versa, and it wouldn't matter. I think you can do the same with *The Entertainer* and *Look Back in Anger*. *The Entertainer* does have the big difference of the stage show in it, but the family natterings might easily be in either play.[13]

The contrast may be illustrated by comparing such plays wherein the subjective has been substituted for the objective and, say, R. C.

[12] Prefatory note to *Plays* (Heinemann, 1957).
[13] 'Building the Play', *Encore*, viii (1961), 33.

Sherriff's *The Telescope* (1956) and *The Long Sunset* (1955), which may be taken as stemming, without any 'new dimension', from the Galsworthy tradition.

The self-centredness and subjectivity, finally, lead towards indifference to, and even dislike of, the audience. John Osborne, who in *The World of Paul Slickey* lashed out at the auditorium, has given us his creed:

> It's possible to write for yourself and to write for a few people at the same time. It's also possible to write for yourself and write for everybody. But it's not my job *as a dramatist* to worry about reaching a mass audience if there is one, to make the theatre less of a minority art. So much of that, in any case, depends on other factors like new buildings, with good restaurants, service and other amenities. If you're going to do what other people think, or say you ought to do, it's a waste of time. Ultimately, after all, the only satisfaction you get out of doing all this is the satisfaction you give yourself.[14]

Says Pinter, 'I don't write with any audience in mind.'[15] Arden agrees: 'When you write a play, you don't think of the audience. I certainly don't. If I do, I put it out of my mind because I find it depressing.'[16] But, as Robert Bolt has wisely pointed out, the attitude thus expressed is perilous; 'Simply to slap your audience in the face,' he warns, 'satisfies an austere and puritanical streak'; 'it is a dangerous game to play'[17] and it is dangerous not only for the individual who practises it but for the theatre as well.

In the work of the young playwrights of 1956–61 there assuredly exists much vigour, and anxious striving, and genuine achievement; but perhaps a true assessment of their qualities and a recognition of the enormous odds against which they are struggling will not come either to them or to us if they are considered solely against the now critically fashionable background provided by Sartre, Brecht, Ionesco and Beckett. Maybe a better perspective and a posing of basic questions— of which clearly the most essential is 'What do we want of the theatre?' —is to be secured by pausing to compare and contrast them, in much greater detail than can be permitted here, with their predecessors at one remove, the playwrights of the Edwardian and early Georgian eras.

[14] 'That Awful Museum', *The Twentieth Century*, clxix (1961), 214.
[15] 'Writing for Myself', *The Twentieth Century*, clxix (1961), 171.
[16] 'Building the Play', p. 33.
[17] Preface to *A Man for All Seasons* (1961), p. xviii.

Note

T. S. *Eliot* (1888–1965, St Louis, Missouri) began dramatic work with the un-finished melodrama *Sweeney Agonistes* (1926–7), published in *Collected Poems 1909–31* (1936). The pageant-play of *The Rock* (1934) was written with E. Martin Browne, who has produced all Eliot's plays; *Murder in the Cathedral* (1935) for the Canterbury Festival; *The Family Reunion* (1939); *The Cocktail Party* (1950), *The Confidential Clerk* (1954), and *The Elder Statesman* (1959), presented at the Edinburgh Festivals of 1949, 1953 and 1958. Browne has an account, 'From *The Rock* to *The Confidential Clerk* ', in *T. S. Eliot: a symposium for his seventieth birthday*, edited by N. Braybrooke (1958). David E. Jones's *The Plays of T. S. Eliot* (1960) is valuable and contains an excellent bibliography.

A recording of *Sweeney Agonistes* (CLP 1924) contains an unpublished scene.

Christopher Fry (b. 1907), began his dramatist's career with *The Boy with a Cart* (1938) and *The Tower* (1939), but came to wider audiences when Martin Browne, then Director of the Mercury Theatre introduced three new poetic plays in 1946: Norman Nicholson's *The Old Man of the Mountains*, Ronald Duncan's *This Way to the Tomb*, and Fry's *A Phoenix Too Frequent*. *The Lady's Not for Burning* (1949) ran at the Globe in 1949, with Gielgud and Pamela Brown in the cast. *Venus Observed* (1950) was at the St. James's in 1950, and *Ring Round the Moon* (a version of Anouilh's *L'Invitation au Château*) at the Globe in 1950. Among later festival contributions were *The Firstborn* (1946), produced at Edinburgh in 1948; *Thor, with Angels* (1949) for the Canterbury Festival of 1949. *A Sleep of Prisoners* (1951) was produced at St. Thomas's Church, Regent Street, 1950. *The Dark is Light Enough* (1954), written for Edith Evans, was at the Aldwych: *Curtmantle* (1961) was first performed at Tilburg. Fry's plays are published by Oxford University Press: *The Firstborn*, *Thor, with Angels* and *A Sleep of Prisoners* are in a collected paperback.

Faber & Faber publish Auden and Isherwood's *The Ascent of F 6* (1936) and *The Dog Beneath the Skin* (1935), Macneice's *The Dark Tower and other radio scripts* (1947) and his translation of *Agamemnon* (1936). The first version of Thomas's *Under Milk Wood* (Dent, 1954) appeared as *Llaregyb, a Piece for Radio Perhaps*, in *Botteghe Oscure* (Rome, 1952).

For earlier verse dramatists, there is a study by Priscilla Thouless of *Modern Poetic Drama* (1934). Denis Donoghue's *The Third Voice* (1959), is a well-documented account though controversial. Eliot's work is treated in Ronald Peacock's *The Poet in the Theatre* (1946), in Raymond Williams's *From Ibsen to Eliot* (1958), and in J. Middleton Murry's *Unprofessional Essays* (1956). Walter Stein has written on 'After the Cocktails', in *Essays in Criticism* (1953), and Raymond Williams on *Under Milk Wood* in *The Critical Quarterly* (Spring, 1959). Works of Shaw, Eliot, Fry and Thomas among others, are given close analysis in J. L. Styan's *The Elements of Drama* (1960). Martin Browne has a brief note on 'The Poet and the Stage' in *Penguin New Writing*, 31 (1947), 81–92. John Arden has written on 'Verse in the Theatre', *N.T.M.*, II, 3 (1961), 12–17.

V

Verse and Prose

KENNETH MUIR

★

THE most important event in the history of modern drama was Ibsen's abandonment of verse after *Peer Gynt* in order to write prose plays about contemporary problems. But the event was often misinterpreted, so that, as Rilke said, Ibsen was misunderstood in the midst of fame. Disciples of Ibsen in France, Germany and England thought they were following the master in writing naturalistic plays on social problems; but Ibsen himself explained clearly what his aim had been. Verse, he thought, had done immense injury to the art of the theatre; art forms become obsolete; and serious dramatists were unlikely to use verse in the foreseeable future. His aim, therefore, in the sequence of plays which began with *Pillars of Society*, was 'poetic creation in the plain unvarnished speech of reality'. To the end of his life he was a poet who wrote prose plays.

If one looks at the history of English drama between 1660 and 1900 one is bound to recognise that it bears out Ibsen's theory. Dryden and Congreve did write successful verse plays, but who would now read *The Mourning Bride* in preference to *The Way of the World* even if we may prefer *All for Love* to *Marriage à la Mode*? All through the eighteenth and nineteenth centuries nearly every good poet tried his hand at poetic drama, but they did not write a single play which is likely to be in the repertory of a National Theatre.

There were several reasons for this failure. Most of the poetic dramas written between 1700 and 1900 imitated literature rather than life; they had no immediate relevance to the age in which they were written;[1] they were completely lacking in the qualities which make the novels of the age so memorable; their authors never learnt the art

---

[1] Cf. Tennyson's *Becket* with *Murder in the Cathedral*.

of playwriting in the theatre itself[2] and they were not enough interested in human beings in action;[3] above all they never evolved a dramatic verse which could give the illusion of men speaking to men or distinguish between one character and another.

One example will serve for all these defects. Robert Bridges sometimes imitated classical drama (as in *Achilles*) and sometimes Elizabethan (as in *Nero*). He never wrote on a contemporary theme and never wrote with a real theatre in mind. One of his better plays, *Palicio*, is ruined by the fact that it is irremediably literary, that its characters are determined by the plot and never begin to come alive, and by its diction. At one point in the play Margaret, who has betrayed the conspiracy of the man she loves, because he has promised that if it fails he will marry her and settle down, is confronted by her irate lover:

MARGARET: 'Twas I betrayed thy men.
GIOVANNI: Ha! thou was't! Was't thou?
    From me, sorceress, thou viper, go from me!
    Traitress, was't thou? Thou wast my secret curse!
    Sent by the devil, wast thou, to destroy me,
    To kill my soul? . . .
    There is not any tyrant or crowned fiend
    Whom I will hate like thee.
MARGARET: Then kill me, Giovanni.   (*swoons.*
GIOVANNI: This dagger in my heart, and I am avenged.
    Nay, nay, O God, I am adding wrong to wrong.
                                        (*Putting dagger back.*
    . . . Alas! What have I done?
    I spake too roughly, Margaret; I was angry:
    I knew not what I said. Margaret, I am sorry.
    Forgive me, Margaret. Nay, I meant it not.
    I am not angry with thee now. I think
    I can forgive thee. Hear me! She doth not hear me.
    She doth not breathe. Her eyes are fixed and sightless.
    Her hands are cold.
    My God, oh, if I have killed her! Margaret, Margaret!

    [2] Tennyson expected Irving to make the necessary alterations to fit Becket for the stage.
    [3] Browning was, of course, interested in character, but it was only in the dramatic monologue that he successfully exploited that interest.

Dost thou not hear?—I have killed her—Margaret!
I do forgive thee. I forgive thee all.
O God, she is dead, she is dead.—Now if I kiss her,
If she can feel . . . She stirs. O, Margaret,
Hear me. I do forgive thee all.

MARGARET: Giovanni:
I did it for thy love.
GIOVANNI: Thank God, thank God.

We may pass over the absurd psychology of this climactic scene.[4]
Bridges apparently approves whole-heartedly of his moronic heroine
and he funks the real conflict between love and honour in his hero's
mind. His sudden changes from hatred to love by way of attempted
suicide are not made credible. But the worst flaw in the scene is the
diction which ranges from the pseudo-poetic to the flatly prosaic.
The succession of *was'ts* and *wasts* in the opening lines, the exclamatory
bathos of the speech after Margaret faints, the rhythmical woodenness
and linguistic poverty of the whole, and the complete lack of imagery
are some of the factors in Bridges' failure.

★   ★   ★

Irish poets, faced with the problem of how to revive poetic drama,
had certain advantages over their English counterparts. Drama to
them was part of a larger strategy of reviving or creating a national
culture. Their subjects, though often legendary, were at the same time
contemporary. What is more important, perhaps, is that Ireland had
been less affected by the industrial revolution.

Of the two leaders of the Irish dramatic movement, Yeats wrote
mainly in verse, Synge in prose. Yeats was writing plays for half a
century. His early ones resemble in style that of his early poems and
they are more lyrical than dramatic in their impact. Then after 1914,
at the same time as he was adopting a more taut and colloquial style
in his lyrics, he came under the influence of Fenollosa and of Nōh
plays in Pound's translation. In this period his plays were condensed,
and his verse was more forceful and colloquial. But it was only in his
old age, in such plays as *A Full Moon in March* and *Purgatory*, that he

[4] Hopkins, writing to Bridges of another play (*Letters*, I, p. 217), said that
the 'characters from men become puppets, their bloodshed becomes a leakage
of bran'.

reached his full stature as a dramatist; and, indeed, T. S. Eliot thought that only in the last play did Yeats solve 'his problem of speech in verse, and laid all his successors under obligation to him'. Yet, in spite of his lifetime of experimentation in poetic drama, Yeats never attempted to attract more than a coterie audience—perhaps because his powers of characterisation were never very great—and his best play, a play that uses the technique of the Nōh play while remaining absolutely modern, is *The Words on the Window Pane*, in which Swift, Stella and Vanessa speak through a spiritualist medium. It is written in prose.

Synge wrote non-dramatic verse of no great merit, but he wisely chose to write his plays in prose. He asserted that 'all art is collaboration' and claimed that he learnt more from overhearing the servant-girls through a chink in the floor than he did from books, although his favourite dramatist was Racine. He found Ibsen's plays 'joyless and pallid', as Yeats did,[5] and he believed that in countries such as Ireland

> where the imagination of the people, and the language they use, is rich and living, it is possible for a writer to be rich and copious in his words, and at the same time to give the reality, which is the root of all poetry, in a comprehensible and natural form.

We should be wrong, however, to assume that Synge merely imitated what he heard. Although the rhythms and the vocabulary of his dialogue are derived from peasant speech, it undergoes a process of transformation. The advantage of the peasant basis was that it enabled him to write a kind of prose poetry which could be accepted as natural. *Riders to the Sea* keeps fairly close to colloquial speech, but in the love scene in the last act of *The Playboy of the Western World*, there is obviously a considerable heightening of ordinary speech, though in the theatre we can still accept it as 'natural':

> If the mitred bishops seen you that time, they'd be the like of the holy prophets, I'm thinking, do be straining the bars of paradise to lay eyes on the Lady Helen of Troy, and she abroad, pacing back and forward, with a nosegay in her golden shawl.
>
> (Penguin edition, pp. 195–6)

This is closer to Rossetti than to the conversation of the Aran islanders.

[5] Joyce, significantly, began his career with a eulogy of Ibsen's last play.

The real heir of Synge was Sean O'Casey who found the material for his early plays in the Dublin slums during the 'troubles'. The inferiority of nearly all his later plays is frequently ascribed to his abandonment of realism. But we may suspect that English critics, who are willing to allow the Dublin proletariat to talk in vivid and eloquent prose and are not prepared to believe in eloquence nearer home, have misunderstood the nature of O'Casey's achievement and the reasons for his undoubted decline. Mrs. Boyle's great lament in the last act of *Juno and the Paycock* echoes word for word the speech of Mrs. Tancred in Act II. Even if we could believe that the speech was naturalistic in itself, it is impossible to suppose that a Mrs. Boyle in real life would have remembered her neighbour's speech with absolute accuracy:

> It's well I remember all that she said—an' it's my turn to say it now: What was the pain I suffered, Johnny, bringin' you into the world to carry you to your cradle, to the pains I'll suffer carryin' you out o' the world to bring you to your grave! Mother o' God, Mother o' God, have pity on us all! Blessed Virgin, where were you when me darlin' son was riddled with bullets, when me darlin' son was riddled with bullets? Sacred Heart o' Jesus, take away our hearts o' stone, and give us hearts o' flesh! Take away this murdherin' hate, an' give us Thine own eternal love!   (Collected edition, i, 87)

The comedy is likewise stylised. Some critics have complained of Boyle's use of 'chassis' (for chaos) and Fluther's repetition of 'derogatory'. Although this may seem exaggerated on the printed page, it justifies itself in the theatre. O'Casey invests all his characters with a wonderful gift of the gab, as in this exchange between Mrs. Burgess and Mrs. Gogan:

> BESSIE: Bessie Burgess doesn't put up to know much, never havin' a swaggerin' mind, thanks be to God, but goin' on packin' up knowledge accordin' to her conscience: precept upon precept, line upon line; here a little, an' there a little. But, thanks be to Christ, she knows when she was got, where she was got, an' how she was got; while there's some she knows, decoratin' their finger with a well-polished weddin' ring, would be hard put to it if they were assed to show their weddin' lines!
>
> MRS. GOGAN: Y'oul' rip of a blasted liar, me weddin' ring's been well earned be twenty years be th' side o' me husband, now takin' his rest in heaven, married to me be Father Dempsey, in th' Chapel

o' Saint Jude's, in th' Christmas Week of eighteen hundred an' ninety-five; an' any kid, livin' or dead, that Jinnie Gogan's had since, was got between th' bordhers of th' Ten Commandments!

(1926 ed., p. 59)

In *Within the Gates* O'Casey abandoned any pretence of realism after he had experimented with expressionism in one act of *The Silver Tassie*. The symbolic use of the four seasons in the four acts of *Within the Gates*, the Chorus of Down-and-Outs, the instructions that the dialogue of the last twelve pages should be intoned, the naming of the characters (Gardener, Dreamer, Atheist, Bishop, Young Whore), the morality technique, and the use of allegory—the Young Whore, for instance, is the illegitimate daughter of the Bishop—are indications of how far O'Casey had moved away from the style of his early plays. A similar technique is used in *The Star Turns Red*, a play which sacrifices art to ideology both in plot and characterisation, but which contains one superb scene. In it, against a chorus of the lame, the halt and the blind, is debated the question of whether religion is the opium of the people.

O'Casey has tried deliberately to write poetic drama in prose. If his early model was Synge, his later models were Strindberg and O'Neill. He surpasses O'Neill in eloquence, but in nearly all his later plays he seems to be eloquent in a dramatic vacuum. But one may be tempted to suspect that it was the merits rather than the defects of his plays that banished them from the professional stage.[6]

* * *

Bernard Shaw's plays were disliked by the poets. Although he was Irish and wrote one play for the Abbey Theatre, Yeats thought that he wrote 'with great effect without music, without style, either good or bad' and that he eliminated 'from the mind all emotional implication'. Shaw to him was a sewing-machine that clicked and shone and smiled.[7] Pound described him as a tenth-rate artist. Eliot, in his 'Dia-

[6] The best of the next generation of Irish dramatists was Denis Johnston, who wrote one interesting impressionistic play—*A Bride for the Unicorn*—and one masterpiece—*The Moon in the Yellow River*—somewhat in the manner of Chekhov, but with broader comic scenes. His later plays have been disappointing.

[7] Yeats and Shaw both admired William Morris, though for different reasons, and they loved the same actress, also for different reasons (*Autobiographies*, p. 283).

logue on Dramatic Poetry' (1928), remarked that 'Shaw has a great deal of poetry, but all stillborn; Shaw is dramatically precocious, and poetically less than immature'. But in his later essay 'Poetry and Drama' Eliot likened Shaw's prose style to that of Congreve.

The idea that he was a mere propagandist, one who used the stage as a platform and his characters as mouthpieces for his own ideas, was encouraged by Shaw himself in some of his early prefaces. But when Allardyce Nicoll spoke of him as a follower of Robertson, Pinero, Jones and Ibsen, Shaw, then an old man, protested. His real masters, he asserted, were Shakespeare, Mozart and Wagner.

It is now obvious, if not to dramatic critics, that Shaw was not in any sense a naturalistic dramatist; that the element of fantasy far outweighs the touches of realism; that he writes a prose which, even in his last feeble plays, is unique in its compound of lucidity, precision and eloquence; that his plays have been preserved from the fate that has overtaken Pinero and Jones, partly because of his superior intelligence but more because of the timelessness of his style;[8] that his long speeches are set pieces constructed with great art; and that very few of his characters can be regarded as mouthpieces for his own ideas. Eric Bentley, easily the most perceptive of Shaw's critics, is perfectly right to stress the way in which in *Major Barbara* the truth emerges from the conflicting opinions of Barbara, Cusins and Undershaft, and that none of these characters expresses Shaw's own views without qualification.

There are, of course, weaknesses in many of Shaw's plays. His love scenes are generally embarrassing (like that of Vivie and Frank in *Mrs. Warren's Profession*); his portraits of poets (for instance Marchbanks and Octavius) are unintentionally sentimental; he spoils some of his best scenes by tasteless buffoonery (such as the trial of St. Joan); and he can be long-winded and tedious, as in the middle parts of *Back to Methuselah*. But these and other flaws should not blind us to his greatness. Has any dramatist, since Shakespeare, written so many good plays?

Shaw was at first liberated and afterwards spoiled by his own success. It enabled him to experiment, but it ended by allowing him to get away with much inferior work. When he wrote *Man and Superman* he inserted the Hell scene in a well-constructed comedy from which it could easily be detached. (The Hell scene contains some of his best

[8] The only other play of the period which has not significantly dated is *The Importance of Being Earnest*.

writing but at this stage of his career he could not expect that the whole play would be performed.) In *Heartbreak House* the element of symbolism first becomes pronounced. The play was clearly intended to be a representation of the impact of the 1914–18 war on capitalist England. Shaw's avowed model was Chekhov, though it has more in common with Strindberg, to the translation of whose plays Shaw devoted his Nobel prize money. Its value lies in its cleansing wit, in its moral force, and in its vein of genuine poetry. The following passage from the last act illustrates what may be called the Shavian poetic imagination:

> HECTOR: And this ship that we are all in? This soul's prison we call England?
>
> CAPTAIN SHOTOVER: The captain is in his bunk, drinking bottled ditch-water; and the crew is gambling in the forecastle. She will strike and sink and split. Do you think the laws of God will be suspended in favour of England because you were born in it?
>
> HECTOR: Well, I don't mean to be drowned like a rat in a trap. I still have the will to live. What am I to do?
>
> CAPTAIN SHOTOVER: Do? Nothing simpler. Learn your business as an Englishman.
>
> HECTOR: And what may my business as an Englishman be, pray?
>
> CAPTAIN SHOTOVER: Navigation. Learn it and live; or leave it and be damned.   (*Complete Plays*, p. 801)

The method of *Heartbreak House* is carried further in most of the later plays, and they lack the brilliance and power of the masterpieces. The three political plays (*The Apple Cart*, *On the Rocks* and *Geneva*) are all set in the future; and so too are such fantasies as the later parts of *Back to Methuselah*, *The Simpleton of the Unexpected Isles* and *Too True to be Good*. In the last of these all the characters are allegorical—the Clergyman-Burglar (Lost Faith), the Invalid (the Sick World), the pious Sergeant who reads Bunyan, Sweetie (the Lower Centres made vocal by the discoveries of Freud and Lawrence) and the Atheist who has lost his faith in rational determinism. Shaw was right to recognise his affinities with the author of *Everyman*.

*   *   *

Meanwhile there had been attempts to revive poetic drama in England. Stephen Phillips, for example, though negligible as a poet, had an inside knowledge of the theatre and a certain facility. In the first years of the century he wrote a number of verse plays which had some success on the stage and which deluded responsible critics— Colvin, Churton Collins and Archer—into comparing him with Sophocles, Racine and Dante. We can now see that he was entirely derivative, that his language exhibits the putrescence of a dead romanticism, that his blank verse was flabby, and that even his characters were wooden.

Most of the other poets were influenced in their different ways by the Abbey Theatre. John Masefield, for example, tried in his first full-length play, *The Tragedy of Nan*, to find an equivalent for Synge's poetic prose. It is written in dialect and the plot is laid in the early nineteenth century when one could literally be hanged for stealing a sheep. In spite of a melodramatic plot, of some lapses into sentimentality, and of a gaffer who acts as a maundering chorus, it remains Masefield's most effective play and it provided Lillah MacCarthy with an opportunity which she took superbly. It was not Masefield's fault that the dialect he chose was less expressive than the speech of Irish peasants and that as a result his attempts to lift it into poetry exhibit a sense of strain not apparent in Synge's work. Masefield's later experiments in non-dialect prose (*Pompey the Great* and *The Faithful*), in rhymed verse (*Good Friday* and *Philip the King*), and in regular and free blank verse (*A King's Daughter* and *Tristan and Isolt*) were less successful. Laurence Binyon has the negative virtues that his blank verse is not obviously derivative, it never lapses into romantic tushery, and it does not call attention to itself. But it is lacking in personality; it contains no vivid imagery, no illuminating phrases; it is somewhat academic. Gordon Bottomley, who wrote better blank verse than any of the Georgians, became less and less dramatic; so that, in his later rhymed plays, which were performed by verse-speaking choirs, what action there was came to us through a haze of beautiful words. These poets and many others wrote not for ordinary playgoers but for 'poetry-lovers'; their plays were for the most part performed by amateurs; their themes were mostly archaic and without the contemporary relevance which Celtic themes had at the Abbey Theatre; they never found a suitable verse medium; and there was some justification for Yeats's description of one of them that he was a sheep in sheep's clothing.[9]

[9] Flecker's *Hassan*, written mostly in prose, did have a considerable success in

There is some irony in the fact that Thomas Hardy, who was in some ways more successful in solving the problem of how to write modern dramatic verse, did not write his epic drama for the stage. The blank verse of *The Dynasts* and *The Tragedy of the Queen of Cornwall*, stiff and awkward as it often is, and sprinkled with odd words, escapes the romantic anonymity of style so prevalent in poetic drama before the First World War. At his worst, where he is indulging in philosophical commentary on the action, Hardy writes in a strange jargon:

> Things mechanized
> By coils and pivots set to foreframed codes
> Would, in a thorough-sphered melodic rule,
> And governance of sweet consistency,
> Be cessed no pain, whose burnings would abide
> With That Which holds responsibility,
> Or inexist.

This indigestible passage comes just after the death of Nelson, a scene which, in spite of clumsiness, does come across with genuine poetic power:

> Yes, Hardy; yes; I know it. You must go—
> Here we shall meet no more; since Heaven forfend
> That care for me should keep you idle now,
> When all the ship demands you. Beatty, too,
> Go to the others who lie bleeding there;
> Them you can aid. Me you can render none!
> My time here is the briefest.—If I live
> But long enough I'll anchor . . . But—too late—
> My anchoring's elsewhere ordered! . . . Kiss me, Hardy:
> I'm satisfied. Thank God, I have done my duty!

It would be quite easy to find fault with several of these lines—the inversions in the sixth line, for example—but it is refreshing to read Hardy after the more obviously 'poetical' dramatists discussed in this section.

$$\star \qquad \star \qquad \star$$

---

the West End; but this was due more to the things it had in common with *Chu Chin Chow* than to its real merits. Its pseudo-oriental language did offer a solution of how to write poetic drama in prose, but from the nature of things it was a solution which was useless to other dramatists.

The most important figure in the attempt to revive poetic drama in the thirties was T. S. Eliot, whose greatness as a poet and eminence as a critic have made his plays the central topic of discussion, a centrality they might not have achieved on their merits alone. His first full-length play was not written until he was in his middle forties, but he had been considering the problems of poetic drama for many years. The best of his early essays were concerned with Elizabethan and Jacobean dramatists whose style left their mark on his early poems. His attack on Gilbert Murray's translation of Euripides has a wider target than appears at first sight. In 'A Dialogue on Dramatic Poetry', one of Eliot's spokesmen, E, argues that 'the perfect and ideal drama is to be found in the ceremony of the Mass'; and G declares that 'we must find a new form of verse which shall be as satisfactory a vehicle for us as blank verse was for the Elizabethans'. By this time he had written the fragmentary *Sweeney Agonistes* in which he had experimented in poetic rhythms close to some forms of colloquial speech—

> I gotta use words when I talk to you
> But if you understand or if you don't
> That's nothing to me and nothing to you—

and in choruses which imitated Jazz lyrics and the Savoy operas. In *Murder in the Cathedral* he claimed to have modelled his verse on that of *Everyman*, though some of the best dialogue is not; and the great choruses perhaps owe most to Walt Whitman and Saint-John Perse's *Anabase* which he had just translated. The prose speeches of the Knights at the end were intended, as Eliot later admitted, 'to shock the audience out of their complacency'; but although they achieve that end they destroy the unity of the play.

In his later plays from *The Family Reunion* to *The Elder Statesman* Eliot was gradually evolving a form of verse which would not be noticed as such in the theatre. He succeeded in his aim; but the price he had to pay was very heavy. There are other reasons for the weakness of these plays, but much of their dialogue would have been better expressed in prose:

> You've changed your name too, since I knew you.
> When we were up at Oxford, you were plain Dick Ferry.
> Then when you married, you took your wife's name
> And became Mr. Richard Claverton-Ferry;
> And finally Lord Claverton.

Eliot states his own aim as

> finding a form of versification and an idiom which would serve all
> my purposes, without recourse to prose, and be capable of un-
> broken transition between the most intense speech and the most
> relaxed dialogue.

In practice the development of this unobtrusive verse has coincided
with a steady decline in poetic power; and though the two things may
be unconnected one cannot help feeling that the Elizabethan practice
of alternating verse and prose is preferable to Eliot's use of verse for
prosaic matters. No one thinks that Hamlet is being 'poetic' when he
changes from prose to verse at the end of Act II.

Eliot is now very critical of *The Family Reunion* and his sympathies
have switched from Harry to the totally unsympathetic Amy. He is
right to point out the structural weakness of the play and the awkward-
ness of the chorus of aunts and uncles. One is less certain about the
need for apologising for the lyrical duets he uses three times in the
course of the play. Eliot suggests that the member of the audience 'is
putting up with a suspension of the action in order to enjoy a poetic
fantasia'. But it is just not true to say 'that they are hardly more than
passages of poetry which might be spoken by anybody'. They are a
means—and a very effective one—of showing the *rapport* between
Harry and Mary (afterwards destroyed) and between Harry and Agatha.

AGATHA: Only feet walking
  And sharp heels scraping. Over and under
  Echo and noise of feet, and the eye
  Seeing the feet: the unwinking eye
  Fixing the movement. Over and under.
HARRY: In and out, in an endless drift
  Of shrieking forms in a circular desert
  Weaving with contagion of putrescent embraces
  On dissolving bone. In and out, the movement
  Until the chain broke, and I was left
  Under the single eye above the desert.
                (1947 ed., p. 107)

Whatever we may think of these passages, the normal verse of the
play is a remarkably successful medium both for the trivial conversation between the aunts and uncles and for the more intense speeches
of the hero and Agatha, and even for the speeches of Downing, the

chauffeur. The later plays show a gradual deterioration. The verse, as verse, is as skilful as ever; but there are fewer and fewer passages in which it rises above the prosaic—a few speeches of Celia in *The Cocktail Party*, a single scene in *The Confidential Clerk*, and a few lines, perhaps, in *The Elder Statesman*. In trying to make poetic drama acceptable to an ordinary audience, Eliot has gone to the limit of compromise. The result has been that although the plays have been enjoyed at a superficial level, the deeper meanings have gone unrecognised by most of the audience. We may well ask what is the use of writing about sainthood and vocation if the audience goes away from a performance believing it has been watching a drawing-room comedy almost worthy of Noël Coward.

* * *

Although Eliot's later plays were derived, if remotely, from Aeschylus, Euripides, Menander and Sophocles, he tried to graft poetic drama on the popular form of modern drawing-room comedy. But Auden and Isherwood believed that the pantomime, the music hall and the revue were the popular theatrical forms of our time, and they tried, particularly in *The Dog beneath the Skin*, to make use of them for their own purposes. They were also influenced, it would seem, by the plays of Brecht, then little known in England. The man disguised as a dog and the doggerel of the opening scene are reminiscent of pantomime, and some of the scenes are like revue sketches. Much of the political satire has dated, but the scenes in Paradise Park and the hospital are still reasonably effective. The writing is very uneven, there is no attempt at characterisation (Auden, indeed, argued that types rather than characters are desirable in poetic drama), much of it reads like an undergraduate skit rather than serious satire, and not one of the scenes is worthy of the fine poetry of the choruses. *The Ascent of F6* is superior in almost every way: it has a better plot, there is some rudimentary attempt at characterisation, there is some good verse[10] and better prose (notably in the speech of the Abbot) and the

---

[10] e.g.   O you, who are the history and the creator
Of all those forms in which we are condemned to suffer;
To whom the intelligent and necessary is also the just;
Show me my path, show all of us, that each upon
This mortal star may feel himself the danger
That under his hand is softly palpitating. (pp. 72–3)

theme is complex and significant. Critics have rightly complained that Auden is too eclectic in his style, and F. R. Leavis and others have pointed out that in the scene on the mountain where sublimity is required Auden provides only a serious parody of Shakespeare:

> O senseless hurricanes,
> That waste yourselves upon the unvexed rock,
> Find some employment proper to your powers,
> Press on the neck of Man your murdering thumbs
> And earn real gratitude! Astrologers,
> Can you not scold the fated loitering star
> To run to its collision and our end?   (p. 104)

But the critics are less justified in their complaints that Auden never makes up his mind what the subject of the play really is. It can be taken as an adventure story, a race to reach the summit of the mountain; or as a satire on imperialism; or as a satire on the boredom of suburban life which demands heroes in whose exploits the bored can experience a vicarious excitement; or as a play about the hero's mother-fixation; or, finally, as a tragedy of spiritual pride. The play is about all these things, and Auden and Isherwood display considerable skill in appealing on these different levels and in creating a sort of unity out of such diverse themes.[11] But the play, and its weaker successor, *On the Frontier*, achieved only a coterie audience.

Louis MacNeice's feeble stage play, *Out of the Picture*, is very much in the Auden manner, and so too are some of his radio plays. The best of them, *The Dark Tower*, was so successful that it seemed for a while that the real future of verse drama would be on the radio. Yet its value depends not on the quality of the verse, which would seem undistinguished in quotation, but on a brilliant exploitation of the medium. MacNeice has, in one respect, been underrated. He is not even mentioned in the most substantial book on modern poetic drama, *The Third Voice*, although his translation of *Agamemnon* seems to me greatly superior to Pound's *Women of Trachis* (which is praised at some length by Denis Donoghue) and although in it he solved the problem of how to write dramatic verse which is natural, modern and speakable. A brief comparison will illustrate the lively impropriety of Pound's version and the straightforward propriety of MacNeice's. This is the dying Herakles:

[11] Cf. E. M. Forster's review of the play in *The Listener*.

Misery. I'm going out
and my light's gone.
          The black out!
I understand perfectly well
where things have got to . . . Go, son,
call all my seed and their kindred
and Alkmene, ill-starred for the empty name
of the Godhead, my mother,
so they can get my last report
of the oracles, as I know them.

This is part of the herald's speech in *Agamemnon*:

If I were to tell of our labours, our hard lodging,
The sleeping on crowded decks, the scanty blankets,
Tossing and groaning, rations that never reached us—
And the land too gave matter for more disgust
For our beds lay under the enemy's walls.
Continuous drizzle from the sky, dews from the marshes,
Rotting our clothes, filling our hair with lice.

                              (pp. 31–2)

The comparison is weighted against MacNeice in that this passage does not come from one of the great passages in the play, whereas the death of Herakles is the climax of *Women of Trachis*; and yet is it not apparent that Pound slides from modernity to archaism, embarrassing to actor and audience, while MacNeice provides us with a satisfying translation which nevertheless could have been written only after Eliot?

A word should be said of one of the most original plays of the inter-war period, Stephen Spender's *Trial of a Judge*. Spender is an intro-spective poet and by no means a born dramatist; but in this play— which presents the dilemma facing a liberal judge on the eve of the Nazis' seizure of power—he hit on a powerful theme and a dramatic technique for putting it across. What is more, the verse (at least in the speeches of the hero) is unexpectedly effective on the stage. The play is not a complete success because both the villains and the com-munists are stereotypes, and because the verse they are given to speak is feeble.

Christopher Fry, the last of the verse dramatists to be considered, has been unlucky in his critics. The verbal pyrotechnics of *A Phoenix Too Frequent* and *The Lady's Not for Burning* led to such extravagant estimates of his achievement as a dramatist that there was an inevitable reaction. Critics complained that his imagery was decorative rather than organic, that he was drunk with words, that he was lacking in seriousness, that his lines were often impossible to scan, that his plays were badly constructed, and his characters puppets. Whether Fry took these criticisms to heart or developed away from the exuberance of youth, in *The Dark is Light Enough* he pruned his style so much that it became colourless. But in *Curtmantle* (1961), written after a lapse of seven years, he achieved a style of remarkable power. Two passages will illustrate Fry's development; the first is from *The Lady's Not for Burning*:

> When he was born he gave an algebraic
> Cry; at one glance measured the cubic content
> Of that ivory cone his mother's breast
> And multiplied his appetite by five.
> So he matured by a progression, gained
> Experience by correlation, expanded
> Into a marriage by contraction, and by
> Certain physical dynamics
> Formulated me.

This is a witty use of scientific language to describe the life of a scientist; but there is nothing in the language to differentiate the speaker from others in the same play. The passage is metrically unsatisfactory because the actress is compelled to ignore the division of the lines. One is tempted to wonder whether it would lose anything by being printed as prose. Fry's imagery and phrasing are often charming, but they call attention to themselves rather than to the theme of the play.

Here, by contrast—and the contrast is not merely between tragedy and comedy—is a passage from *Curtmantle* in which Becket is reluctant to become Archbishop:

> I haven't said so.
> But listen to the things I fear. However much
> We both imperatively want it otherwise,
> You're dividing us, and, what is more, forcing
> Yourself and me, indeed the whole kingdom,

Into a kind of intrusion on the human mystery,
Where we may not know what it is we're doing,
What powers we are serving, or what is being made of us.
Or even understand the conclusion when it comes.
Delivering us up, in fact, to universal workings
Which neither you nor I wish to comply with
Or even to contemplate.   (p. 22)

This is admirable dramatic verse and *Curtmantle* would be Fry's best play, and one that shows that he is still developing, if its structure had matched its verse.[12]

★   ★   ★

During the last decade a large number of new dramatists have appeared on the scene. Some of them—Wesker and Osborne, for example—are most successful when they are most realistic. But many of the others have experimented in different kinds of unrealistic drama. Beckett's *Waiting for Godot* is the representation of a situation rather than of an action. It is a prolonged music-hall turn, a tragi-comic allegory of what the existentialists call *délaissement*. Few of the speeches are more than five or six words in length, but they are arranged in rhythmical patterns, skilfully varied in repetition, and in some passages the influence of Joyce is apparent. N. F. Simpson writes surrealist farces, reflecting in a distorting mirror the absurdity of accepted ideas. Harold Pinter, like Simpson influenced by Ionesco, uses dialogue superficially colloquial to express neurosis, madness and terror. There is not a single speech in *The Birthday Party* and *The Caretaker* which could not be spoken by ordinary people in real life, but the total effect is Kafkaesque and terrifying The bewilderment of the tramp employed as a caretaker, the ritualistic speeches of McCann and Goldberg in the last act of *The Birthday Party*, and Aston's tremendous monologue at the end of the second act of *The Caretaker* are examples of 'poetic creation in the plain unvarnished speech of reality'.[13]

[12] Among other verse dramatists may be noted Ronald Duncan, Anne Ridler, Patric Dickinson and Andrew Young.

[13] John Mortimer's *What shall we tell Caroline?* and John Arden's *Serjeant Musgrave's Dance* may also be mentioned.

These plays have been successful in the West End; and, in spite of the long runs of *The Cocktail Party* and *The Lady's Not for Burning* there does not seem any immediate prospect of a revival of verse drama in the theatre. Even on the radio the outstanding poetic success since the war was Dylan Thomas' prose play, *Under Milk Wood*. Holbrook has recently complained[14] that it is 'a tedious piece of verbal "ingenuity", "redeemed" only by its innuendos and salacious jokes'; that its style is derived and debased from *Ulysses*; that Thomas's ' "vitality" of language is really an immature "draft" effervescence', and that it is a failure, morally, dramatically and artistically. Thomas' real crime, we may suspect, is that the play was unforgivably successful. The jokes are often genuinely funny; the style is only occasionally derived from Joyce—it is mostly watered-down Thomas; and a process of simplification, but not vulgarisation, was necessary if a radio audience was to follow it at a first hearing. Thomas quite properly submitted to his medium—as his betters, Shakespeare and Molière had to do—and the result is a masterpiece, one of the very few radio plays which deserve the title.[15]

It is essentially a poetic play in prose. Yet it could be argued that the two best poets of our time have failed to write plays as great as their non-dramatic poetry not because of a failure of appreciation in their audiences, nor because of the economics of the theatre, nor even a failure on the part of the poets to find a suitable dramatic verse. The fact is that, despite Yeats's assumption of 'masks' (of Crazy Jane or Michael Robartes) and despite Eliot's belief that all poetry is dramatic, they both lacked the power of creating vital characters. They, much more than Shaw, used their characters to express themselves. In *The Cocktail Party*, for example, Eliot could imagine Celia, but most of the other characters seem to me to be caricatures; and it is difficult to believe in any of the characters in *The Elder Statesman*, and one would not find them very interesting even if one could believe in them.

The best plays of the present century—two by Synge, six or seven by Shaw, two or three by O'Casey—have all been in prose; and this confirms Ibsen's prophecy that prose would be the principle dramatic medium in the foreseeable future. Audiences are accustomed to prose and for the most part seem to regard verse as vaguely unnatural. A poet who wishes to write verse plays has difficulty, therefore, in over-

---

[14] *The Modern Age* (ed. Boris Ford), pp. 417 ff.
[15] Another is Beckett's *All that Fall* (1957).

coming the uneasiness and inhibitions of his audience. But we have not yet had a fair test. We have not had since the age of Shakespeare a great poet who was also a good dramatist. If one were to emerge there is little doubt that he would find the audience he needed.

Note

Anton Chekhov (1860–1904). *The Seagull* was produced by the Moscow Art Theatre in its first season (1898), and his other great plays were written in the next six years. The standard translation is by Constance Garnett (Chatto & Windus, 1923 and 1935) from which all quotations are taken. Penguin Books has published a new translation by Elisaveta Fen (1959).

Constantin Stanislavski (1863–1938). He was co-founder and Director of the Moscow Art Theatre. Translations include *My Life in Art* (1924), *An Actor Prepares* (1936) and *Building a Character* (1949).

N. F. Simpson. He is a schoolteacher turned dramatist. *A Resounding Tinkle* won a prize in *The Observer* competition and was first produced at the Royal Court, London, in 1957. A one-act version was performed there the following year, together with *The Hole*. *One Way Pendulum* was performed at the end of 1959 and transferred to the Criterion Theatre. Revue sketches by Simpson were performed in London in 1959 and in 1961 a one-act play, *The Form*.
Faber published *One Way Pendulum* (1960), and French *The Hole* and the one-act version of *Tinkle* (1958); quotations are from these editions. A fuller version of *Tinkle* appeared in *Observer Plays*, ed. K. Tynan (1958) and the Penguin *New English Dramatists, 2* (1960).

John Whiting. Born at Salisbury in 1917, he trained as an actor. His first play was *Penny for a Song* (1951) and his most recent *The Devils* (1961). Three plays were published by Heinemann in 1957, and *The Devils* in 1961.
Whiting has an interview in *Encore* (1961) and pages 'From my Diary' in *The Twentieth Century* (1961).

Eugène Ionesco. A French-speaking Roumanian living in Paris, he was born in 1912. *La Cantratrice chauve* was his first play to be performed (1950) and *The Lesson*, the first in English (1955, at the Arts Theatre Club). Translations, mostly by D. Watson, have been published by Calder & Evergreen (7 vols; 1958–67). Quotations are from this translation. There is a Penguin paperback (1962) of three plays, *Rhinoceros*, *Chairs* and *The Lesson*.
M. Esslin's *Theatre of the Absurd* (1962) and R. Coe's *Ionesco* (1961) should be consulted; the latter contains an admirable bibliography. Ionesco's criticism has been collected as *Notes and Counter-Notes* (1964).

General. Recent articles are G. Hauger, 'When is a Play not a Play', *T.D.R.* (1960); R. W. Corrigan, 'The Theatre in Search of a Fix', *T.D.R.* (1961). and P. Brook, 'Search for a Hunger', *Encore* (1961).

For *Pinter* see note to Chapter I, and for *Beckett* note to Chapter VII.

VI

Back to the Text

R. D. SMITH

★

At first sight the title may seem rather catchpenny, but I don't think it is, even though this article contains more general argument than detailed textual criticism. There is so little attention paid to what new playwrights actually write, and so little chance of experiencing their work in the theatre, that an effort must be made, if their very real achievement is to be appreciated.

All the arts are suffering from a decline in critical standards through the pressure of mass journalism. The theatre, sharing the general difficulty, has its own problems that make it specially hard for a dramatist to have his work received on the serious level at which he has created it. In the mass-circulation paper, a 'personality' gets drunk on a television screen; a princess has a night out at a theatre; a long-established stage marriage breaks up; an actress has a baby with the press snooping round; and a play, and possibly a dramatist (not to mention an actor) at the beginning of his career, may fail or succeed with no more reason than a new detergent firm may boom or bankrupt. In the literary weeklies, dramatists are tested by 'social' or 'political' touchstones (Black Mark—Whiting and Dennis); or worse, by the fashion of the season, they are 'in the movement' or 'old hat' (Black Mark—Rattigan and Fry). Even the few serious critics strive to find symbolical, allegorical interpretations that reduce the rich substance and intellectual complexity of a good play to one tidy, topical 'explanation'. The theatre, long exiled from the serious arts, needs intelligent criticism; as things are it's not surprising that theatre people are wary of what they're being offered.

'Personally, I loathe all abstract discussions about the theatre. They bore me,' said Sir Laurence Olivier.[1] Harold Pinter declared 'I

---

[1] Cf. A. Pryce-Jones, 'Sir Laurence Olivier or Larry', *Theatre Arts* (1961), p. 14.

certainly don't write from any kind of abstract idea. And I wouldn't know a symbol if I saw one:' [2] John Arden, in his introduction to *Serjeant Musgrave's Dance*, takes pains to tell us that the play is *not* symbolic, and John Whiting has modestly explained how *Saint's Day* started with a particular object, a mural in a house, and the extraordinary feeling it gave him.[3]

Dramatists, with novelists, poets, composers and painters, are suffering from the pressures of finance and publicity which force art into fashionable distortions. The Venice Biennale is more a guide to the international money market than to what genuinely contemporary artists are doing. Pictures and sculpture from Korea, Poland, Venezuela, England, Norway are indistinguishable in style and intention, and a special ad-man's prose, poetical and pseudo-scientific at once, has been created to sell the products to the business world. Novelists, and even poets, are clumped together in schools and movements by critics who so save themselves the bother of finding out what each individual writer is saying. (This labelling is very different from the forming of a coterie by artists themselves when they are working on a common problem, or towards a common end.) Labels like Lucky Jim, Angry Young Men, Kitchen Sinks, Fifties' Poets, New Wave, induce general chatter about abstractions, and encourage people to fill newspaper columns with polemics on hypothetical modes of behaviour. More and more people work up an intellectual and moral sweat without the exertion of actually reading and experiencing a work, and seem to prefer to the created original the printed criticism it promotes, and even the criticism of the criticism.

*　　*　　*

If it is true that in art we need to get back to the paint and the stone, and in poetry and prose to the text, then in the theatre it is most urgent to get back to the play as the author has written it. And this presents problems peculiar to the dramatist. For however difficult it is for an original novelist or poet to be generally appreciated, a text is readily available and there are always some readers who do read and understand and appreciate. A dramatist, whose 'text' is only fully experienced in stage performance, is at the mercy of many confusing, concealing or distorting influences. The 'front-office' Big Brother puts on pressure for box-office considerations: supporters of the Actors' Theatre theory,

[2] *Twentieth Century* (1961), p. 174.   [3] Cf. *Encore* (1961), p. 14.

or the Producers' Theatre theory, use the author's text as a basis for personal exhibitionism: the Lord Chamberlain weakens and suppresses by censorship: the 'theatre-going public', anxious to be 'taken out of itself', stays away if it feels it's going to be disturbed, and most of the intelligentsia are sniffy in the fashionable manner: critics too often are peering through keyholes, or grinding axes, while some of their colleagues, political Jack Horners, if they cannot pull out of the text luscious plums of social exhortation, strike the play off the menu, and say what a bad boy the dramatist is.

Of course, dull or wilful productions, and hostile criticism, will not entirely obscure real talent, but complete lack of financial backing will and does. Theatres, following the lead of the Royal Court and Theatre Workshop, are giving us increased chances of getting to know the new dramatist. And some brave publishers are taking chances in putting out the texts of plays. It is generally possible to get hold of a text: the problem is to read it meaningfully. For the text of a play, like a musical score, is not comprehended by the untrained reader, and except, possibly, to the really gifted person will never, at a reading, yield up all its subtleties and profundities. Even actors and producers, despite their expertise, make bad mistakes when reading plays, and the reader who is not practised in the theatre will have to train himself to enlarge his imagination before the text of the play will flower for him. The text of a play is more than the words on the page. The things implied are as important as the things uttered. The décor and costumes and lighting give overtones and undertones to apparently simple statements. The placing of characters on a stage, the prominence they are given, the way they may illuminate a scene though they never speak, all these points are difficult to take in the study. They are difficult, but immensely worth working for.

A useful approach to the problem is by assessing the reasons for one's disappointment after seeing or hearing a well-known text performed on screen or radio. The film of *The Importance of Being Earnest*, seeking to make the best of its brilliant cast, shot one character delivering a crack and then cut to the reaction of the character to whom it was addressed. This had the effect of killing the joke stone-dead: in place of verbal wit we were invited to admire actors' virtuosity. Bad television directors have still not learned this valuable lesson, and tend to make passable comic lines unbearable by this trick of over-emphasis.

A play by Chekhov on radio or television is less than half what it is in the theatre. One is glad to have the half because half of Chekhov is better than the whole of most contemporary hacks, but once a play by Chekhov (or by any creative stage dramatist) has been fully experienced in the theatre, its transfer to another medium can only be a let-down. Similarly, reading say *The Cherry Orchard* without awareness of the possibilities of the full theatrical context can easily lead to misinterpretation of Chekhov's meaning. Even directors can isolate a single speech and build an 'interpretation' of the play round its misreading.

Trofimov, the eternal student, says:

Humanity progresses, perfecting its powers. Everything that is beyond its ken now will one day become familiar and comprehensible; only we must work, we must with all our powers aid the seeker after truth. Here among us in Russia the workers are few in number as yet. The vast majority of the intellectual people I know, seek nothing, do nothing, are not fit as yet for work of any kind. They call themselves intellectual, but they treat their servants as inferiors, behave to the peasants as though they were animals, learn little, read nothing seriously, do practically nothing, only talk about science and know very little about art. They are all serious people, they all have severe faces, they all talk of weighty matters and air their theories, and yet the vast majority of us—ninety-nine per cent. —live like savages, at the least thing fly to blows and abuse, eat piggishly, sleep in filth and stuffiness, bugs everywhere, stench and damp and moral impurity. And it's clear all our fine talk is only to divert our attention and other people's. Show me where to find the crèches there's so much talk about, and the reading-rooms? They only exist in novels: in real life there are none of them. There is nothing but filth and vulgarity and Asiatic apathy. I fear and dislike very serious faces. I'm afraid of serious conversations. We should do better to be silent.   (p. 39)

This speech in isolation can be made to bear the meaning that Trofimov is a forerunner of the C.P.S.U., and that the other characters are worthless and contemptible: if it came from certain modern plays that might well be the right interpretation. In an imperfectly imagined context of a nineteenth-century Russia filled with lovable eccentrics the speech can be made to indicate an atmosphere of pathetic helplessness in which all the main characters are to be admired and

pitied equally: if it came from a play by N. C. Hunter that might be
the right interpretation. Clearly neither is right for Chekhov, who
loathed both preaching and sentimental indulgence, and who always
insisted on the need to emphasise the comic elements in the plays.

Take the governess Carlotta Ivanovna. In the theatre she is a powerful character, and important to the mood of the play. On radio or on
the screen she practically disappears. Why? Because in the theatre,
even when off the scene, she is *there*, so that when she speaks her infrequent words have a detonating effect. In the text she enters Act I
with at least eight other people and a pet dog, and says one line, 'My
little dog eats nuts, too.' One move before she enters again, has two
lines, and exits. In Act II she has three short speeches, in Act III she
does a few conjuring tricks, and in Act IV she speaks less than forty
words. I venture to think a similar character in a quite new play would
not be readily valued at a reading for the powerful creature she is:
and if she were not so valued then the total effect of the new play
could not be assessed.

★   ★   ★

The difficulties to overcome in reading a play are comparable with
the difficulties in getting a play well produced, but despite all the
difficulties, and wonderful to think, over the last few years, we have
enjoyed in Britain as well as in Europe, a renaissance in theatre writing.
Unfortunately, the gossip and fashion journalists who need labels and
slogans for their work (Hell-raising Peter O'Toole, the Drunken
Behans, and so on) have been helped in their bill-sticking and shouting
by some of those serious critics and journalists, who are concerned
with the social impact of plays and the political responsibilities of
playwrights.

They have made great play with three labels that I propose to take a
look at, for I think they have done the theatre some damage, by turning
away potential audiences. These labels are Commitment; Non-Communication; Anti-Human Pessimism.

There is a whole volume about Commitment, and many interesting
and some sensible and valuable things are said in it.[4] Tynan's punch-up
with Ionesco was good clean fun, and instructive too [5] But I cannot

[4] J. Mander, *The Writer and Commitment* (1961).
[5] *Observer* (22 June–13 July, 1958).

escape the conclusion that Committed critics from their understand-
able, indeed noble, platform for survival, are arguing for a narrowing,
not a deepening and broadening of, artistic experience: Zhdanov and
Mrs. Gurney are waiting in the wings. Their philosophies range from
sentimental humanism to mechanical marxism: what's missing is the
dialectical tension we experience in Brecht. As John Whiting says,
'The movement has a heart. No doubt about that. All the throbbing
emotionalism proves it. We are asked to admire its virility. I am pleased
to do so. It is that little tiny head that worries me.' [6]

Non-Communication and Pessimism, like policemen, patrol in
pairs, with Anti-Human Pessimism and Reactionary on call if needed.
The trouble with Non-Communication is that the plays it is commonly
applied to (*Godot*, *The Chairs*, *The Caretaker*) communicate trium-
phantly in a great many languages, and in countries with very different
social systems and values.

It would be interesting to do an Empsonian analysis of 'non-
communication' as used by modern critics: it is essential to distinguish
some of the many meanings the word is being made to carry.

All periods of drama, of course, abound in examples of 'non-communication', where one character does not understand what another
character is saying. The riddle that isn't solved and the working that
isn't comprehended are basic theatre ploys: so are mistaken identities,
foreigners who hash the language, changes of costume to simulate
changes of sex, failure to recognise places for what they are, talking to
oneself, talking to deaf people, dumb people who can't talk and
characters so self-absorbed they do not know what other people are
thinking and feeling.

A basic form of 'non-communication' is the private language, nicely
illustrated in *The Roaring Girl*, by Middleton and Dekker. Moll, the
pioneer feminist and the lady of the title, falls in with a bunch of
crooks, whom she invites to 'cant' with her:

> TRAPDOOR: Ben mort, shall you and I heaue a booth, mill a ken or
> nip a bung, and then wee'l couch a hogshead vnder the Ruffe-
> mans, and there you shall wap with me, and Ile niggle with
> you . . .
> SIR BEAUTEOUS: Nay, nay Mol what's that wap?
> DAPPER: Nay teach mee what niggling is, I'de faine bee niggling.

---

[6] *Encore* (1959), p. 15.

MOLL: Wapping and niggling is all one, the rogue my man can tell you.

TRAPDOOR: 'Tis fadoodling: if it please you . . .

MOLL: Come you rogue sing with me.

> A gage of ben Rom-bouse
> In a bousing ken of Rom-vile.

TEARCAT: Is Benar then a Caster,
> Pecke, penan, lap or popler,
> Which we mill in deuse a vile.

BOTH: Oh I wud lib all the lightmans.
> Oh I woud lib all the darkemans,
> By the sollamon vnder the Ruffemans,
> By the sollamon in the Hartmans.

TEARCAT: And scoure the Quire cramp ring,
> And couch till a pallyard docked my dell,
> So my bousy nab might skew rome bouse well.

BOTH: Auast to the pad, let vs bing,
> Auast to the pad, let vs bing.   (V. i)

The gentlemen dandies' frisson at their complicity on hearing these thieves canting corresponds exactly to the frisson that delighted the Belgrave gentry and outer-suburbans when Behan, Littlewood and Willis Hall, moving west from Theatre Workshop and the Royal Court, gave them a tour round low life in prison, the army and the spielers. An earlier generation relished Kipling's soldiers, a later one still uses 'pad' with similar satisfaction. Ted Kavanagh in *I.T.M.A.* created a language of private phrases that the whole radio community was overjoyed to share, and he it was who popularised the Marx Brothers' type of surrealism, pioneered the verbal extravaganza, and made respectable the then out-of-date pun:

Q. Who was that ladle I saw you with last night.
A. That was no ladle, that was my knife.

This playing with language certainly inspired the Goons, who have managed to use many forms of 'non-communication' for commercially successful communication with audiences of all kinds. With his improvised jabberwocky phantasias Professor Stanley Unwin has even persuaded a famous firm to pay him for his poetic brand of 'non-communication'.

But the current usage of 'non-communication' is mainly concerned with more sombre situations and tends to mix up speech-tricks that are age-old in the practice of comedy, with a variety of individual and personal idioms used, each in his uniquely individual and personal way, by the poet-dramatists, Samuel Beckett, Eugène Ionesco and Harold Pinter, and in an eclectic and derivative way by a number of lesser, mainly comic writers, of whom N. F. Simpson is the funniest and best-known.

In his *A Resounding Tinkle*, *The Hole* and *One-Way Pendulum* we see a lightweight inspiration, supported by considerable technical virtuosity, working a number of fashionable themes for satire (bourgeois family life, personal obsessions, emotional insecurity, freak philosophies) with a coruscation of verbal tricks. He has learned from all these forerunners, and from Will Hay too, and he is specially fond of lists of improbable words, sometimes simply for the pleasure they give, as with Auden, and sometimes for mickey-taking, as in his twice-employed parody of the Anglican service.

This is from *A Resounding Tinkle*:

PRAYER: Let us sing because round things roll:
RESPONSE: And rejoice that it might have been otherwise.
PRAYER: Let us give praise for woodlice and for buildings sixty-nine feet three inches high:
RESPONSE: For Adam Smith's *Wealth of Nations* published in seventeen seventy-six.
PRAYER: For the fifth key from the left on the lower manual of the organ of the Church of the Ascension in the Piazza Vittorio Emanuele the Second in the town of Castelfidardo in Italy:
RESPONSE: And for bats. (p. 24)

Good undergraduate rag-day stuff: while in *The Hole* he means the trick to carry more weight:

ENDO, SOMA [*and*] CEREBRO (*together; without a break*):—which was and is and shall be; in which shall be comprehended the sprat and the Black Widow; in it the sole and the carp shall swim together, the swordtail and water-flea; with the gudgeon shall float the mackerel, with the roach the guppy; duckweed shall be there, and foaming moss; neither shall the water at seventy-five degrees Fahrenheit be at variance with the water at forty degrees Fahrenheit, or eschew it. And the freshwater shall be salt and the salt-water fresh, and no distinction shall be made between them, for all are of one aquarium, and there is no other aquarium, but this.

(p. 20)

But commentary on Simpson by means of quotation outside the full theatre context can be misleading. Like Beachcomber (another founding father), he is fertile in preposterous names and funny situations that can be simply laughable, or can be punishingly ironic. The physical fact of the hole and the people looking into it gives the play a compelling centre. In *A Resounding Tinkle* the elephant in the garden (like the off-stage Carlotta) fascinates us, though we never see or hear it, because it simply is there. The weighing machines in *One-Way Pendulum* with their fifteen-stone-ten-pound-odd-man-out, are irresistible: so, when realised on the stage, is this stage direction:

> MR. GROOMKIRBY *appears downstage Right. He crosses laboriously with a faint suggestion of sternly repressed stealth from Right to Left in front of the living-room set.*
> *He is carrying the front end of a very long, very high oak panel which completely masks the living-room set as it passes across.*
> *On the panel are the words THIS WAY UP. They are stencilled upside down at the bottom.* MR. GROOMKIRBY *disappears off Left but the panel continues to pass across. On it, as a kind of trade mark, is the figure of Justice—blindfolded and with sword and scales—also upside down. Above it, upside down, are the words: BUILD-IT-YOUR-SELF. SERIES NINE—FAMOUS INSTITUTIONS. NUMBER SEVEN: OLD BAILEY.*
> *When the other end of the panel comes into view it is seen to be carried by* STAN.
> *He looks less neat than he did, has obviously been working hard, and looks very much like a forced volunteer.* (pp. 39–40)

All this makes me laugh a great deal, but I do not experience any of the emotional and intellectual disturbance that occurs when an artist is deeply involved with his material. Rattigan in *The Browning Version* and *The Deep Blue Sea* is more moving and goes deeper, and I am surprised that some good critics, including the perceptive and scholarly Martin Esslin, include Simpson among the authors they classify as belonging to 'The Theatre of the Absurd'. Esslin says:

> Basically the Theatre of the Absurd expresses the loss of feeling that the world makes sense, and can be reduced into an integrated

system of values—which is due to the decline of religion—that had been apparent since the end of the First World War, and the decline in the belief in the substitute religions of nationalism, faith in progress and socialism, in the cynical disillusionment of the period after the Second World War.   (p. 177)

I am sure that Citizen Simpson is consciously affected by this situation, and aware of the evils arising from it, but in his writing he seems to me to stand rather with the social plays of Osborne and Wesker, and even, despite their completely different methods of using language, with the religious plays of Fry, than with the time-haunted genius of Beckett, the life-preserving struggle for sanity of Ionesco, or with Harold Pinter's passionate analysis of people at the edge of their being, if not at the end of their tether.

For Simpson (like Nigel Dennis) speaks of a world that is crazy, frustrated and hypocritical, from the satirist's position of intellectual and moral normality. He stands at a centre, with values that are conventionally acceptable, and it's from this centre he snipes at the follies and weaknesses that surround him. So Fry values the world from a moral base made firm by conventional religion. Bolt and Wesker attack capitalist society with the confidence of passionate, rational Socialists, and Osborne screams abuse at it from a steady, keenly-felt pain. They all (I think essentially this goes for Adamov too) can consciously use their art to promote ideas that, they believe, express emotions that they know they have. It seems pointless even to use a word like 'non-communication' about them or their characters, except in one of the simple (or similar) technical nuances I mentioned above. However, there are some very nonsensical usages:

> At a time when words carry little meaning, become barriers rather than channels of communication, film arrives as a language still fresh and potent enough to enable us to touch reality.[7]

Here indeed is an infant crying in the night, and with no language but a cry. I don't know how he obtains a seat in the circle or a copy o Sight and Sound, but I'll bet he doesn't do it all by signs. Words may have started as cries, *expressing* emotion, or as part of a unit of speech *expressing* ideas, but at a later stage of sophistication they came, when

[7] B. Sulik, 'Recording Reality', Tribune (1 December, 1961).

in fixed order, also to *communicate* ideas, while still expressing emotions and ideas. By this function we and our society have developed, and are still developing. If we find ourselves at a time when words ever 'carry little meaning, become barriers' we can be sure society will be in such a state that the arts, film included, will not exist at all.

The dramatists' frustration is not with 'words', with 'the language', but with the speech habits of a particular class, that bourgeois middle-class that makes up the theatre-going public. It's here that their problem of 'non-communication' starts. In Britain the frustration is acute because we have a made-up received speech that originated with the creation of the minor public schools for the purpose of providing a new category of 'gentleman' that could be guaranteed conformist in all respects to the interests and values of the ruling class. The popular taunt about 'R.A.D.A.' speech was justified in so far as actors and actresses had to eradicate their native dialects before they could find employment: the phrases 'talking cut-glass,' 'bay-window' or 'Third Programme' express a similar process in other walks of life. The effect of this type of change in speech-habits (when it is not purely a technical skill for particular technical needs) is to induce psychological insecurity, social timidity, political reaction and emotional thinness.

Mankowitz (in an open discussion on modern theatre) accurately expressed all this, as it involves contemporary writers:

> In Oxford-English, so-called, the synthetic official language of the country, we find all the frigidity, all the sterility, all the absolute utter deadness, the blankness, the inability to communicate the deepest fires of human experiences.[8]

Though the speech situation in Britain, where it is the decisive 'placing' mark of class, is specially acute, the general bourgeois situation in relation to culture is so sterile that Beckett and Ionesco in France (both out-landers of course, and aware of other languages) have been driven to extreme linguistic shifts.

They—and this is common to most of the post-war dramatists— have developed a language in which the emptiness of conventional speech is charged with a new emotion. Fry tried this first, let it not be forgotten, by the conventional poetic method of heightened speech, of calling on traditional nineteenth-century poetic effects to transcend

---

[8] Reported in *Encore* (1957), p. 30.

the flatness of everyday talk. His successors, feeling that Fry's experiment wasn't working, and also having different things to express, tried a different method. They decided (again) to wring the neck of rhetoric. Where he blew up the language into rainbow bubbles, they fired it into hard-cutting jewels. He extended, they compressed. He flew away from the monotony, repetition, emptiness or bourgeois speech; they immersed themselves in the destructive element. With them, and especially with Beckett, Ionesco, Pinter, words charged with meaning are not barriers against communication, but locks for the channels of communication, raising emotion to greater heights and directing meaning to a richer flow. While their lesser colleagues work in rhetoric, these giants produce from themselves poetry. As W. B. Yeats said, 'Out of the quarrel with others we make rhetoric, out of the quarrel with ourselves poetry.' Byron wrote to Miss Millbanke, 'Poetry is the lava of imagination whose eruption prevents an earthquake.' Yeats, the maker, remembered the shaping, the craft. Byron mentioned only the therapeutic value of the 'expression'. Their statements are complementary, not contradictory.

> I believe that . . . a writer must possess a mixture of spontaneity, of subconscious impulses, and of lucidity; a lucidity which is unafraid of whatever the spontaneous imagination may give birth to. If one were to insist upon lucidity as an *a-priori* condition, it is as though one were to dam up the sluice-gates. The waters must be allowed to come flooding out; but *afterwards* comes the sorting, the controlling, the understanding, the selecting.
>
> (*Ionesco, reported by Edith Mora*)[9]

This shaping process can be called craftsmanship. It is true a great many plays by young dramatists have been botched through lack of skill, but no one seriously denies the craftsmanship of Beckett or Ionesco or Pinter: many are deaf to their spontaneous imagination, their 'quarrel with themselves', to the 'lava of their imagination'. These critics are people who force on language a metaphysical dualism, the same dualism that vitiates Brecht's theory of how audiences should and/or do respond. (If they identify = feel, then they won't think = act.) They demand of the dramatist plain logical statements. But language is rarely either emotional or logical. A play like a poem carries its meaning in its totality, emotion and thought are fused.

[9] Quoted by Coe, p. 6.

John Whiting and John Arden, who with Pinter are our most
original playwrights, suffer from such critics and audiences. Audiences

find it hard to make the completely simple response to the story that
is the necessary preliminary to appreciating the meaning of the play.
Their habits of playgoing have led them to expect that they are
going to have to begin by forming judgments, by selecting what
they think is the author's 'social standpoint' and then following it to
its conclusion.

John Arden's technique to defeat this 'deadness behind the eyes' (in
Osborne's phrase[10]) is to turn to the fable and the ballad where 'we
draw our own conclusions':

If the poet intends us to make a judgment on his characters, this will
be implied by the whole turn of the story, not by intellectualised
comments as it proceeds. The tale stands and it exists on its own
right. If the poet is a true one, then the tale will be true too.[11]

John Whiting ('I have always written on moral problems of a
humanist kind, not of a religious kind') says:

I construct on a sort of thematic basis, almost a subconscious
thing, where words gain a significance—a word like hat, or horse—
to the characters within the play. This is the texture of the play, and
it doesn't seem to me to be frightfully important that an audience
should recognise it. It is merely a method of writing.[12]

I have heard (at the Edinburgh Festival 1960) the twelve-note com-
poser Humphrey Searle say the same thing to enquiries about just
how he used his tone-rows. All these artists are appealing for an
appreciation of the whole text, the text in its full context, not a bit of
the text tricked out and isolated for its overt prose meaning, or its
technical dexterity.

Not that close attention to the logical meaning alone would not be
an improvement on much of contemporary practice. I remember
people talking confidently, but against the text, of *The Deep Blue Sea*,
and describing the author's daring in writing of a doctor who had been
disgraced for abortion, or critics writing of Aston in *The Caretaker*

[10] *Entertainer*, p. 72.
[11] *Encore* (1960), pp. 25–6
[12] *Encore* (1961), pp. 26 and 18.

having had 'his frontal lobes removed'. And there is the misinterpretation, much more important because more damaging to an understanding of his whole work, of Sartre's clinching line in *Huis-Clos*
'L'enfer, c'est les autres', the others being not the human race in general,
but the betrayers who make up the characters in the play. Hell is their
own act of betrayal with which they have to live for eternity. When
critics attacked Sartre for 'pessimism', for lack of faith in human beings
in general, they were seizing on a suitable text, not experiencing the
impact of the whole play.

There is no virtue and may be much harm in getting facts wrong,
but facts are only part of the total text of the play. Blindness and deaf-
ness to the emotional content and the total meaning can be more misleading than inaccuracy on a point of fact. And to call *Waiting for Godot*
or *The Chairs* or *The Caretaker* plays of 'non-communication' because
the characters of the plays at certain points in the action do not choose
to, or cannot, communicate with each other, is pointless unless the term
is strictly defined and used only to describe certain technical means
used by the dramatist for the purpose of communicating with the
audience.

However, the general use of the word is less technical than emotional.
It carries a feeling of despair, the view that the world and the human
situation is so hopeless that everyone is isolated, helpless, doomed, and
that we are all invited to hand in our cards:

> The Smiths, the Martins, can no longer talk because they can no
> longer think; they can no longer think *because they can no longer be
> moved, can no longer feel passions*; they can no longer be, they can
> 'become' anybody, anything, for, having lost their identity, they
> assume the identity of others, become part of the world of the im-
> personal; they are interchangeable.[13]

This is where the 'Anti-Human Pessimism' label is stuck on. A look,
beyond the label, at the goods, suggests that we are involved in the old
paradox that has been fully thrashed out in classical criticism, when
considering the way tragedy functions.

*   *   *

There is no doubt that the action in the plays of these dramatists is
by no means cheerful, and their characters seem to have very little

[13] E. Ionesco, 'La Tragédie du Langage', *Spectacles* (1958), tr. J. Undank,
T.D.R. (1960), p. 13.

future to look forward to. Beckett's Didi and Gogo say they will hang themselves tomorrow if Godot doesn't come: Pinter's Stanley (*The Birthday Party*) is taken away, depersonalised and helpless, possibly to a mental home, possibly to execution: Davies (*The Caretaker*) is ejected from his last refuge through his own inescapable weaknesses: Ionesco's plays ring down their curtain on people changed to monsters or automata; on rape and murder; on various forms of suicide.

Partly because Ionesco's temperament is nearest both to despair and to madness, his plays offer extreme examples of 'Anti-Human Pessimism' expressed through 'Non-Communication'. In this the paradox is most acute, because his inner struggle is violent and his philosophic view of life not organised. A reading of Beckett's great short study of Proust reveals the depth and cohesion of Beckett's 'philosophy', and his compassion is apparent throughout his work. Pinter offers a reasonable explanation of what his plays are about. He knows that the room, an image central to much of his work, is a haven of security, a hearth, a shelter, a womb. It may, we feel, be broken up by violence, violence that may be physical or emotional. Of the people in the room he has said:

> Obviously they are scared of what is outside the room. Outside the room there is a world bearing upon them which is frightening. *I am sure it is frightening to you and me as well . . .* (My italics: his solitaries communicate universally.)[14]

And after being taxed with leaving his characters in a vacuum, by not telling us enough about them he wrote:

> The desire for verification is understandable but cannot always be satisfied. There are no hard distinctions between what is real and what is unreal, nor between what is true and what is false. The thing is not necessarily either true or false; it can be both true and false. The assumption that to verify what has happened and what is happening presents few problems I take to be inaccurate. A character on the stage who can present no convincing argument or information as to his past experience, his present behaviour or his aspirations, nor give a comprehensive analysis of his motives is as legitimate and as worthy of attention as one who, alarmingly, can do all these things. The more acute the experience the less articulate its expression.

(Royal Court Theatre Programme, March 1960)

[14] Interview with K. Tynan, B.B.C. Home Service (28 October, 1960).

Ionesco is no less lucid in analysing his own emotional state while creating, but his analysis is mainly hindsight. Beckett and Pinter know beforehand something of where they are going: only a little, probably, but still something. Ionesco appears to be saving himself in the very act of writing.

Beckett's characters remain at their darkest moments anguished human beings: Beckett, when intellectually at his most pitiless, feels and suffers with them. Pinter's characters talk our daily language and engage our compassion: their plight could be our plight. Ionesco is further out, way out. If the critical case for 'Non-Commitment' and 'Anti-Human Pessimism' can be established, Ionesco offers the soundest grounds for argument. I propose to look at *Jacques* not only because I have produced it in the theatre, but because if you equate the intellectual and emotional effect of the play with the amount of cheerfulness and hope expressed by the characters in the plot, then it can only be interpreted as an irrefutable example of decadence, despair, non-communication and anti-human pessimism.

Jacques sits mute while his family cajole and bully to force from him his consent to marry. He maintains silence, resisting emotional and social blackmail. After a deadly assault by his sister, he reluctantly consents, then immediately rejects the offered bride because she has only two noses. A bride with three noses is produced: he is left with her: both feel alone, disorientated, rejected. In a great *scène à faire* by means of a rhythmic dialogue full of sexual imagery she seduces him. He has successfully resisted intellectual and social pressures, but is enslaved (cf. Strindberg) by a woman. The family enter like obscene monsters celebrating a ritual. The families begin as conventional middle-class figures: Jacques struggles for his personal integrity, his social independence, and fails: everyone ends as less than human.

The diction, which starts as a parody of social conversation, transforms itself into a private language of personal imagery. This change from conventional reality into terrible fantasy is Ionesco's normal method. Donald Watson, who has so brilliantly translated most of the plays, lists his principal verbal tricks as 'banality, exaggeration (to include repetition and inconsequence), illogicality, dislocation and elevation' (Foreward, ii. viii). These one discerns at a reading, but in performance they are enhanced by a consummate technical command of all the devices of the theatre. The dramatic and poetic use of 'props' (cf. Cocteau) counterpoints and augments the verbal effects; and vice versa. The chairs (*The Chairs*), the coffee-cups (*Victims of Duty*), the corpse (*Amédée*), the furniture (*The New Tenant*), the eggs (*The Future Is In Eggs*) all take on a terrible uncontrolled life of their own: in *Jacques* it is the language that takes flight.

The Lesson ends in rape and murder with another victim, his forty-ninth, waiting at the door. In *The Chairs* the old couple commit suicide and their message is never delivered. In *The Future Is In Eggs* the characters, already degraded in the earlier play, *Jacques*, become cyphers.

The plays start in everyday reality: they end in a looking-glass world. When the curtain rises, chairs and tables are chairs and tables: when it falls, they have taken on an independent life of their own. Inanimate banal objects have become living magical forces. An identical trans-formation comes over language, which flowers into a liberating jungle of exotic fantasy. Actors and producers must proceed accordingly. To quote Watson again:

> Most important of all perhaps is Ionesco's rhythm. It is this rhythm of language, moulding and moulded by the rhythm of the action that is for me the greatest unifying force in his art as a drama-tist.   (Foreword, ii. XI)

Beckett has said 'It is the shape that matters',[15] and Ionesco 'The cohesive unity that grants formal structure to emotions in their primi-tive state satisfies an inner need and does not answer the logic of some structural order imposed from without' (Preface, i. VIII–IX). Critics allowed that he 'communicated' successfully in *Rhinoceros*, because they were able to pin a neat social-political label on his horned beasts: Ionesco was against the mass pressures in capitalist and communist life that force us to conform to herd-standards; the Nazis, the Com-munists? In fact this easy identification of 'meaning' only shows up the inadequacies of the play, which never achieves the organic unity of his best work. Ionesco's craftsmanship makes the play theatrically effec-tive: but there is a gap between the original impulse and the craftsman-ship. The carpentry (the strict order imposed from without) necessary to construct a full-length play was skilful indeed, but the impulse, the 'inner need', was being over-stretched.

In his best plays we are aware of an unbearable anguish: what is communicated is a sense of release. The characters may be doomed,

15 Quoted in Esslin, *Theatre o the Absurd* (1962), p. 40.

but the audience, having experienced with them the deepest despair, comes out of the theatre shaken and elated. The clinical study of despair and depression we have endured lightens our own anxieties and fears. We experience a catharsis, a catharsis often set off by comedy. It is not perversity that causes him to call his plays 'a comic drama', 'a tragic farce' and so on. He is being precise in describing (manic-depressive?) extremes of emotion. Briefly he is fleetingly aware of a secure joy:

> Of course, this state of consciousness is very rare; this joy and wonder at being alive, in a universe that troubles me no more and *is* no more, can only just hold; more commonly the opposite feeling prevails; what is light grows heavy, the transparent becomes dense, the world oppresses, the universe is crushing me. A curtain, an impassable wall stands between me and the world, between me and myself; matter fills every corner, takes up all the space and its weight annihilates all freedom; the horizon closes in and the world becomes a stifling dungeon. Language breaks down in a different way and words drop like stones or dead bodies; I feel I am invaded by heavy forces, against which I can only fight a losing battle . . . But in this anxious situation I do not quite give up the fight, and if, as I hope, I manage in spite of the anguish to introduce into the anguish, humour,—which is a happy symptom of the other presence—this humour is my outlet, my release, and my salvation.
>
> (Preface, i. vii–viii)

Salvation is perhaps the key word: in *Godot* we are reminded that one thief was saved. At the beginning of the play Didi says 'And I resume the struggle': and at the end Didi and Gogo do not hang themselves. The tree has leaves on it: the rope is not used:

ESTRAGON: Well? Shall we go?
VLADIMIR: Pull on your trousers.
ESTRAGON: What?
VLADIMIR: Pull on your trousers.
ESTRAGON: You want me to pull off my trousers?
VLADIMIR: Pull ON your trousers.
ESTRAGON: (*realising his trousers are down*) True. (*He pulls up his trousers. Silence.*)
VLADIMIR: Well? Shall we go?
ESTRAGON: Yes, let's go. (*They do not move.*)

They do not move, they remain; they are themselves, *human*, and they survive.

In Pinter (when he is not writing commercially, which he does very well) a terror we may all feel, may come through the door we all know:

> LEN: There is my table. That is a table. There is my chair. There is my table. That is a bowl of fruit. There is my chair. There are my curtains. There is no wind. It is past night and before morning. There is the coal-scuttle.
> This is my room. This is a room. There is the wall-paper, on the walls. There are six walls. Eight walls. An octagon. This room is an octagon.
> There are my shoes, on my feet.
> There is no wind.
> This is a journey and an ambush. This is the centre of the cold, a halt to the journey and no ambush. This is the deep grass I keep to. This is the thicket in the centre of the night and the morning. There is my hundred watt bulb like a dagger. It is neither night nor morning. (*The Dwarfs*, p. 95)

It is neither night nor morning. A man must find himself without the support of groups, or labels, or slogans. Beckett, Ionesco and Pinter, engaged in finding or saving themselves, remove their characters from immediate social contexts. This does not make them Reactionary, Anti-Human Pessimists or Non-Communicators; in my view they are committed more deeply than many writers who aggressively claim a virtue in being committed. All writers are men, all men are committed, like it or no. Artists have the special social value of helping each of their fellow-men in his personal commitment.

The question then is simply for an author to discover truths and to state them. And the manner of stating them is naturally unfamiliar for this statement itself is the truth for him. He can only speak it for himself. It is by speaking it for himself that he speaks it for others. Not the other way round.

Beckett, Ionesco and Pinter have reached out to audiences throughout the world. They share the anguish and perplexity of the times, but it is the very personal quality in their writing that has allowed them to transcend social and linguistic frontiers. In the early days of the

Nazi regime, from Lübeck prison, Julius Leber, who died long years later in a concentration camp, wrote:

> The situation is such that in this place each man must find his way, hold himself up, and develop strength by himself. 'Here the heart is weighed in the balance, no one intercedes for him': this holds true here much more than on the battlefield. For here all pathos and high passion are lacking. Here the heart is put into the scale without any makeweight. Here one can delude oneself about nothing, absolutely nothing, for one is always alone within four bare walls that in the long months become as bright as a mirror of the soul.[16]

To be concerned with this moment of truth is not to be obscure or pessimistic or reactionary. The way to the moment of truth is not signposted. The playwright, like any other artist, is a pioneer. As Picasso said: 'I seek only one thing: to express that which I want to express. I do not seek. I find.'

Therefore the 'message' of this kind of play is the play itself. Since the author has no other way of saying what he has to say the critic must take particular care not to limit the scope or deny the originality or the uniqueness of the work, by shoving it into a pigeon-hole already labelled, or by extracting quotations that can be made to add up to a neat 'prose' message.

★   ★   ★

To conclude, a play must be judged not only verbally: it must be judged temporally and visually as well. The bucket in *The Caretaker* is a bucket: it catches water when the roof leaks. It is not a symbol. It has no meaning outside the total context of the play. Only a bad reading (and how many have there been) would ignore the charge of human feeling that animates these mis-called 'pessimistic' plays.

> Compassion's the thing. That's why I think I like *Waiting for Godot* more than anything I've seen since the war. I don't know why so many people call it a depressing play. Beckett writes about suffering in a way that makes me feel exhilarated—that I must get up and go out and do what I can.[17]

says Robert Shaw. He being actor and novelist has the advantage of being trained in two different disciplines.

[16] *Dying We Live* (1956), p. 138.
[17] Interview, *London Magazine* (1960), p. 34.

But reading a play is not a simple matter. The text must be worked on as a whole. 'There are times when anyone writing for the theatre longs for the control over performance that a score and the presence of a conductor dictate in music.' [18] No such external discipline exists, so we have to improve our own inner discipline. Perhaps Dr. F. R. Leavis might have a go. 'The theatre is the only art which lacks an articulate form of scholarship. So it is always being mistaken by its audience for something it is not.' [19] We can change all that by a scrupulous attention to and respect for the total, authentic, unique text.

[18] J. Whiting, *Twentieth Century* (1961), p. 200.
[19] *ibid.*, p. 196.

Note

Existentialism. Sartre's concise *Existentialism and Humanism* (tr. P. Mairet, 1948) is suitable as an introduction; H. J. Blackham, *Six Existentialist Thinkers* (1952), is a recent general study; K. F. Reinhardt, *The Existentialist Revolt* (1952), written from a Catholic standpoint, has a very good bibliography. Anthologies include W. Kaufmann, *Existentialism from Dostoevsky to Sartre* (1956), and R. Bretall, *A Kierkegaard Anthology* (1946).

Henrik Ibsen (1828–1906). His *Collected Works* in translation were edited by W. Archer in eleven volumes (1906–7): quotations are taken from this edition. *Seven Famous Plays* were published with introductions by P. F. D. Tennant (1950). The Oxford University Press are publishing a new translation, with full editorial aids, by J. W. McFarlane (1960–   ).

Recent studies are J. Lavrin, *Ibsen: an Approach* (1950) and McFarlane, *Ibsen and the Temper of Norwegian Literature* (1960).

Luigi Pirandello (1867–1936). Dent published two selections (1922 and 1923) and Dutton two one-act plays (1928). E. Bentley edited five plays as *Naked Masks* (1952). A new translation of *Six Characters* by F. May was published in 1954 from which quotations are taken.

Jean-Paul Sartre. Born in Paris in 1905, Sartre is novelist, philosopher and editor of *Les Temps Modernes*, as well as dramatist. His first play was *Les Mouches* (1942). Hamish Hamilton has published translations: *Crime Passionnel, Men without Shadows, The Respectable Prostitute* (1949); *The Flies* and *In Camera* (1946), *Kean* (1954) and *Nekrassov* (1956). *No Exit and three other plays* was published by Vintage Books (1955), *Altona* with two others by Penguin (1962).

A volume of *T.D.R.* (Spring, 1961) is largely devoted to Sartre; Iris Murdoch's *Sartre* (1953) is a perceptive assessment of his thought.

Jean Anouilh. Born in Bordeaux, in 1907, Anouilh wrote his first play in 1932. Translations have been published by Methuen (from which quotations are taken); two volumes of plays are published by Hill and Wang.

E. O. Marsh, *Jean Anouilh* (1953) is a comprehensive if lightweight survey.

Samuel Beckett. Born in Dublin in 1906, he has lived in Paris since 1932, writing poems and stories and then plays. His English reputation was established by the production of his first play, *Waiting for Godot*, at the Arts Theatre Club, London, and the Criterion in 1955; since then, *Fin de Partie*, or *Endgame* (1957), and *Krapp's Last Tape* (1958) have been produced at the Royal Court Theatre, and *Happy Days* (1961) at Cherry Lane Theatre, New York. His plays have been published by Faber & Faber from which editions quotations are taken.

Hugh Kenner's *Samuel Beckett: a Critical Study* (1961) and F. J. Hoffman's *Samuel Beckett: The Language of Self* (1962) are recommended. Ruby Cohn has written a study, *The Comic Gamut* (1962) and M. Esslin edited a volume of criticism in the *Twentieth Century Views* series (1965).

For *Ionesco* see note to Chapter VI.

VII

Dipsychus Among the Shadows

H. A. SMITH

★

The Two Voices

Each of us has surely felt at moments that the substance of the world is dream-like, that the walls are no longer solid, that we seem to be able to see through everything into a spaceless universe made up of pure light and colour . . . When you fail to go beyond this first stage of *dépaysement*—for you really do have the impression you are waking to a world unknown—the sensation of evanescence gives you a feeling of anguish, a form of giddiness. But all this may equally well lead to euphoria: the anguish suddenly turns into release; nothing counts now except the wonder of being, that new and amazing consciousness of life in the glow of a fresh dawn, when we have found our freedom again . . . Of course this state of consciousness is very rare; this joy and wonder at being alive, in a universe that troubles me no more and *is* no more, can only just hold; more commonly the opposite feeling prevails: what is light grows heavy, the transparent becomes dense, the world oppresses, the universe is crushing me. A curtain, an impassable wall stands between me and the world, between me and myself; matter fills every corner, takes up all the space and its weight annihilates all freedom; the horizon closes in and the world becomes a stifling dungeon.

This description of 'two fundamental states of consciousness' is taken, not from the writings of the mystics, but from an essay on his own plays by Eugène Ionesco (*Plays*, i.). It could in fact be paralleled time and again in the world's mystical literature, and might itself be called mystical, but for one highly significant proviso. The mystic is concerned not only with the existential fact of his experience, but with its 'truth'; he finds in it an unassailable sanction for his belief in a 'spiritual reality' existing beyond, or immanent in, the phenomenal world. Ionesco, on the contrary, while recognising its central importance for himself, since it provides 'the starting point' for his plays, explicitly rejects any relationship between his experience and a 'structural order' or system; he is simply indicating, he says, 'a mood and not an ideology'. And the mood itself, with its alternation of opacity and transparency, anguish and laughter, impresses him only with a sense of absurdity and futility, of the world as 'a baseless and ridiculous sham' and life (to quote the sub-title to *The Chairs*) as 'a tragic farce'.

Ionesco's dilemma (if rarely pushed to this extreme of paradox) is of course familiar enough in modern literature, no less in drama than elsewhere, and it would hardly be too much to claim that an awareness of the 'two fundamental states of consciousness'—a discontent with the one, and a struggle, usually although not always frustrated, towards the other—has been endemic in the dramatic writing of the last hundred years. It is there in the mountain, with its riddling message, which draws Ibsen's Brand to his aspiration and his death, in the Moscow which vainly beckons Chekhov's Three Sisters, in the mysterious Mr. Godot ('Godet? Godin?') who keeps Beckett's tramps transfixed in their inextinguishable but unrealisable hope. It summons John Osborne's Luther to Worms, and Robert Bolt's More (less equivocally in this case, in spite of the play's title) to his death. It recurs in the figure of Orpheus (again a symbol of promise and death) which has haunted the imagination of Cocteau, Anouilh and Tennessee Williams. And the double awareness is equally apparent in the work of such writers as Strindberg, W. B. Yeats, T. S. Eliot, Christopher Fry, Giraudoux, Obey and Hugo von Hofmannsthal. In the light of this, the old claim, long since outdated, that modern drama is dominated by naturalism or social realism, is seen to be ludicrous. But by 'double awareness' I do not mean simply that many of the best modern dramatists have been poets; that they have seen beyond the limits of the camera-eye, have created their own imaginative worlds, and found appropriate symbols for them. I am thinking specifically of a metaphysical awareness—but an awareness which (for many, although by no means of course for all) is no longer sustained by positive faith or intellectual conviction, so that it survives only as a *feeling*, something which can be undeniably sensed but no longer confidently affirmed.

Now the problem of the religious consciousness which has lost the support of religious belief has been investigated, perhaps to the point of weariness, in relation to non-dramatic literature, but its implications or the drama have not been so closely studied. Clearly, the indeterminacy will affect not only the dramatist's whole view of life, but his whole approach to his play; not only must there be mental adjustment, but his technique and craftsmanship will have to learn new ways. Words themselves are affected. When meanings become dubious, the counters that express them tend to lose their solidity and sharpness of edge, and they must be made to carry a weight of irony and ambiguity. Or they must be used more modestly and sparingly, and be supplemented by mime, music, lighting and a variety of other devices which can evoke a sharp impression but avoid the specious hard intellectual clarity which words can so easily convey; the sentence must lose its sententiousness. Character, too, is shaken out of its old categories and loses its firm lineaments, as the question-mark which follows the old query, 'What is man?' becomes enormously enlarged. The traditional line between illusion and reality tends to dissolve, and, if the basic absurdity can give rise, at one and the same time, to both anguish and laughter, the distinction between comedy and tragedy becomes blurred. And underlying all this is a fundamental conflict which, if not peculiar to the modern period, has emerged as especially characteristic of it. The nature of the conflict is clearly suggested in the first act of Ionesco's play, *The Killer*. When Bérenger enters the 'radiant city within a city' it recalls to him with a vivid sense of immediacy the five, six or ten times perhaps in his life when he has felt a similar joy and radiance within himself, and he is caught up into a kind of ecstasy as he looks around him and believes that in the city he has at last found 'the projection, the continuation' of the universe inside himself. His own inward experiences have filled to overflowing the secret reservoirs of his mind with joy and conviction, and he feels the loss of them so badly that they surely cannot be an illusion. But he feels the need for the inward impulse to project itself, and fulfil itself objectively, and he says, 'When there's not total agreement between myself inside and myself outside, then it's a catastrophe, a universal contradiction, a schism.' The contradiction, however, now seems to be resolved, and as he touches the walls of the radiant city, he says, 'It's concrete, solid, tangible. . . . No, no, it's not just a dream, this time.' But Bérenger never takes up residence in the 'radiant district'. We learn later that it has been turned into a hell by an insatiable murderer who terrorises and kills everyone he finds in it, and at the end of the play he kills Bérenger himself. Now there is nothing new, of course, in the association between death and beatitude. The river of death flows beside the

Eternal City in both the Bible and Bunyan, and in mystical literature, the 'dark night of the soul', which is a kind of spiritual death, must often precede the moment of illumination. What *is* new is the riddle which Ionesco keeps poised over us throughout the play: reality or illusion, vision or waking dream? No explicit answer is given, but the irony and ambiguity in Ionesco's approach are perceptible from the start. Bérenger finds the walls of the city 'concrete, solid, tangible', but there are no walls on the set, and the stage direction reminds us that he is touching empty space. Equally significant is the fact that he totally fails to establish communication with the Architect who has actually designed the 'radiant city'; the Architect patently regards his ecstatic outpourings as romantic gibberish. There is no reason at all to conclude that this was the way in which Ionesco regarded them himself. Admittedly there is a touch of the comic in the high-pitched, near-hysterical tone in which Bérenger rhapsodises about the city, and this no doubt indicates a degree of naïveté in his expectations. But when he describes how his moments of transfiguration faded into the light of common day, and tells us, 'I was overcome with the immense sadness you feel at a moment of tragic and intolerable separation', his experience is clearly akin to Ionesco's own, and is obviously deeply *felt*. But when we ask, 'Is it also to be *believed*? Does it tell us anything about the nature of ultimate reality?' we are faced only with a mocking void or a sniggering motiveless destroyer.

Any dramatist possessed of the 'double awareness' referred to earlier who looks out upon the world around him is liable to feel, as Ionesco does, a sense of 'catastrophe, universal contradiction, schism'. But absurdity may still pursue him if he tries to break out from this ntolerable impasse into some kind of transcendent 'other'. And this is not to be seen simply as a contemporary version of the old charge of the fideists against the sceptics: that faith must necessarily seem foolishness to those who have never experienced it. All the marks of faith may be there—the nostalgia of the spirit, the sense of loss, guilt or dread, even the occasional attainment of ecstasy—everything except the essential conviction which gives the faith its direction and dynamic. What we are faced with, in fact, is the characteristic absurdity of the existentialist choice: the choice which must be made, but in a context which lacks meaning. The dramatist who, feeling the force of this dilemma, represents one of his *personae* as making the 'leap' which crosses the line of intersection between the timeless and time, is obliged to portray him equivocally. Is he the hero or saint, climbing to a superhuman wisdom? Or is he the fool, obsessed by the most fatal of all illusions? Or is he, like Icarus who felt impelled to fly into the sun even though the melting of his wings must inevitably plunge him into the sea, hero and fool both? It is with this conflict, as it has found expression in some of the most notable plays of the last hundred years, that this chapter will be primarily concerned.

In suggesting that the dilemma is inescapable in the modern world, I do not of course claim that everyone is in the grip of it; only that everyone (or everyone who thinks) must be aware of it, so that it forms an essential part of the contemporary climate of opinion. How inescapable it is becomes immediately apparent in the clouds which descend upon our vocabulary as soon as we even begin to discuss the subject. I have myself felt the need to hedge such terms as 'truth', 'spiritual reality' and even the neutral anonymous 'other' with half apologetic inverted commas, and the difficulty is of course a quite fundamental one for the practising dramatist. T. S. Eliot, who is a notable exception among the playwrights I shall be dealing with in that he takes his stand on the traditional rock and rejects the shifting sands, has been just as perplexed as they have by the problem of communication. In *East Coker*, for example, after developing a series of images portraying the two states of consciousness, he breaks off to say:

> That was a way of putting it—not very satisfactory:
> A periphrastic study in a worn-out poetical fashion,
> Leaving one still with the intolerable wrestle
> With words and meanings

—and the problem may be seen again (to take just one example from the many pages he has devoted to the 'wrestle with words and meanings') in the sense of uneasiness he has felt in his use of symbols with a metaphysical import, such as the Eumenides in *The Family Reunion* and the Guardians in *The Cocktail Party*. Robert Bolt, in *A Man for All Seasons*, writes from a very different standpoint from that of Eliot, but he faces much the same problem of communication. The play is concerned with a great sixteenth-century Christian and Catholic who gives up his life for a religious conviction—a conviction which Bolt himself ('not a Catholic nor even in the meaningful sense of the word a Christian' [1]) cannot share. And he is convinced that the major part of a

---

[1] R. Bolt, Preface, *A Man for All Seasons* (1961), p. xiii.

modern audience cannot share it either. Sir Thomas More's choice, he says in his Preface, was, though not easy, perfectly simple. He enjoyed the society in which he lived and could contribute much to it, but for him:

> the English Kingdom, his immediate society, was subservient to the larger society of the Church of Christ, founded by Christ, extending over Past and Future, ruled from Heaven. There are still some for whom that is perfectly simple, but for most it can only be metaphor.

And he adds, 'I took it as a metaphor for that larger context which we all inhabit, the terrifying cosmos. Terrifying because no laws, no sanctions, no *mores* obtain there.' Now it might well be asked how one view of the ultimate nature of things can be taken as a 'metaphor' for one radically opposed to it, and it should perhaps be said in passing that Bolt's phrases roll out much too glibly, so that one suspects that he had the wit to catch the prevailing mood without himself being deeply agitated by it. But the prevailing mood certainly is there, and Bolt's difficulty is one shared by many of his contemporaries: that a revolutionary change of outlook has made many long-treasured inherited concepts, and the traditional words for them, no longer viable and not always even fully intelligible.

Some of the effects of this upon contemporary theatrical practice will be touched on later, but before considering the consequences of the breakdown of established values, we must first glance, as briefly as possible, at the process of disintegration itself. The metaphor which Robert Bolt uses for the 'superhuman context' in *A Man for All Seasons* is the sea. He chooses this because for him the cosmos is terrifying and perhaps empty, and the sea, he says in the Preface, is 'the largest, most alien, least formulated thing I know. . . . Society by contrast figures as dry land.' It is instructive to compare this with the use of the same metaphor by Sir Thomas Browne in his *Religio Medici*, written in 1635, precisely a hundred years after the execution of More:

> Thus is man that great and true Amphibium, whose nature is disposed to live, not onely like other creatures in diverse elements, but in divided and distinguished worlds.[2]

For Browne the issue is already not so simple as it had been for More;

[2] *Religio Medici* (ed. 1901), p. 56.

the shock of the Copernican revolution was in course of being assimilated, the earth could no longer be seen as the centre of things, and Heaven too was inevitably pushed further away. Browne has to face 'sturdy doubts and boisterous objections' within himself, but his serenity is not seriously impaired; amphibious man can still move as happily in the sea of faith as on the dry land of reason. And this confidence is on the whole maintained in the late seventeenth and eighteenth centuries, although there is a significant shift of emphasis. Traditional Christianity, strongly supported by the Platonism with which it was frequently suffused, had placed its stress on divine transcendence; the light of eternal truth cast its shadows into the cave of mortal life, but in the terrestrial world it could be seen only as through a glass, darkly. In the eighteenth century the supernatural gives place more and more to the natural, and Browne's amphibian almost loses the use of his sea-legs. God is seen as the great artificer who controls the majestic ordering of Nature or even becomes a part of that order, and the light of truth is identified with Nature:

> Unerring Nature, still divinely bright,
> One clear, unchanged, and universal light.[3]

By the end of the century a further stage is reached, when Nature itself is seen as sentient and animate, interfused with 'a motion and a spirit which impels All thinking things, all objects of all thought',[4] and Coleridge in *The Eolian Harp* rejoices in 'the one Life within us and abroad'. It should be noted however that increasingly throughout this process the City of God—the pilgrim's promised land—has been losing its firm objective externality and has tended to become, no longer a place, but a state of mind, or even, in Bolt's word, a metaphor. And how precarious the state of mind itself is may be poignantly seen in Coleridge's great *Dejection Ode*, in which, like Ionesco in *The Killer*, he meditates upon 'the moment of tragic and intolerable separation' when the 'reconcilement of the external with the internal' [5] has broken down.

The real collapse, however, came in the mid-nineteenth century. The golden dream of a divine and beneficent nature was shattered by the biologists, and even before the advent of Darwin, Tennyson was

---

[3] A. Pope, *Essay on Criticism*, ll. 70-1.
[4] W. Wordsworth, 'Tintern Abbey', ll. 101-3.
[5] S. T. Coleridge, 'On Poesy or Art', *Biographia Literaria* (ed. 1907), ii. 258.

K

turning in horror from a 'nature red in tooth and claw'. In his poem *The Two Voices* he says:

> That type of Perfect in his mind,
> In Nature can he nowhere find.

But the inward sense of perfection too was being deprived of its traditional support, since the Christian revelation was being assailed on all sides. The note of perplexity which characterised the age can be heard in the title of Tennyson's poem, and its typical figure can be seen in Arthur Hugh Clough's Dipsychus, the twi-souled or twi-minded man, forever engaged (to borrow a phrase from Clough's friend Arnold) in 'the dialogue of the mind with itself'. Matthew Arnold's own poetry provides perhaps the most lucid comment on the dilemma of his time, and—although the process of disintegration has gone considerably further in the hundred years since he wrote it—it is interesting to find that he was already conscious of many of the problems which preoccupy the present-day playwright. He finds himself

> Wandering between two worlds, one dead,
> The other powerless to be born.[6]

(These lines could provide an epigraph for *Waiting for Godot*.) He is troubled, too, by the problem of non-communication, and the sense of being incarcerated in a self-enclosed world ('For most men in a brazen prison live' [7]), and he feels the weight of a metaphysical loneliness. He suggests, in his poem *Isolation*, that at one time all men were part of a single continent, but now we are all solitary islands, severed from each other by 'the unplumbed, salt, estranging sea'. It will be observed that the sea, which was man's natural element for Browne, and was still a promise of hope for Wordsworth ('Our souls have sight of that immortal sea') has become as uncompromisingly alien for Arnold as it was to be, much later, for Bolt.

Vision or Waking Dream?

The mid-twentieth-century Dipsychus was to face further problems which his mid-nineteenth-century predecessor could hardly foresee, but his fundamental dilemma originated in that time, and the first significant expression of it in the theatre is to be found in the work of

---

[6] M. Arnold, 'Stanzas from the Grande Chartreuse', ll. 85–6.
[7] M. Arnold, 'A Summer Night'.

a dramatist who was both a contemporary of Arnold and also the first of the moderns: Henrik Ibsen. *Brand*, which was written in 1865, may well seem to us more 'modern' than it did to Ibsen's own contemporaries, since it is the earliest existentialist play and seems to have been directly inspired by his reading of Kierkegaard. Brand's 'All or Nothing' reflects the uncompromising absolutism of Kierkegaard's 'Either/Or', and the satire on the Mayor and the Dean is in line with Kierkegaard's own contemptuous rejection of a 'Christendom' which is too materialistic or passionless or lazily easy-going to accept the total spiritual commitment of Christianity. Kierkegaardian too is the emphasis on a pledging of the will, a supreme act of decision which brings in its train a series of further decisions, so that the willing must be constantly renewed:

> It is Will alone that matters!
> Will alone that mars or makes,
> Will, that no distraction scatters,
> And that no resistance breaks.
> (*Brand*, p. 75)

But (and this is the crucial point, since all the rest could be found in any high, severe statement of the Christian ideal) the leap of faith is a 'leap into the absurd'. It may be at odds not only with the rational but with the ethical as well; the religious choice may offend the moral conscience. In his book *Fear and Trembling* Kierkegaard considers the case of Abraham and Isaac: God's requirement that he should sacrifice his son was bound to be morally abhorrent to Abraham, but it was a command that he could not deny. Kierkegaard in his own life incurred considerable odium because in response to what he regarded as a similar requirement he broke off his engagement with Regina Olsen, and there are parallels to this in Ibsen's play when Brand, in pursuit of his 'All or Nothing', not only leaves his mother to die unconsoled, but sacrifices the lives of his wife and son.

It seems reasonable to conclude then that in *Brand* Ibsen was setting out to dramatise the paradox of the existential choice, and it may well be that his reading of Kierkegaard directly suggested to him the possibility of a new drama. Kierkegaard examines the problem of Abraham in dramatic terms. He compares the proposed sacrifice of Isaac with the seemingly parallel cases of Iphigenia and Jephtha's daughter, and suggests that in each of these two the father would be subordinating a narrower ethical impulse (his duty to preserve the life of his child) to a more universal one (his duty to save his nation in its hour of need). In each case 'the tragic hero remains within the ethical'; his sacrifice will arouse pity and terror, but his motive will be universally applauded and understood. But there is need for 'a new category if one would understand Abraham'. His decision to sacrifice Isaac is not actuated by any intelligible higher principle; it is a leap into faith—beyond the realm of the ethical—but also a leap in the dark. Except within the context of this inexplicable faith, Abraham 'is not even a tragic hero but a murderer'. If he is mistaken, 'he suffers all of the pain of the tragic hero, he brings to naught his joy in the world, he renounces everything—and perhaps at the same instant debars himself from the sublime joy which to him was so precious that he would purchase it at any price'. Hence, Kierkegaard concludes, 'though Abraham arouses my admiration, he at the same time appals me'.

Brand is a drama of this 'new category'. Ibsen was not a Christian, and may well not have accepted Kierkegaard's view of faith. But he was aware of the irresistible tug of the imagination towards an autonomous world of spirit, beyond the jurisdiction of normal ethical laws, and he was also aware of its enveloping mists and possibly fatal dangers. And his troubled uncertainty as he approaches this height is akin to that of Keats, when, in *The Fall of Hyperion*, he is summoned by the 'veiled Shade', Moneta, to climb the altar-stair which can bring either death or a dying into life. In Moneta's words,

> The poet and the dreamer are distinct,
> Diverse, sheer opposite, antipodes.
> The one pours out a balm upon the world,
> The other vexes it.

The distinction is a vital one, but how, in these rarefied regions, is one to be sure of one's own status with regard to it? And the question hangs heavily over Keats: Is he the true poet with the authentic vision, or is he the dreamer, in the grip of an illusion which 'venoms all his days'? This same fundamental ambiguity seems to me to lie at the heart of *Brand*. We admire Brand, but we are also appalled by him. He lives heroically, with unfaltering integrity, in a dimension of being which is beyond the reach, or even the comprehension of the Mayor, the Dean, the Sexton or the Schoolmaster. But although he wants to serve the world, he only vexes it, and since, while inflicting intolerable anguish upon his wife Agnes, he retains enough of his own humanity to suffer

terribly with her, he venoms his own days as well. And the absolute
assurance of his 'All or Nothing' is turned, ironically, at the end, into a
despairing question. The last scene of the play, when he is left alone on
the mountainside, is a landscape of the 'absurd', conventional no doubt
in its imagery and lacking the strange originality of Kafka's *The Castle*,
but taking us into the same kind of metaphysical twilight. Stumbling
through the mists, Brand is beguiled or taunted by equivocal ghost-like
voices, and he is compelled to ask himself:

> Were those visions but the vain
> Phantoms of a fever'd brain?
> Is the image clean outworn
> Whereunto Man's soul was born? (p. 247)

He had believed that he had been called to the mountain by God, but it
is in fact the mysterious 'troll', the mad gipsy-child Gerd who both
urges him on and brings down the avalanche that kills him. And in his
final despairing cry:

> Shall they wholly miss thy Light
> Who unto man's utmost might
> Willed——?

we see him precisely in the situation depicted by Kierkegaard in the
words quoted earlier; he has renounced everything, brought to naught
his joy in the world, and yet even so debarred himself from the 'sublime joy' so precious to him that he would purchase it at any price.

The central paradox in *Brand* is to be found in Agnes's warning to
her husband: 'He dies Who sees Jehovah face to face' (p. 162). The
strongest impulse in the religious consciousness is to see God—but the
sight of God kills. This may of course be interpreted in traditional
terms. Brand's death may be a penalty for *hubris*: the contemptuous
rejection of the inevitable limits of the human condition such as we
find in Marlowe's *Faustus*. Ibsen returned to the theme of *Brand* in two
of his latest plays, *The Master Builder* and *When We Dead Awaken*, and
in all three a man of creative mind—Brand the prophet, Solness the
master-builder, and Rubek the sculptor—aims at the superhuman and
is guilty of inhumanity to those nearest to him. Again, these three
plays may deal, half-satirically and half-tragically, with the theme of
Romantic aspiration, and what Ibsen himself calls 'the great, painful

joy of striving for the unattainable'.[8] Solness sees Hilda Wangel as a 'troll' because, like him, she had felt 'how the impossible seems to beckon and cry out to one', and—very much like the 'troll' Gerd in *Brand*—she directly incites the master-builder to climb to the height from which he plunges to his death. But, as has been hinted already, part at least of the storm and stress of the Romantic period was due to the fact that the sense of infinite aspiration could find no definite goal (compare the calm confidence with which Milton is content to leave everything to the 'will of Heaven' and the 'perfet witnes of all judging Jove'). By the time that Ibsen came to write, the vague mood of divine discontent had crystallised into an ironic recognition of an inescapable paradox. The man who has the purity of imagination to be repelled by the corruption and compromise of the commonplace world is also impelled to reject it, but he can have no conviction that the summons away from it is the voice of God. Brand is tempted to his fatal height by the mad gipsy-child, Solness by a young woman who as a child had responded with rapturous devotion to his great moment of epiphany, Rubek by the 'dead' madwoman Irene who now, like Ionesco's killer, carries a knife, but who as a young girl had inspired his masterpiece, called (with suitable irony) 'The Day of Resurrection'. All three of these invite comparison to the young boy, with his equally riddling message, in *Waiting for Godot*, and in each case the choice that is offered is seen to be noble, necessary, foolish, futile and possibly fatal. The end of Ibsen's last play, *When We Dead Awaken*, precisely repeats the end of *Brand*; Rubek and Irene are overwhelmed by an avalanche as they approach the top of the mountain. On their way up, they are told by the bear-hunter, Ulfhejm, that they will come to a tight corner, 'where you can neither get forward nor back. And then you stick fast. . . ! Mountain-fast, as we hunters call it' (xi. 448). This image—'mountain-fast', up on the heights but stuck there—admirably illustrates the dilemma involved in the existential choice and the 'leap into the absurd'. Ibsen clearly recognises this dilemma, and makes it the central theme, in all three of the plays I have referred to. *Brand* (which is, incidentally, much more spacious than the other two, and avoids their crude allegory) can then be regarded as the first, although by no means the last, of a 'new category' of plays.

[8] Written on 20 September, 1899, in a hotel visitor's book at Gossensass: quoted by Tennant, p. 466.

The Hell of Make-Believe

Ibsen still felt free to create his characters on a massive scale, as though cut out of stone. But since he wrote the process of disintegration has moved one very significant stage further on. C. E. M. Joad presented it for easy comprehension in his *Guide to Modern Thought* in 1933:

> Copernicus abolished the primacy of man's planet in the universe, Darwin abolished the primacy of man within his planet, materialistic psychology abolished the primacy of mind within man. (p. 41)

Already in the nineteenth century man, for many, was losing his secure identifiable status as a 'child of God', and Sartre in our own time has said, 'There is no human nature, because there is no God to have a conception of it. Man simply is' (p. 28). But if man has also lost his long-recognisable, self-regulating coherent identity as a 'rational creature', what *is* he? Is he to be seen merely as a kaleidoscope of rotating but often irreconcilable impulses? If not only the outward centre of a God to whom all his endeavours are ultimately directed but also the inward centre, whether of Right Reason or the more modest regulative and co-ordinating reason, have disappeared, then he is indeed a shadow among shadows. Now it is true that it has always been possible to *conceive of* human life in these terms. We all know the trance-like experience when we sit in a crowded café and the buzz of talk—the earnestly engaged as well as the simply frivolous—suddenly seems as meaningless as the clatter of water over stones. The Duke's superb speech in *Measure for Measure* regarding man's life as 'an after-dinner sleep', and Prospero's more famous meditation on the 'baseless fabric' and the 'insubstantial pageant' are in tune with this. But the inveterate habit of mind which persuades us that the whole process (universal or individual) is purposive makes it very difficult for us to live daily with the concept (that 'we are such stuff . . .') as an undeniable fact of existence. A number of recent dramatists have so accepted it, and it has both posed new problems for them and created new theatrical opportunities. Pirandello of course seized upon the essential novelty forty years ago. If we are all in the normal course of things constantly donning different masks and playing a variety of roles, not because the role has any ultimate significance, but for its own sake or because we have no choice but to play it, then 'all the world's a stage' ceases to be a metaphor and the old distinction between 'theatrical illusion' and

'real life' breaks down. In *Six Characters in Search of an Author* Pirandello actually reverses the usual assumption; the imagined stage-figure
may be '*more* alive than those who breathe and wear clothes' (p. 9). A
character is always 'somebody' while a man may very well be 'nobody' (p. 56). And the imagined Father explains this to the real
Producer in these terms:

> . . . thinking back on those illusions which you no longer have . . .
> on all those things that no longer *seem* to be what they *were* once
> upon a time . . . don't you feel that . . . I won't say these boards . . .
> No! . . . That the very earth itself is slipping away from under your
> feet, when you reflect that in the same way this *you* that you now
> feel yourself to be . . . all your reality as it is today . . . is destined to
> seem an illusion tomorrow? . . . if we (*again pointing to himself and
> to the other* CHARACTERS) have no reality outside the world of
> illusion, it would be as well if you mistrusted your own reality . . .
> The reality that you breathe and touch today . . . Because like the
> reality of yesterday, it is fated to reveal itself as a mere illusion
> tomorrow. [In contrast our reality] doesn't change! You see . . .
> That's the difference between us! Our reality doesn't change . . .
> It can't change . . . It can never be in any way different from what
> it is . . . Because it is already fixed . . . Just as it is . . . For ever! For ever
> it is *this* reality . . . It's terrible! This immutable reality . . . It should
> make you shudder to come near us!   (May, pp. 57–8)

There is too much pressure of feeling behind these lines for them to be
taken merely as an exercise in paradox, and Pirandello seems to be
saying that, when the illusions of yesterday which concerned us so
much at the time now don't even seem to exist for us any more, life
is a fatuous comedy, and only art can give it a degree of stability and
permanence.

This Pirandellian theme of life itself as (not in its older sense of *as if*
but inescapably *as being*) charade or masquerade was taken up in the
thirties by Jean Anouilh and has been exploited through a series of
plays with astonishing virtuosity, wit, verve and theatrical resource.
Anouilh's characteristic method is to take the world of the theatre, with
its traditions, conventions, and the backstage or off-the-boards life of
theatre-folk, as an image for the world at large. The effect is to hold up
the mirror, not to nature, but to a series of other mirrors, poised at a
variety of angles, so that the ensuing reflections and refractions create
the curiously wraith-like impression felt in a hall of mirrors. He shows

us actors and actressses slipping into diverse roles as easily off the stage as on. He uses the device of the play-within-a-play in many different ways: sometimes to suggest an ironical contrast between inner and outer action, as in *Colombe*, sometimes to show the assumed parts merging into 'real life' experience, as in *La Répétition*, sometimes to satirise the universal habit of fantasy-building by showing his characters spinning a whole elaborate drama around themselves, with convincing settings and paid actors, as in *Léocadia* and *Le Rendez-vous de Senlis*. His exploitation of theatrical and literary tradition is equally varied: the *commedia dell' arte*, Marivaux and Musset are drawn upon to create a world of delicate or dazzling artifice; *Roméo et Jeannette* invokes devastating comparisons with the impassioned idealism of *Romeo and Juliet*; *Antigone*, while retaining the tragic sense of heroic suffering to be found in Sophocles, reinterprets it in a modern context; *Eurydice* retells the noble legend of Orpheus against a background of shabby squalor.

But there is of course a more serious concern in Anouilh, besides that of playing puppet-master in a world of shadows. Even in the *pièces roses* the laughter always has an edge of irony, and in the *pièces noires* the dominant notes are of revulsion at the spectacle of human degeneracy and pity for innocence lost or caught in the trap. The subject most commonly treated in the plays is love, and if we think only of the myriad fantasies of the lover, the multiple roles of the artful seducer, and all the tricks and self-deceptions of the sexual game, love obviously provides rich, and richly entertaining, material for a dramatist who envisages life as a masquerade. But love also arouses, if not more potently, at least more widely and frequently than any other kind of experience, an awareness of the 'two states of consciousness', of what Ionesco calls the 'heavy' and the 'light'. Not only in the Neo-Platonic dream of the sonneteers, but in a long line of poets, love has been associated with Eternity and the search for Perfection. But as the reverse side of the same coin (or one so like it that it is often difficult to distinguish the counterfeit) there is the sense of corruption, the self-disgust, and the drag of the corporeal involved in 'the expense of spirit in a waste of shame'. Now this 'double awareness' is just as much Anouilh's theme as the theme of 'life as theatre'; it merges into it but also dominates it, giving it a seriousness which it would not otherwise possess. The world of make-believe is also the world of compromise and corruption, and Anouilh effectively emphasises this (in *Ardèle*, for example, or *La*

Répétition, or *Colombe*) by juxtaposing with a mannered pattern of behaviour and a glittering artifice of background a naked, unashamed *naturalism* of language which startles by its cynical candour.

The corruption and the make-believe are seen together in the loose, sprawling moral shabbiness of the Father's amorous reminiscences in the last act of *Eurydice*, and M. Henri, speaking to Orpheus, makes the appropriate comment:

> You heard your father speaking about life just now. Grotesque, wasn't it, lamentable? Well, that was life. That buffoonery, that futile melodrama, is life . . yes, that heaviness, that play-acting, is truly it.   (p. 184)

Contrasted with this is the intent singleness of purpose of Orpheus, with his 'thirst for eternity', and his determination that if love (in its 'eternal' sense) is irreconcilable with life, then he will reject life. But the only alternative can be death, with no promise of a 'dying into life'. Anouilh's own attitude would appear to be summed up in these words from *L'Alouette*:

> In this loneliness, in the desert of a vanished God, in the privation and misery of the animal, the man is indeed great who continues to lift his head. Greatly alone.   (p. 31)

The issue is presented even more starkly in what is surely the strongest of Anouilh's plays to date: *Antigone*. In response to the weary, jaded reasonableness of Creon, Antigone makes her 'leap into the absurd', and her affirmation of 'All or Nothing' is just as uncompromising as that of Brand:

> You with your promise of a humdrum happiness—provided a person doesn't ask too much of life. I want everything of life, I do; and I want it now! I want it total, complete; otherwise I reject it!
>   (p. 58)

When Antigone, for no explicable motive ('For nobody. For myself'), decides to 'say no, and die', she is making, very precisely, the existentialist choice. She chooses death because only by dying can she achieve her selfhood, or, as Sartre puts it, choose herself: 'Man is nothing else but what he purposes, he exists only in so far as he realises himself' (p. 41). But she must also suffer the anguish of 'the absurd' because there is no 'intelligible heaven' (Sartre, p. 33) in the light of which her choice can be justified or explained. It is instructive to compare her situation with that of Celia in *The Cocktail Party*. Celia too has rejected a world of corruption and compromise, but her choice ('the awful daring of a moment's surrender', as Eliot calls it in *The Waste Land*) is a surrender to God, and her immolation on the ant-heap is a martyrdom sanctified by faith. Antigone's choice, on the other hand, is entirely her own, and she has to bear the whole terrible responsibility alone.

Anyone, however, who regards her decision simply as wild romanticism, absurd in the ordinary sense, should remember that Creon's political 'reasonableness' is urged in defence of an order whose symbol is a stinking, fly-infested corpse, lying dishonoured and unburied and a prey to dogs and rats. At the time the play was written, that order was identified with the Nazi tyranny, but the stinking corpse can now be seen as a symbol of all the piled-up corpses of Passchendaele, Auschwitz and Hiroshima, of all the purges, massacres and tortures of our century which hang like a physical weight of guilt upon the imagination of the modern writer. Man's body, pulled down from its dignity as the temple of God or the seat of Right Reason, and further degraded and devalued by political barbarism, comes then to be regarded as an incubus, suffused with the reek of its own mortality. Thus Anouilh's Orpheus feels a weight on his shoulders like a beast which grows heavier and heavier and beats on the nape of his neck as though to strangle him. Sartre, in his short story *Le Mur*, analyses the state of mind of a political prisoner awaiting execution: 'I felt . . . a sort of weight, a filthy presence against me; I had the impression of being tied to an enormous vermin'.[9] John Osborne's Luther (speaking in a voice more appropriate to the twentieth century than the sixteenth) faces the familiar modern dilemma: 'I listened for God's voice, but all I could hear was my own' (p. 101). However, whether in his leap of faith he chooses God or chooses himself, he feels an enormous sense of relief—as though 'a large rat, a heavy, wet, plague rat' (p. 63), which he had sensed beneath him, had been purged away. And Beckett, in his novel *The Unnamable*, feels it necessary to downgrade the legend of Prometheus, so that he is in danger of being gnawed to death, not by an eagle, but by 'an old satiated rat'.[10] Very much akin to this image of the incubus is that of the close, confined room, isolated from the world without (and sometimes also cluttered with impedimenta within)

---

[9] Quoted by Kaufmann, p. 235.
[10] *Molloy, Malone Dies, The Unnamable* (1959), p. 305.

such as we find in Ionesco's *The Chairs* and *The New Tenant*, in Pinter's *The Caretaker*, in Beckett's *Endgame*, in Sartre's *Huis Clos*, and, most impressively of all perhaps, in Sartre's later play, *Les Séquestrés d'Altona*, where the half-demented Franz communes behind permanently closed shutters with the 'crabs' in the ceiling. Franz's situation—seeking refuge in a fantasy, which is partly involuntary but also partly deliberate self-deception, from an intolerable burden of guilt which is not only his but that of his whole family, and, in a sense his whole generation—is perfectly summed up in some lines by T. S. Eliot from *Murder in the Cathedral*:

> In the small circle of pain within the skull
> You still shall tramp and tread one endless round
> Of thought, to justify your action to yourselves,
> Weaving a fiction which unravels as you weave,
> Pacing forever in the hell of make-believe
> Which never is belief.   (p. 85)

Magnanimous Despair

The characteristic dilemma of Ionesco, Sartre, Anouilh and, as we shall see, Beckett, is that while they say No to the 'hell of make-believe', they cannot (as Eliot does) say Yes to an 'intelligible Heaven'. It is however completely misleading to suggest that their attitude is therefore one of decadent submission to an irresponsible nihilism. The 'No' of Ionesco's *Bérenger* in *Rhinoceros*, and of Anouilh's Antigone and Jeanne d'Arc, no less than that of Bolt's More or of Osborne's Luther, is an *affirmation* of the self; pushed to the point at which its inviolability is threatened, it feels impelled to cry: 'Here I stand. I can do no other.' And just because the impulsion to make the stand is so irresistible, the self craves desperately for an order of absolute values which will both fortify it and make it explicable. Hence, as Sartre says in his essay *Existentialism and Humanism*, 'The existentialist finds it extremely embarrassing that God does not exist' (p. 33).

Iris Murdoch, in her excellent book on Sartre, says that he 'describes very exactly the situation of a being who, deprived of general truths, is tormented by an absolute aspiration' (p. 69). This situation, as we have seen, has now been treated in a good many plays, but it has found consummate expression only in one: the most comprehensively and profoundly evocative play of the last thirty years, *Waiting for Godot*. Beckett's great achievement was to create a new, workable and entirely relevant parable about man and the universe at a time when the old certainties about both had given place (in a sense unforeseeable by Wordsworth) to 'fallings from us, vanishings, dark misgivings of a creature moving about in worlds not realised'. Pope described man as 'the glory, jest and riddle of the world'; T. S. Eliot has spoken of the human condition in terms of 'the boredom, the horror, and the glory'. Beckett's two tramps live in daily consciousness of the boredom and the horror; they are wryly aware of the jest, and are dumbfounded (although not defeated) by the riddle, but they have no sight of the glory. There remain for them 'only hints and guesses, hints followed by guesses', and these demand an appropriate language. The polished, well-rounded periods not only written but spoken by Shaw and many of his generation had disappeared with the rational assurance which had given shape to them, and—although poetry was needed—the formal grace of established verse-rhythms was equally out of place. Beckett's problem was similar to that of Eliot in his search for a verse-form which could admit ordinary speech while being able to rise where necessary to the intensity of poetry, but he has, I think (while dispensing of course with verse), solved the problem more satisfactorily than Eliot. He has succeeded in *fusing* the ordinary and the poetic, and in establishing an ironical counterpoint between a surface triviality or banality and overtones which are infinitely varied in their power of suggestion and often vast to the point of cosmic in their implication. Beckett faces us at the beginning of his play with 'the thing itself', the 'poor, bare, forked animal' which is 'unaccommodated man', and although the deserted roadside with its single tree has a monotonous, menacing stillness (more intolerable in its way than the buffeting storm), there is much to recall the heath-scenes in *King Lear*. The Fool, Poor Tom and Lear are all outcasts from society, and they all (since Edgar's sufferings enable him to play Poor Tom with complete conviction) have the penetrative clairvoyant 'madness' which can look beyond the upholstery of illusion which supports civilised life to man as he basically is. And their language is appropriate to this; there is the same technique of ironic unexpectedness as we find in Beckett. The speeches of Lear and Poor Tom, for all their apparent inconsequence, have a gnomic quality, a frequent wisdom in the 'matter with impertinency mixed', which surprises, and so stirs, the imagination. Similarly, the 'crazy' jests of the Fool have an astonishing shrewdness and point, and when he takes over from the other melancholy

Fool in *Twelfth Night* the half-doggerel song ('With hey, ho, the wind and the rain') there is the same contrast between the largeness of implication—summing up the whole condition of unaccommodated man—and the seeming poverty of the vehicle used to convey it.

In *Waiting for Godot* Beckett deploys an equal range of resource. The brief, barely articulate exchanges between Estragon and Vladimir often seem on the level of music-hall patter, but they can also rise to a ritual, antiphonal quality:

ESTRAGON: All the dead voices.
VLADIMIR: They make a noise like wings.
ESTRAGON: Like leaves.
VLADIMIR: Like sand.
ESTRAGON: Like leaves . . .
    Silence.
VLADIMIR: They all speak together.
ESTRAGON: Each one to itself.
    Silence.
VLADIMIR: Rather they whisper.
ESTRAGON: They rustle.
VLADIMIR: They mumur.
ESTRAGON: They rustle.
    Silence.
VLADIMIR: What do they say?
ESTRAGON: They talk about their lives.
VLADIMIR: To have lived is not enough for them.
ESTRAGON: They have to talk about it.
VLADIMIR: To be dead is not enough for them.
ESTRAGON: It is not sufficient.
    Silence.

Or there is the sudden, intensely moving, leap from the trivial to the momentous:

[ESTRAGON *is leaving his boots at the edge of the stage*]
VLADIMIR: But you can't go barefoot!
ESTRAGON: Christ did.

There is also the use of what may be called the transfigured cliché. Pozzo tells the tramps, as though beginning a fairy-tale, 'I woke up one fine day as blind as Fortune'—and the conventional simile takes on poignancy as Pozzo's individual blindness is identified with the blindness of the world-process. Akin to this is the frequent playful but

pregnant jump from a trivial verbal connotation to a more absolute
and final one. Thus Vladimir suggests to Estragon that they should do
their exercises, and proposes, 'What about a little deep breathing?',
but Estragon replies, 'I'm tired breathing'. Or, when Estragon has
been kicked by Lucky and Vladimir protests angrily, 'He's bleeding',
Pozzo comments, 'It's a good sign.' Even puns can be made to serve
the same purpose. Lucky's ineffectual dance is called, among other
things, 'The Hard Stool', and while this can be associated with the
penitential stool and with the actual stool which he carries for Pozzo,
there seems also to be the suggestion that Lucky has the same anguished need for purgation as Osborne's Luther. But perhaps Beckett's
most characteristic device is his intimate wedding of speech and mime.
We can see how each serves the other in the dialogue immediately
preceding the entrance of Pozzo and Lucky in both acts. In Act I
Estragon asks if they are 'tied' to Godot, Vladimir replies, 'No question
of it', but in fact they remain uncertain. A few moments later we see
Lucky indubitably tied to Pozzo. In the second act Estragon is staggering about and asks despairingly. 'Do you think God sees me?' Vladimir
says, 'You must close your eyes' (with the obvious association of
prayer); Estragon does so, but his staggering gets worse, and Vladimir
cries out, 'God have pity on me!' (The irony of this may be more fully
appreciated if we recall for a moment Browning's blithe assertion of
implicit faith: 'Love shut our eyes and all seemed right'.) Then Pozzo
enters, irretrievably blind. In each case there is use of both parallel and
contrast. The tramps' commitment to Godot, and their blind faith,
painful though it is, is less painful than the servitude of Lucky and the
darkness of Pozzo—and our eyes confirm this impression even more
than our ears. Again, Lucky stands unforgettably in the centre of the
stage, weighed down by all the impedimenta which Pozzo has thrust
upon him, and Estragon asks 'Why doesn't he put down his bags?'
And, once more, behind the naïve curiosity of the question, there is
the universal implication: Lucky can't put down his bags because the
human condition requires that we should 'fardels bear', and 'grunt and
sweat under a weary life'. The mime, enhanced in its effect by the
speech, becomes a visible and powerful poetic image.

The play works so much by the power of suggestion, often elusive,
ambiguous, hinting and guessing at more than it knows, that any attempt at analysis is in danger of imposing a neat allegorical pattern
upon what is really far-ranging symbolism. But it does seem to me un-

mistakable that Beckett has the 'double awareness' that we have found
earlier, and that he is presenting in *Godot* the 'two fundamental states
of consciousness': Pozzo–Lucky is incarcerated in the world of time,
while Estragon–Vladimir is committed, however forlornly, to the
timeless. Pozzo is preoccupied with time. He talks importantly about
his 'schedule', and 'cuddles' his precious watch to his ear. But although
he grows expansive about time in his most eloquent speech in the first
act, it is already linked closely to mortality. Vladimir puts his ear to
Pozzo's fob, but hears the 'tick-tick' of his heart; his heart, we are told
earlier, 'goes pit-a-pat', and he grows faint and fearful without his
vaporiser. The point is reinforced with a triple pun: his watch is 'a
half-hunter with a deadbeat escapement'; time pursues, if not always
perceptibly, and the only escape is the silenced heart. In the second act
he cries, 'Have you not done tormenting me with your accursed
time?' and he sees the pitiful brevity of the whole process: 'They give
birth astride of a grave, the light gleams an instant, then it's night once
more.' (Vladimir later identifies grave and womb.) But his way of
occupying the time before he reaches this pass is with the same kind of
'play-acting' as we find in Anouilh, and his implied role of circus-
ringmaster accentuates this. He addresses Vladimir and Estragon with
a formal old-fashioned courtliness, and is anxious to know the effect
as a performance of his speech about the evening. (We find much the
same in the two tramps of course; they are constantly playing little
games with each other—but *they* do it quite self-consciously, to 'pass
the time' while they wait for something beyond time.) Pozzo even
judges Lucky's thinking in aesthetic terms: 'He . . . used to think very
prettily once.' But there is nothing 'pretty' about the anguished in-
coherence of Lucky's speech, and the Pozzo–Lucky relationship can
perhaps be explained in terms of Shakespeare's sonnet:

> Poor soul, the centre of my sinful earth,
> [Foiled by] these rebel powers that thee array,
> Why dost thou pine within and suffer dearth,
> Painting thy outward walls so costly gay?

Lucky is the mind of man, defeated in its impossible battle to shore up
the splendours of Pozzo's 'fading mansion'. Pozzo cannot do without
Lucky, for all his abuse and misuse of him, and when Lucky becomes
dumb, Pozzo becomes blind, a wretched beast without discourse of
reason. But Lucky can also be seen in contemporary terms as the final

collapse of discursive reason to explain the mystery of the universe. His long speech jumbles together many of the themes touched on elsewhere in the play: God, death, hell, divine justice or love ('with certain exceptions for reasons unknown'—like the *one* thief saved), or life as a game—with the constant repetition of 'the tennis' (suggesting an incongruous mixture of bourgeois green lawns with the pointless to-and-fro of the ball, and the spectators' heads jerking like automata in films of Wimbledon), but for all his pitiful efforts to give it a specious intellectual respectability by falling back upon older theological or newer scientific jargon, the speech becomes more and more meaningless and more and more haunted by images of death ('the great dark . . . the great cold . . . the skull alas the stones'), until at last it becomes unendurable both to Pozzo—who at one time had admired Lucky's thinking—and to Vladimir and Estragon, to whom it is irrelevant. (Is it too suspiciously plausible to suggest that the enmity between Lucky and Estragon represents the long conflict between faith and reason? Faith has taken some hard knocks from reason—Lucky's kick; but reason is impervious to faith—Estragon's kicks in return, which hurt only himself?)

If Lucky is 'mind at the end of its tether', Pozzo-Lucky is 'all mankind', Cain and Abel, murderer and murdered—or at least all mankind subject to Time, and finally returning, sightless, voiceless and constantly falling, to Time's womb which is also her grave. The plight of Vladimir and Estragon is not so hopeless as this, even though they have chosen 'the absurd'. When Pozzo falls, he can't get up, or stay up, without their help, but for them it's 'child's play', a 'simple question of will-power'. And while the Pozzo-Lucky relationship is one of tyrant and slave, Vladimir and Estragon are friends, who need, cheer and comfort each other. They are of course distinguished (along the lines of Eliot's distinction within the poet between the man who suffers and the mind which creates); it is Vladimir who wills, aspires, and recalls them to their 'waiting', while Estragon takes the beatings, feels most acutely the agony of their long crucifixion—and also wants to eat, sleep, and above all forget. (But everyone in the play forgets—Pozzo, the Boy, even, it seems, Godot; Dipsychus can only be sure of the here-and-now self.) They are however essentially at one, and although they disclaim anything heroic or even conspicuous in their stance—Vladimir says, 'We are not saints, but we have kept our appointment', and Estragon adds that there are 'billions' like them—

L

they certainly have some of the marks (or, in Beckett's own joke, the odour) of sanctity about them. But if they are saints and pilgrims, they seem infinitely remote from beatitude. They breathe an air which is 'thoroughly small and dry', and suffer all the

> Desiccation of the world of sense,
> Evacuation of the world of fancy,
> Inoperancy of the world of spirit.[11]

Or, to go back to an earlier parallel, it is as though they had journeyed as far as the Valley of the Shadow, and then got stuck there. Bunyan observes, very acutely, that 'now poor Christian was so confounded, that he did not know his own voice'. This is the plight, not only of Vladimir-Estragon, but of all the Dipsychus-figures, from Brand onwards, who need to trust to their own (now unsupported) voice, but who are often so confounded that they cannot recognise it. Vladimir and Estragon even, momentarily, take Pozzo for Godot, but here they are simply slipping into the most common anthropomorphic error. 'Man, proud man, dressed in a little brief authority', has often called himself 'Lord', and the 'Lord God' was a natural enough assumption from this, particularly when the divine terrors and favours often seemed to be dispensed in the same arbitrary way. Pozzo, we may be sure, is not Godot—but we are never told who or what Godot is. Beckett does not indeed leave his pilgrims without hope. Godot's messenger appears not once but twice, but even under the pressure of the most earnest entreaties his answers remain evasive and equivocal. And finally the 'faith' of Vladimir-Estragon, like the 'love' of Marvell's poem, seems to be 'begotten by despair upon impossibility'. But it is a 'magnanimous despair' for all that, since the faith, like the love, is genuine.

One way of not being defeated by the cosmic irony is to laugh at it. It is this ability to laugh—to enjoy the absurdity of the spectacle while still feeling its full pressure—that most distinguishes the attitude I have been dealing with from the older kind of romantic aspiration which looked before and after and pined for what is not. At the end of *Waiting for Godot* Estragon takes the cord from around his waist in order to hang himself, and his trousers fall down. Vladimir tells him to pull them up; the implication seems to be that there is a loss of spiritual

[11] T. S. Eliot, 'Ash Wednesday', *Collected Poems* (1936), p. 94, and *Four Quartets* (1944), p. 11.

dignity in giving up the struggle. It is tragic that spiritual dignity should have to be sustained with such a poverty of resources, but it is ridiculous too. This capacity to see absurdity even on the flanks of despair gives realism and fortitude to the tragic farces of Ionesco and the tragicomedy of Beckett.

Note

Sean O'Casey (born John Casey, 1880, in Dublin) turned playwright when over forty. *The Shadow of a Gunman* was accepted by the Abbey Theatre in 1923, and a year later *Juno and the Paycock* was successful enough for O'Casey to live by writing. In 1926 *The Plough and the Stars* caused a riot, *Juno* was awarded the Hawthornden Prize, and O'Casey came to England. *The Silver Tassie* (1928) was produced in England in 1929. Of his later plays, *Within the Gates* (1933), *The Star Turns Red* (1940), *Red Roses for Me* (1942) and *Oak Leaves and Lavender* (1946) have been described as modern morality plays. Along with them have appeared four fantastic comèdies, *Purple Dust* (1940), *Cock-a-doodle-Dandy* (1949), *The Bishop's Bonfire* (1955) and *The Drums of Father Ned* (1960). A Collected edition of the plays is published by Macmillan, who also provide, in the St. Martin's Library paperbacks, *Three Plays* (1957)—*Juno and the Paycock*, *The Shadow of a Gunman* and *The Plough and the Stars*—and *Five One-Act Plays* (1958). O'Casey's autobiography is in six volumes, from *I Knock at the Door* (1939) to *Sunset and Evening Star* (1954). There is a good study by David Krause of *Sean O'Casey, The Man and his Work* (1960).

W. Denis Johnston (b. 1901) was a co-Director of Dublin's Gate Theatre, before joining the B.B.C. in 1936. He served as a B.B.C. War Correspondent, 1942–5, and was a Programme Director for TV in 1946–7. Since 1961 he has been Head of the Theatre Department, Smith College, Massachusetts. Johnston published an autobiography, *Nine Rivers from Jordan* (1953). Jonathan Cape have published two volumes of his *Collected Plays*.

The following chapter is chiefly concerned with O'Casey and Johnston. For study of the early Abbey dramatists Una Ellis-Fermor's *The Irish Dramatic Movement* (1939, second edition 1954) remains the most valuable appraisal. For the earliest period of the Abbey it is useful to compare Lady Gregory's *Our Irish Theatre* (1913) and Gerard Fay's *The Abbey Theatre* (1958). *Ireland's Abbey Theatre* (1951) is an 'official history' by Lennox Robinson, and Peter Kavanagh's *The Story of the Abbey Theatre* (1950) is entertaining. The only 'history' of the Gate Theatre is the diverting but unreliable autobiography of Micheál Mac-Liammóir, *All for Hecuba* (1946). In *Abbey Plays, 1899–1948* (Dublin, At the Sign of the Three Candles, undated) Brinsley MacNamara has provided a useful dated list of 'first nights'.

A. E. Malone's *The Irish Drama* (1929) is a respectable study by a practising critic. and Peter Kavanagh's *The Irish Theatre* (Tralee, 1946) the fullest general history, For something less than history and more than fact the text is Yeats's *Dramatis Personæ* (1936). See also his 'An Introduction for My Plays' in *Essays and Introductions* (1961). Daniel Corkery's *Synge and Anglo-Irish Literature* (1931; 1947) is crucial for the understanding of Synge's impact on an intelligent Irish Catholic mind.

Macmillan publish Yeats's *Collected Plays*, and Synge's *Collected Plays* are available in the Penguin edition.

VIII

The Irish Theatre: Retrospect and Premonition

JOHN JORDAN

★

IT is commonplace, and has been so, long before the coming of the anti-Establishment snipers of the sixties, to assert that the English Theatre since Shakespeare has survived on injections of Irish vitality. And the glittering names are rolled off: Congreve, Farquhar, Sheridan, Goldsmith, Wilde, Shaw, Synge, O'Casey . . . an inaccurate listing which provides plenty of material for perverse jokes.

While the Irish are happy to accept this tribute to a dubiously national 'genius', and the English in making it, happy to torment each other, one important fact in Irish (and English) cultural history is conveniently forgotten. And that is, that of all the names listed, only the last two, Synge and O'Casey, wrote originally for a native Irish Audience. Which in turn reminds us that the opening of the Abbey Theatre in 1904 was the culmination of five years' work, chiefly by Yeats and Lady Gregory, to establish an Irish Theatre: a theatre, which would be distinctly recognisable in kind from the existing English Theatre, a bedraggled reflection of which was all that Dublin knew.

I re-state these facts for the purpose of giving them a rather different emphasis than is usual. For few if any have pointed out that an 'Irish Theatre' as such, while possibly a useful prop to national pride, did not and does not imply high artistic achievement. In fact the wonder of the Abbey is that it achieved anything at all, given its self-imposed limitations of subject matter and of repertoire.

Only recently has Edward Martyn, George Moore's 'Dear Edward', received serious scholarly attention.[1] Martyn is important in many extra-theatrical contexts, but he has a special significance in his in-

[1] From Sister Marie-Thérèse Courtney, *Edward Martyn and the Irish Theatre* (New York, 1956), and Jan Setterquist, *Edward Martyn* (Upsala, 1960).

effectual efforts to direct the Irish Dramatic Movement into cosmopolitan channels. It may fairly be said that if Martyn had remained in collaboration with Yeats and Lady Gregory, the course of the Abbey would have been radically different. Without him and without his insistence on the importance of looking outwards, not towards England, but towards Europe, the Abbey was to be almost from its inception a theatre for peasant plays. No one has ever claimed that Yeats's verse plays provided more than a fraction of the repertoire. During the first five years (December, 1904–January, 1910) the largest single contribution came from Lady Gregory. The most important contribution came from Synge, whose *Deirdre of the Sorrows* was first performed, posthumously, in 1910.

Between the first performances of the Irish Literary Theatre in 1899, and the death of Synge in 1909, there is roughly a decade of original Irish dramatic activity. And it all hinges about Synge, a most dangerous model, since he was a dramatic genius working in apparently easy-to-be-copied modes. (The extent to which Synge impressed himself on Dublin audiences as being the very quintessence of the Abbey may be illustrated by the fact that as late as 1949 a Dublin comedian could raise a laugh on an inept parody of the Synge idiom.) In fact, Synge's imitators have not survived. Nor with the exception of *The Playboy of the Western World* has Synge's own work, so far as Irish urban audiences are concerned. The Irish have never really liked Synge, and they accept *The Playboy* only as they might accept a technically skilful comic dramatist like the late George Shiels, or as they do accept at present the principal Abbey comic dramatist John McCann.

It is not my place to attempt here an evaluation of Synge.[2] But it may be granted that although he found his material in real peasants and fishermen and tramps, seen against real landscapes, he was in no sense a 'realistic' or 'naturalistic' writer. Nor, on the other hand, was he a decorative fantasist. He combined in his art something, certainly, of the naturalistic writer's minuteness of observation, with something, it is true, of the fantasist's ebullience. But essentially, he was an orchestrator of significant myth, a poetic dramatist in the way that Ibsen and Chekhov were poetic dramatists, and so his plays demand that kind of attention from ear and brain and heart, which appears to have been lost in the English-speaking theatre three centuries ago.

[2] A useful recent survey is Alan Price's *Synge and Anglo-Irish Drama* (1961).

Among his own people *The Playboy* passes as a comic extravaganza, and of his other plays they see only occasional professional performances of *In the Shadow of the Glen* and *Riders to the Sea*.[3]

When one considers that first decade of the Irish Dramatic Movement and abstracts from it the work of Synge, there is very little of theatrical importance left. The early verse plays of Yeats might be cited, but though they were performed by the Abbey Theatre and its antecedents, they belong properly to the history of the revival of verse drama, and of course to the history of a poet's mind. They have had no progeny worth recognising in the Abbey itself, and only the work of Austin Clarke in the Irish Theatre as a whole.[4]

There were of course the little plays of Lady Gregory, but no amount of special pleading can present this heroic woman's dramatic achievement as of major importance.[5] She was a worthy craftswoman and an unblinking recorder of human foible, but perhaps only her short play *The Gaol Gate* (1908) breaks the local barrier.

By 1910 the Abbey had failed as the cradle of a new verse drama, and it had had only one dramatist, Synge, of European stature. With a few insignificant exceptions, the repertoire was composed of new plays by Irish authors, the majority of which now seem either trivial or dreary. But although officially the door was barred to Ibsen, he was coming in by reason of his influence on the new so-called 'Cork Realists', Lennox Robinson, T. C. Murray and R. J. Ray. These young men made genuine attempts to apply a limited number of Ibsenite lessons to the realities of Irish life. Murray alone remained faithful to the depiction of the peasant-farmer. He alone in a long and tiresome history of kitchen interiors, contrived to attempt tragedy, the tragedy of the inarticulate engulfed by nemesis. His best plays, *Maurice Harte* (1912), *Autumn Fire* (1924) and *Michaelmas Eve* (1932), may be included in that small body of Abbey drama which might be mentioned in the context of Synge and O'Casey. Here it is apposite to stress a fact, which in a survey of the theatre of any other country might seem at the best to be a pietistic irrelevance and at the worst a bigoted red herring. Murray was a Catholic, and with the exception of a rather lesser writer for the theatre, Padraic Colum, the first Irish

---

[3] A recent Irish TV production of *The Well of the Saints* raised protests that took one back sixty years.

[4] *Collected Plays* (Dolmen Press, Dublin, 1962).

[5] As in Elizabeth Coxhead's *Lady Gregory* (1961).

Catholic dramatist worthy of critical consideration. It may be seen later why I introduce a sectarian distinction.

Of the other two 'Cork Realists', nothing can be said of R. J. Ray, whose plays were never published and, I was informed by Lennox Robinson in 1954, 'had been lost'. Robinson himself, a man of erratic and versatile talent, turned from the depiction of peasant-farmer life, and found more congenial material in the new bourgeoisie, and later in the dying Ascendancy. He is important not only for some of his own work, but as the originator of certain characters who in the many plays of many lesser writers were to become types. His own achievement is honourable and varied. His Parnell play *The Lost Leader* (1918), his Ibsenite *The Round Table* (1922) and his two-act Pirandellian experiment *Church Street* (1934) are sufficient evidence of a talent which in another city, and in another theatre, one not so devoted to cosseting the frivolous, might have achieved minor international status.

For by the twenties not only had Realism conquered, so also had Comedy. When Robinson's sombre and almost despairing *The Round Table* was revived in 1927, he had re-written it with a happy ending. But in the meantime O'Casey had arrived.

★   ★   ★

When O'Casey's first play *The Shadow of a Gunman* was first produced in 1923, the Irish Dramatic Movement was, dating from the first performance of the Irish Literary Theatre, almost a quarter of a century old. So far as I know, no one has thought it worth while to reflect on an astonishing lacuna in the existing achievement, a lacuna all the more astonishing given the official clerical image of the soul of Ireland. I mean of course that after twenty-five years of a native theatre there was not a single play of merit which might be described as distinctively Christian in tone, not a single play which communicated effectively the unceasingly proclaimed spirituality of the Irish Catholic. (One might except *Riders to the Sea*, but Synge's masterpiece reflects a kind of spiritual resignation not easily distinguishable from the stoicism of any traditional fishing community.)

I have mentioned T. C. Murray as the first Irish Catholic dramatist of importance. But no one of his plays might be described as deeply 'Christian'. It is not of course important that any play, as such, should be Christian or Catholic or Taoist. It is, I think, important that the theatre should reflect, in some manner, the deeper even if unexpressed feelings of a society. And though the situation has changed a little, a very little, since 1923, Ireland has not yet produced even a pale parallel to Claudel for instance, or even to Hochwalder.[6]

Oddly enough, in view of what happened later, it was O'Casey who brought the first wind of Christian feeling to the Irish Theatre. Much of the appeal of *The Shadow of a Gunman* in 1923 lay in its apprehension of squabbling humanity, made aware of itself through sympathy with a rather inane girl (by unromantic criteria) who gets shot through the bosom by British Auxiliaries during the War of Independence. There was appeal too in the horseplay of the foxy young (not old) waster Seamus Shields, and in the strangely off-beat absurdities of the tenement dwellers. Then as now little attention was paid to the poet Donal Davoren, who is a key-figure not only to this play, but to the whole O'Casey canon. Davoren loses the name of action, but in his hatred of dirt and ignorance, in his Dubedat reverence for the mystery of colour and the might of design (O'Casey uses Shaw's phrases) he is the first of a line of O'Casey heroes which has varied little in forty years. When he has learned to respect labour and the people, he will re-emerge in later plays, in *Red Roses For Me* (1942) and *Oak Leaves and Lavender* (1946). But the audiences of 1923 detected nothing at all of the gathering storm in O'Casey. In the following year, 1924, they accepted rapturously *Juno and the Paycock*, relishing especially the antics of 'Jackie' Boyle and 'Joxer' Daly and the poignant, comfortably familiar prayer of Juno to the Sacred Heart.

Few plays I believe have been as misunderstood as *Juno*, which O'Casey describes as a 'tragedy'. The degree of the misunderstanding is such that a good case might be put for the play's being an artistic failure. O'Casey's genius for high farce and for composing super-ficially agreeable gargoyles, is here working at full power, so much so that the play's 'tragic' content is almost submerged. 'Jackie' Boyle and 'Joxer' Daly cajole and whine and preen and jack-act and inevit-ably convulse complacent and aware alike. But O'Casey was not concerned with the provision of high farce and lovable clowns. He was scalded at heart by the experience, over forty years, of hunger and disease and brutality, and above all of what they may do to the human spirit. Here he first posits a grouping of the redeemable and a grouping of the unsalvageable. And of course he carries further here a dramatic

---

[6] Robert Speaight, in his *Christian Theatre* (1960), lists only one Irish dramatist, Paul Vincent Carroll. Since this chapter was written Brian Friel's *The Enemy Within*, a sensitive restrained study of St. Columba of Iona, has had moderate success at the Abbey. Friel is to be watched.

method he has never forsaken: the juxtaposition of zany antics and significant melodrama, the tensions between which no sensible producer can afford to ignore.

If O'Casey's early audiences were any way disturbed by his first two plays, their unease may have been offset by the fact that the first dealt in a sympathetic way with the recent War of Independence (though even here there are signs of ambivalence) and the second with the very recent Civil War (here partisan passions may have been quietened by Juno's prayer). But in his third play, *The Plough and the Stars* (1926), the devil revealed himself. What so shocked those first audiences was O'Casey's presentation, among other things, of marital strife in the home of a man who fought in 1916, and of drinking, drabbing and looting while the heroes held the General Post Office. The drabbing was especially offensive, and to crown the play's infamy, a prostitute was presented on the stage.

Thirty-five years later the disorder over *The Plough* may arouse indulgent smiles among the old and incredulous indignation among the young. But in fact the demonstrators had an odd perverted inkling of some of the truth about O'Casey: he detested sham, and had no scruples about revealing the dichotomy in official mythologies. I cannot see that there was any other alternative for him, when shortly after he left for London.

The Plough and the Stars remains, I believe, a magnificent play, and unique in the canon for its resolution of a problem which O'Casey had not tried to and would not solve elsewhere. There is again the dual grouping of the redeemable and the unsalvageable, but here for once the unsalvageable catch some of the light that surrounds the good stock and some of the reflected lustre of a revolution in which O'Casey was emotionally deeply involved. The clowns and blatherers participate in the newly born terrible beauty.

But for this writer *The Plough* must give place to O'Casey's first play written outside Ireland, *The Silver Tassie*, published before ever produced, in 1928, a significant year in the Irish Theatre.

★   ★   ★

Apart from a few productions of Shaw, Ibsen, Eugene O'Neill and Shakespeare, the Abbey held fast to its isolationist policy. Edward Martyn had died in 1923, but shortly before the war he had founded The Irish Theatre, a company designed expressly for the presentation,

among other work, of 'foreign masterpieces'. The venture lasted a few
years and was succeeded by The Drama League, founded by Yeats
with Lennox Robinson, and wholly dedicated to 'foreign masterpieces'. Neither of these two organisations could in any sense be
described as professional. But in 1928, as if Edward Martyn's ghost
were knocking on the door, Messrs. Hilton Edwards and Micheál
MacLiammóir founded the first Irish company dedicated to the
presentation of the best of world theatre ancient and modern, and of
such Irish plays as were beyond the scope or outside the perspective
of the Abbey. It is important to remember that by now the Abbey
was a state-subsidised theatre (which it has remained). There is something slightly mad in the fact that by 1930 everyone appeared to
recognise what or what was not an 'Abbey' play. Anything bold or
experimental or fresh-minted, was likely to be *not* 'Abbey'. Plays
about match-making, domineering parents, sharp practice, gombeen-
men (depicted usually as lovable rogues), sprinkled with eccentric
aunts, cretinous Civic Guards, comic chancers, etc.: these were likely
to be considered 'Abbey'. A convention had been established, and it is
a convention that exists still, one which the Directors could hardly
change, even if they wanted to. Audiences would not understand an
upheaval in the theatrical *status quo* consolidated over sixty years.

It was during their second season, at the Peacock Theatre in 1929,
that Edwards and MacLiammóir produced Denis Johnston's *The Old
Lady says 'No'*. Two years later, very surprisingly, the Abbey produced his *The Moon in the Yellow River*. Over the next decade and during the fifties, Gate and Abbey shared, by what could only have been
an accident, the work of putting on Johnston's plays. For what it is
worth Johnston is the only Irish dramatist whose work has *consistently*
been presented by both theatres. There are of course several instances
of Abbey dramatists who have been represented at the Gate by a single
play (etiquette in the matter of infringement has always been strictly
observed by the 'rival' firms: thus it is unlikely that *The Moon in the
Yellow River* would be produced at the Gate, though it seems not to be
an 'Abbey' play).

Given the comparatively small number of this century's Irish
dramatists, outside Synge and O'Casey and Beckett (a very special
case), who might stand up to serious critical examination in the context
of world drama, Denis Johnston's place is very high. There are however, even for an Irishman, great difficulties in approaching his work.

Johnston is an inveterate reviser, constantly tinkering and tampering with the texts of his plays and for years seemingly content to put off any question of definitive versions. This is particularly so of his later plays. While this has meant the existence of a multiplicity of texts, useful for thorough research workers, it also means that we have been left in doubt as to whether the dramatist has stopped writing any of his plays.

At last we have had two volumes of *Collected Plays* which the publishers describe as in their 'definitive form'. There will no doubt be a third volume which may contain *Storm Song* first produced at the Gate in 1933, *A Bride for the Unicorn* first produced at the Gate in 1933, and *The Golden Cuckoo* first produced at the Gate in 1938 but under the auspices of the Earl of Longford (*obit* 1961). I will here confine myself to discussing those plays which are in 'definitive form'.

The earliest of them, *The Old Lady says 'No'*, has never been immediately comprehensible to foreign audiences. Even for Irish audiences it retains difficulty, less because of its quasi-Expressionist form, than because of its weight of allusion. *The Old Lady* has all the marks of a brilliant young man's eclectic reading, and its point of departure, a prologue in the form of a romantic playlet about Robert Emmet and Sarah Curran, can only be savoured fully by those having an acquaintance with Anglo-Irish verse of the nineteenth century, and enough sophistication to be critical of its diction and sentiments. For Johnston's play stands or falls on his ambiguous attitude to Cathleen Ní Houlihan. It is an attitude not unlike that of Joyce's: Ireland is a beautiful young woman, but she is also an ignorant and malicious hag.

The Player Emmet who in delirium becomes the historical Emmet as popularly conceived, is pursued by the dual manifestation of Ireland, now delivered from bondage. But it is clear that the hag, Joyce's farrow-eating sow, has the upper hand. In effect Johnston is contrasting, and not without anguish, the dream and the reality of Independence. This is a sufficiently universal theme. But where even the fully instructed foreigner might be puzzled is in Johnston's final reluctance to throw overboard the romantic trappings, in his half-commitment to the ever-young, ever-beautiful image of Ireland. Yet in fact Johnston's unwillingness to ignore the existence of both sides of the coin is less an Irish peculiarity than evidence of his intellectual balance. His first play when considered as an appeal to the mind in theatrical form is eminently satisfactory, for it does not deny the fact of a racial myth that can awaken intensely emotional responses. Much of the play's power in the theatre depends on the audience's capacity to feel stirred by the name of Emmet, by political martyrdom, by the wrongs of old Ireland.

Johnston's second play *The Moon in the Yellow River* examines another aspect of the face of Ireland, and this time he confronts a German engineer with what might seem to be a paradox in the Irish character. The engineer Tausch comes to Ireland to supervise an electrical power scheme. The time is the twenties, but it is not hard to see the play's undiminished relevance. Tausch is incredulous when he learns from his neighbour Dobelle that there is potential disillusionment and sorrow in his custody of the Power House. Tausch's sentimental equanimity is shattered when an extremist Republican organisation attempts to blow up the Power House. His categorical though kindly views on life and people are further affronted when a Government officer shoots down the Republican leader in cold blood. Tausch in fact is any outsider working on assumptions supposedly based on reason, when set down in a world where nothing is as it seems, where reason and dream have equal authority, where violence erupts without warning. This is Ireland as Johnston saw it in the late twenties, and again his attitude is ambiguous. Lanigan the killer and Blake his victim are, as seen by Dobelle, complementary to each other, their fates a natural consequence in the aftermath of political revolution. Tausch (whose Power House is eventually blown up by accident) remains the outsider.

Unfortunately Johnston's play of ideas, fleshed out in urbane and stylish language, depends for dramatic cohesion far too much on a sentimentally presented relationship between Dobelle and his young daughter. But it is admirably constructed and has an air of intellectual excitement and an almost Chekhovian sense of mood-change rare in Irish dramatists.

Denis Johnston in his first two plays revealed himself as the first recognisably critical intelligence to emerge in the theatre of the New Ireland. This is in no way to disparage O'Casey, but merely to suggest that Johnston's mind tended and still does tend to be analytic and judicial (though he passes no final sentences). O'Casey's mind has always been exposed to his feelings, and his capacity for grief and indignation has sometimes precluded intellectual fairness.

Johnston has published three other of his full-length plays in 'definitive' form. His Swift play, *The Dreaming Dust*, which dates back through several re-writings to 1940, is an audacious attempt to combine techniques in the Pirandellian and Morality Play modes. A group of actors have been performing in a Morality of the Seven Deadly Sins, in the unlikeliest of places, Swift's own cathedral, St. Patrick's in Dublin. At the present Dean's suggestion, they play out episodes of Swift's life, each of them giving the character he or she portrays qualities associated with the Sins they have enacted in the Morality. So we have, if we can remember them, two alienation techniques. The characters in the play are established initially as being really actors (played of course by actors) and as being abstractions. Swift becomes an Everyman figure but his final degradation comes as that of a broken Colossus conquered by evil.

But the play in reading is unsatisfactory. The time sequence is unnecessarily complicated, and the technical labour seems unjustified in terms of theatrical impact. Yet Johnston, as no other Irish dramatist since Shaw, has the gift of using the Queen's English, as distinct from urban or peasant dialect or exotic idiom, with an ear for the effect of trope and cadence in the theatre.

Strange Occurrence on Ireland's Eye, produced at the Abbey in 1956, is a tautly constructed semi-thriller in which the central situation resembles that of *Blind Man's Buff* (1936) a 'rewrite' (Johnston's own term) of Ernst Toller's *The Blind Goddess*. While this play has wit and intellectual conviction (which is why I say 'semi-thriller') it can in no way measure up to the dramatist's earlier achievements. Something of the early Johnston may be scented in *The Scythe and the Sunset*, his most recent play, produced at the Abbey in 1958. This, like O'Casey's *The Plough and the Stars*, is set in Easter Week 1916. Unlike O'Casey's play it is primarily a drama of ideas, but of course the 'ideas' are, as in *The Moon in the Yellow River*, adequately embodied in action and character. And interestingly the situation in this recent play is comparable with that of the earlier. Palliser, a wounded Lancer, has been taken prisoner and installed by the Irish insurgents in a commandeered cheap café. The gallant representative of Empire is thrown face to face with a collection of unreasonable persons who are committed or eventually will commit themselves to the revolutionary ideal. In the cut and thrust of the exchanges between Palliser and Tetley the Irish Commandent General, there are atmospheric echoes of the dialogue between Dobelle and Tausch. But Palliser is an unexpectedly worthy opponent of the revolutionary: Johnston's intellectual fairness is perhaps here too much in evidence. Tetley's unblinking idealism has to survive Palliser's wisdom before the event: 'You don't give a damn about liberty. All you care about is a cause. And causes always let you down. Your admirers will find that out before they're finished.'

Twenty years ago statements like that on the Dublin stage might have caused organised protest. Nowadays one-man or organised protests are likely to occur only over supposed blasphemy, indecency or anti-clericalism (the three are not unrelated in the Irish mind). But it is possible that Johnston's audiences failed to perceive the precision and poignancy of his analysis. In effect, this play, like his earliest, is a critique of the New Ireland. And genuine, unmuddled, critiques of the New Ireland are infrequent. Johnston, luckily for himself, has never appeared to feel the need of treating critically the real powers of the Shamrock Establishment, and they of course include the Church. Which brings me to O'Casey, whose playwriting time (outside Ireland) is roughly coextensive with Johnston's.

*   *   *

Louis Macneice has written touchingly about the Dublin of the cultivated Romantic. But for O'Casey 'the catcalls and the pain' were things to fly from, the 'squalor' had no 'glamour' and 'the bravado of the talk' was largely the blather of people who had nothing very much else to keep them in the running as God's children. O'Casey, on a purely human level, was justified in going into what he may have intended to be temporary exile. At least an extended exile was clinched by Yeats's (and his co-directors') rejection of The Silver Tassie, one of the most shocking blunders in theatrical history.

Yeats's rejection was based on artistic grounds. But Dublin's rejection when the play was finally produced in 1935 was based on an extraordinarily limited notion of the Christian message. But that rejection has a further significance for the Irish Theatre. The campaigns against O'Casey have not since ceased, and the venom of the attackers has been equalled by the bitterness of the dramatist whenever he has occasion to deal with the Church in its ugliest manifestation, the pietistic and totally uninformed Catholic. But it is common in Ireland, as elsewhere perhaps, for people without any intellectual background or critical training to take up the cudgels against what they are not equipped to understand.

Of course *The Silver Tassie* is strong meat for those who believe that war necessarily is a tale of heroic deeds and heroic sweethearts and mothers. Harry Heegan's mother is Juno gone bad, his father and his father's butty are Jackie Boyle and Joxer Daly reduced to their true stature. Harry Heegan's maiming on the battlefield is in a sense symbolic of his spiritual gangrene, but that is no more terrible than the atrophy of the faculty of compassion in the world to which Harry returns. At the football reunion of the last act there are all the outward and visible signs of the failure of compassion, the failure to keep in contact with the real: the trite condolences, the cliché jokes, most ghastly of all, since it is 'well meant', the attempt to calm Harry by getting him to play his ukelele and sing a Negro Spiritual, 'Just as he used to do . . . Behind the trenches . . . In the Rest Camp . . . Out in France.' Robert Speaight does not list this play in his *Christian Theatre*, but one would like to know if he has changed his mind about the noble defence he provided in an English Catholic paper that week in May 1935 when Dublin disgraced herself again. I believe that *The Silver Tassie* is not alone O'Casey's best play, but one of the great plays of our time, not for its slightly outmoded second act, nor for its clowns and grotesques, but for its tremendous weight of feeling. 'We must love one another or die.' O'Casey saw that the dead can go on living, and set down his vision with unequalled passion and grief.

Dublin has never seen *Within the Gates*, published in 1933, the first of O'Casey's plays set completely outside Ireland. Yet there is much in O'Casey's park-scape with figures which could find its counterpart in Dublin. Most of those figures have no notion that the life they are living is a mode of death. Their mental pabulum is the more lurid popular press. Their Irish counterparts may have spiritual pabulum, but they are not averse to the other kind when it comes their way. Yet despite the fact that O'Casey's estranged Irish audiences might well care to read about Murder, Suicide, Rape, even Sodomy, in the English press, those same audiences would be unlikely to accept on the stage the figure of the Young Whore (as she is called in the text of 1933: she becomes the Young Woman for the Stage Version of the *Collected Plays* (1949)).

This brief discussion of O'Casey is so often related to the recorded or surmisable reactions of Irish audiences because not alone does it highlight, one hopes, the peculiar love-hate relationship between O'Casey and his only begetter, but also provides indirectly a commentary on the theatrical climate of Dublin. The Young Woman, a cross between St. Mary Magdalen and Bizet's Carmen, with a dash of La Dame aux Camélias, has failed to meet Christ, the evangelic Christ, in cleric and layman, but she clings on to a belief in the mercy of God and the potential glory of His Kingdom on earth. The Irish resemble the English in their dislike of talk about Christ and religion on the stage. But whereas the English dislike springs in many cases from a simple objection to having their social institutions mixed, the Irish dislike springs from a cleavage between their devotional and secular lives. This may be why they are so touchy about stage references to the practice of religion. It is certainly why Ireland has produced no great Christian dramatist, unless it be the reviled anti-clerical O'Casey.

In *Within the Gates* with its chants, its music and song and dance, O'Casey pushed experimentation as far as he was ever to go. He was silent as a dramatist for seven years, and the next full-length published play was *The Star Turns Red* in 1940, which was followed the same year by *Purple Dust*. In the first O'Casey presents an imaginary Ireland of the future, one split between two bodies, the Saffron Shirts, an extreme Right-Wing group of brutal automata, aided by the Church and the Christian Front, and the Workers, led by Red Jim, a figure obviously based on the great Irish Labour leader Jim Larkin. But this so-called Communist play is more than an ode to the triumph of the Red Star (united with the Star of Bethlehem). It is a profoundly compassionate man's unintellectualised tribute to the Utopia he dreams of for those workers whom he sees as the repositories of the life-force. And there is genius in the last act, when the Star turns Red late on Christmas Eve, and the Revolution begins just when the Lord Mayor is having his annual distribution of tea and sugar to the deserving poor.

Purple Dust is a whimsical cock-snook at vulnerable caricatures, two stage Englishmen. Possibly it is O'Casey's least enriching full-length play. Dublin has never seen it, but there have been two productions of *Red Roses for Me* (1942). Here O'Casey returns to Dublin, a Dublin become a metropolitan version of that two-headed symbol which has served countless Irish writers, in Gaelic and English, as an image of Ireland, the slut who is also the 'beauty of beauties'. As Ayamonn Breydon, the enlightened young patriot and Protestant Socialist puts it: 'We pray too much and work too little. Meanness, spite, and common patterns are woven thick through all her glory, but the

M

glory's there for open eyes to see.' Breydon dies in a strike demonstration and another Protestant, an old landlord who plays the fiddle, brings down the curtain on his favourite song, a nineteenth-century sentimental ballad. Indeed the play as a whole just escapes the charge of sentimentalism. This is O'Casey reliving his youth, with a monopoly of enlightenment in the political sphere, just as enlightenment in religious matters is the prerogative of the Protestant rector, clearly modelled on O'Casey's friend, the Rev. Dr. Griffin.

Although there is little in the play to offend Catholics, it reveals how difficult it would have been for O'Casey to have gone on writing within a predominantly Catholic community. His sympathies were never fully with his Catholic townsmen except in so far as they were fellow-victims of capitalism and temporary allies in the nationalist cause.

O'Casey's tribute to wartime England, *Oak Leaves and Lavender* (1946), is an astonishing testimony of his tendency to be dominated by the heart. Some of the speeches in this play might well appeal to the League of Empire Loyalists, though the Socialist-Communist drum is also beaten. Only the old genius for assembling absurdity saves, in part, this jumble of propaganda, hysteria and maudlinity.

In 1949 O'Casey published his first play about the New Ireland, *Cock-a-Doodle-Dandy*. This was followed by *The Bishop's Bonfire* (1955), *The Drums of Father Ned* (1960) and *Behind the Green Curtain* (1961), all of them critiques of the New Ireland, but by their very techniques proclaiming that they are not 'realistic' pictures. Only in the last does O'Casey's significant distortion—a distortion comparable with Ben Jonson's—lead him into aesthetic and imaginative falsity. But *Cock-a-Doodle-Dandy* with its ghastly final cartoon of an island inhabited solely by ancient chancers has the effect of a Morality. And while *The Bishop's Bonfire* and *The Drums of Father Ned* are comparatively gentle in their satire, they yet reflect with disquieting clarity the weaknesses of the Irish laity and clergy. O'Casey has decided to ignore any strengths the Irish may possess, but from his constricted vision he has made at least three recent plays which attain universal relevance. In his eighties as in his forties he is the involved spectator of a battle between corrupt age and untarnished youth, between the lie and the dream, between death-in-life and life. He remains our only proven living master, if, that is, we accept the theatre as the arena of opposing moral forces.

★   ★   ★

The Dublin Gate Theatre, having launched Denis Johnston in 1929, was to produce no other dramatist of major stature. One might produce a small list of respectable plays, but a brief survey cannot afford such luxuries. And if one goes through the lists of Abbey first productions from 1926 onwards there is comparatively little likely to survive our time. Robinson and Murray were established of course by 1926, and there was a long series of canny, pawky plays by George Shiels, which however belong to the history of taste rather than to the history of drama. The mid-thirties saw the emergence of Paul Vincent Carroll, who inaugurated a potential school of Irish Christian drama with *Shadow and Substance* (1937). This mildly 'anti-clerical' play was successful but led nowhere. Louis D'Alton produced some engaging comedies and one quite remarkable tragedy, *Lovers' Meeting* (1941).

But the only genuine new voice of the thirties was Teresa Deevy. I say 'new voice' advisedly. The Irish Theatre has never been the place to look first for investigation of human personality on its subtler levels. Even in Synge the mysterious human being tends to be less important than a controlling myth. Teresa Deevy in two plays, the unpublished *Temporal Powers* (1932) and *Katie Roche* (1936), treated with extreme delicacy the intangibles of human contact. Much influenced by Chekhov and perhaps by Jean-Jacques Bernard, she showed herself a mistress of silence and pause as expressive means of communication and wrote dialogue which plays and reads as if quotidian words had never been uttered before. And in *Katie Roche* as well as in several one-act plays she dealt with the dignity and pathos of immortal longings in the humble, and in the course of a comparatively small output, created the 'Deevy heroine' as one might say the 'Anouilh heroine'. I write about Miss Deevy in the past tense because she has been almost completely silent in the theatre since the late forties. She has had no imitators and that is one indication of her unique quality.

Several plays by Michael J. Molloy produced in the forties showed a gift for a kind of poetic dialogue, much praised but unrelated to our time. The Abbey tends to produce mildly distinguished anachronisms, and its audiences cannot bear very much reality. Seamus Byrne's *Design for a Headstone*, produced in 1950, dealt with I.R.A. prisoners interned by the Irish Government. It is a confused rambling piece of some power and caused a minor disturbance. I mention it because it was a genuine attempt to deal honestly with an immediate and urgent issue, which is rare in Ireland.

But the two Irish dramatists who have said most to the world in the post-war period owe nothing to the Abbey. Brendan Behan and Samuel Beckett are as unlike as their social and intellectual backgrounds, but they both found their first Irish audiences in the minuscule Pike Theatre Club.

Behan's case is peculiar. On the strength of two plays he has gained international fame. But neither of these plays show any gift for construction or traditional sense of form. The reasons for his success are quite different, and they have much to do with the unmistakable tang of his personality. Behan shows great ability in the recreation of human oddity, and an almost Dickensian flair for the humorously macabre element in a situation. These two aspects of his talent might sustain both his plays in the absence of traditional form. But what gives them their dynamic is the dramatist's own passion for life and his hatred (of a different temperature from O'Casey's) of sham, injustice and puritanism. *The Quare Fella*, first produced in 1954, is an astonishing play to have come out of Ireland, where the issue of capital punishment hardly touches the consciousness of the people. It is worth recording that a production at the Abbey was received with the joyous hand-clapping normally reserved for the rickety farces of John McCann. What matters in the long run is that Behan by treating a supra-national issue struck a blow for those in Ireland who believe that unless the Irish Theatre abandons its parochialism, it is likely to perish from excess of self-regard.

The Hostage was originally a play in Gaelic, *An Giall*, produced in Dublin in 1958. The original was a far simpler affair and the cry in Dublin is that *The Hostage* is as much Joan Littlewood as Brendan Behan. If that is true, only one comment can be made: Miss Littlewood must have an uncanny knowledge, for a foreigner, of Dublin's underworld. Officially there are no brothels and no prostitutes in Dublin, male or female. But one does not need to be vicious to know that Behan's brothel and its inhabitants are an authentic composite picture of Dublin's diminished but hardy underworld. And the whole point of the play is that 'the hostage' and the orphanage-bred skivvy should play out their doomed love-affair in the centre of a corrupt but not uncharitable world. Behan makes no moral judgements about this world. He reserves his darts for the hypocrites and time-servers.

But these two plays are not, in themselves, adequate evidence of Behan's ultimate importance. Both suffer from an air of improvisation, and the battery of personality can run down. But one looks forward to Behan's *Richard's Cork Leg* as one looks forward to Beckett's *Happy Days*. (Since this was written Faber have published *Happy Days*, 1962.)

★   ★   ★

To write briefly of Beckett may seem impertinent. There is no evidence of an Irish theatrical ancestry, though the muted inconsequential plays of his friend Jack B. Yeats may be an influence. Beckett has made himself French, and one thinks of him as Irish only in relation to his early poems and fiction. But it is a measure of the gap between a provincial theatrical city like Dublin and a theatrical capital like Paris, that it is inconceivable that Beckett could have found even moderate commercial success in his native city. A good deal of Beckett's success in Paris, London and New York has been due to the valiant plugging of authoritative critics. In Dublin there are no critics of sufficient authority and boldness of judgement to ensure the survival of the experimental. No Dublin critic earns his keep from reviewing plays.

When Alan Simpson produced *Waiting for Godot* in 1955 at the Pike Theatre, he had Vladimir and Estragon played as two Dubliners in the O'Casey tradition. This was effective as a concession to his audience's theatrical experience, but an unworthy distortion of Beckett's intention. To localise *Godot* is to fall into the trap of sentimentality, and to run the risk of echoes obscuring the bleakness of the play's central theme. The protagonists alternately hope and despair, but they are condemned to waiting. All that, ultimately, sustains them is their relationship with each other, half-desperate and half-erotic. Pozzo, as I read the play, is a symbol of what men believe to be merciful providence, but which in fact is an unmerciful sell. The slave Lucky is in fact the unlucky one, because he has harnessed himself to a figment, of which the only counterpart in reality is a decaying industrialist, himself doomed to madness and degradation. If the play has any Christian overtones they are in the figure of the Boy. But nothing in the play warrants interpreting the Boy as other than a projection of vestigial faith in Christianity. If the play as a whole is to be conceived as in any way a celebration of mankind, the tribute lies in the refusal of Vladimir and Estragon to cease to wait. They have a courage the other side of despair. And Beckett in his marvellously effective use of trivial props and of Chaplinesque antics creates a kind of obscure allegory of human activity from birth to grave. It is a terrible and extreme vision only rendered tolerable by Beckett's exquisite feeling for the rhythms of speech, his gift for the occasional phrase or sentence of verbal splendour. No one in our time has more fully realised the power of words in the theatre.

Endgame has never been played professionally in Dublin. And I doubt if it ever will be. This variant on a theme of *Godot* cannot be played about with, for the setting of the play in itself predicates a commentary on the universal human plight. It is a modern Noah's Ark, only that Hamm and his binned-up parents and his three-legged black toy dog will never reach dry land. Hamm's incessant bleeding figures man's suffering in a world symbolised by the perpetually floating Ark. Clov's departure from the Ark is impossible because, although he attempts it, the human generations cannot avoid an inherited destiny.

There is no hope whatever in this play, and the harmonies of language are rarer and bleaker. But again Beckett shows himself as an unparalleled master of maximum effect through economy of means.

But as I have suggested Beckett belongs to the French Theatre, not the Irish. None of the younger Irish dramatists shows a trace of his influence and perhaps that is good. Irish despair, like the Irish climate, is peculiar to the country.

To give a list of white hopes in the Irish Theatre would be unwise. But I will mention a handful of names not because of their special brilliance but because for various reasons they represent departures from the mould. James McKenna with *The Scatterin'*, because he wrote sympathetically about Dublin teddy-boys and so enlarged the scope of Irish dramatists; James Douglas with *North City Traffic Straight Ahead* because he wrote that unusual Irish thing, a play about the personal problems of recognisable human beings; James O'Toole with *Man Alive* because he tried with some success to co-relate Christian teaching with the problem of uncreative bread-winning; John B. Keane because his several plays indicate a desire to broaden a scope within which he might well have confined himself; Hugh Leonard whose *Passion of Peter Ginty* showed a lively invention, if less keen a sensibility.[7]

That roll-call, and the reasons given for inclusion of the several names, sums up this writer's general feeling about the Irish Theatre. In its narrowness of scope and shallowness of treatment it cannot at

[7] Patrick Galvin's *Cry the Believers* has been produced at the Eblana Theatre, and reveals a powerful and fearless talent in the treatment of sex and religion.

present be included as a component of the living European Theatre. Its classics are treated as museum-pieces and its new plays, or most of them, demonstrate that in Ireland the theatre is an appendage to society, not an integrated part of it. We have no serious plays about politics or religion or sex. And for the most part serious treatment of these topics is taboo. My title, and the reasons for it, should be clear.

Note

Quotations and references in Chapter IX are made from and to the following editions: Paddy Chayefsky, *Television Plays* (New York, 1955); Alun Owen, *Three Television Plays* (1961); Reginald Rose, *Six Television Plays* (NewYork, 1958); John Osborne, *A Subject of Scandal and Concern* (1961); Harold Pinter, *A Night Out* in *A Slight Ache and Other Plays* (1961); *Six Granada Plays* (1960), and *New Granada Plays* (1961); John Mortimer's *David and Broccoli* and *Call Me a Liar* are in *Lunch Hour and Other Plays* (1960); Ted Willis, *Woman in a Dressing Gown and Other Television Plays* (1959); Alun Owen, *The Rose Affair*, printed in *Anatomy of a Television Play*, ed. J. R. Taylor (1962). *The Television Playwright* (1960) contains ten B.B.C. plays selected by Michael Barry, with an introduction and notes by Donald Wilson; the playwrights represented are Willis Hall, Ken Hughes, Nigel Kneale, Leo Lehman, Ian MacCormick, Elaine Morgan, Colin Morris, John Mortimer, Michael Voysey and Donald Wilson.

Critical writing about television, apart from weekly journalism, inevitably dates more rapidly than criticism of the stage. But among general handbooks may be noted Jan Bussell's *The Art of Television* (1952), Mary Crozier's *Broadcasting—Sound and Television* (1958) and Roger Manvell's *The Living Screen* (1961). Paul Rotha has edited *Television in the Making* (1956), and Arthur Swinson provided a manual on *Writing for Television* (1955). *The Armchair Theatre* (1959) is a collection of essays by writers interested in different aspects of the medium. *Contrast*, the quarterly of the British Film Institute, has appeared from August, 1961. In 'Television Drama: the Medium and the Predicament', *Encore*, IV (1958), 30–7, Michael Elliott gives a clear account of technical problems and opportunities, concluding with a view of the future when plays can be satisfactorily recorded and lighting and cuts be managed with the same control now customary in films. And in *Twentieth Century* (1961) John Arden has an article, 'Delusions of Grandeur', in which he discusses the differences between writing for television and theatre.

Since the first edition of this volume of *Stratford Studies*, the only author of note who has continued to explore the television medium in Britain is Harold Pinter, with a brilliantly comic and frightening piece on the marital relationship, *The Lover* (1963), and a farcically cruel study of the undermining of a man's self-confidence, *The Tea Party* (1965). Stuart Hood's *A Survey of Television* (1967) is the best account of the organizational background to the television of the last few years.

IX

Television Drama

J. L. STYAN

★

AN assessment of television drama must measure it against the nature of the medium, against what it can do and what it cannot. Journalistic criticism has failed to do this, but the publication of the British Film Institute's quarterly *Contrast*, although still journalist-centred, holds out some hope that there will now be space and time to consider television more responsibly as an artistic medium. The poverty of critical standards has been due to the pressure of too prolific a medium and too scant a commentary: conveyor-belt drama and conveyor-belt criticism have defeated the best of intentions, and vast audiences have reduced criticism to chit-chat. It is not that the medium is complex, only that it has confused the critical consumer by having to purvey too many goods. The voraciousness of the medium for dramatic material, calling for an average of thirty-five hours a week of drama of one kind or another in Britain alone, or an annual average of 2,000 plays or other dramatic pieces on all channels, staggers the imagination and confounds a cool assessment. Yet with an instrument as powerful as television, this is a desperate state of affairs, and casts a shameful reflection on its critics in their public responsibility.

★   ★   ★

A comparison with the other dramatic media, theatre, cinema and radio, will briefly suggest some of television's technical limitations and serve later to put its dramatic achievement into perspective.

The primary element of live theatre missing from television is that of dramatic space, without which a whole dimension of meaning must be absent. On the stage, the placing of an actor in his surroundings, the spatial relationship between one actor and another, and especially that between the actor and the spectator, encourage degrees of sympathy and understanding, identity and response, between the character and his audience. This quality contributes directly to the experience of the play, and is acknowledged by the good playwright in his writing. Stage space *around* a character gives him identity: a Hamlet set apart from the Danish court, a Cordelia drawing away from her sisters. Although a television play can have more than twice as many sets as an average three-set play, this lends only an illusory sense of place, and no real sense of space.

The size of the television screen is relatively the same as the cinema's from where the spectator is sitting, but because of the difficulties of definition, and the ineffective reduction of the life-size figure of the actor in long-shot, television drama must be sardine drama. The importance of this for the kind of scene which demands dynamic grouping will be apparent. Movement must constantly be strangled, until grouping loses significance; stress falls on the tight close-up, until its power, used sparingly in the well-made film, dwindles into monotony. The visual emphasis of television drama can be neither theatrical nor cinematic. The kind of scene natural to it is one in which a duologue is at its centre; more than three characters become a visual embarrassment rather than a visual asset. Shots which make for forceful television tend to be dialogue shots, with crisp verbal exchanges—the questioning of a witness by a counsel, for example—especially if a sharp musical punctuation can replace dramatic gesture and movement. Where movement is called for, it must be slow and deliberate, else it will break the barriers of the small screen and be laughable. It will be movement forwards into focus, or backwards out of it, rather than from side to side: the spectator cannot comfortably watch ping-pong acting. Even the strong stageworthy gestures of sitting and standing must be so gently done as to blur their effect, and a contrast of levels in the setting, even to the simple extent of having one actor standing and another sitting, cannot be sustained for long.

Related to this tiresome limitation of space is another limitation destructive of time. It is not merely that an actor cannot change his set or his costume without a necessary linking scrap of dialogue or padded business to make it physically possible—this, after all, is equally imposed upon a naturalistic stage play. It is that the camera eye is a single rigidly controlled and very blinkered eye, which must show *one thing at a time*. By contrast, we quickly assimilate the temporal effect of a full and complex stage picture in great and multifarious detail. The ironies of group behaviour are missing from television drama, and panning the camera, however quickly, to catch reactions one by one is no substitute for a richly orchestrated stage.

The film's one eye can overcome this limitation, partly because of the variety of its camera angles, but particularly because it can introduce dramatic cuts into its edited film. Roughly, the ratio of cuts on film is ten to television's one. Cuts on television cannot 'explode', to use Eisenstein's word, and dramatic tempo is only created, if at all, through the speaking of the words. Hitchcock enjoyed his experiment with the 'ten-minute take' when he made his film of Patrick Hamilton's *Rope*, and Shirley Clarke has since used it in her film of Gelber's *The Connection*; but the tension this evinces must smother many kinds of play which want a less brooding treatment. Sydney Newman's 'Armchair Theatre' producers have recently practised a camera technique whereby the eye follows the actor from one set to the next, but only for those scenes which will sustain a rapt attention. Television time is chronological time indeed, as television space is photographic space.

A flight of the imagination is difficult to achieve, and the free play of blind radio's dream and fantasy world is denied it. Mental images are pinned to what the eye can see, and are not readily granted the release with which Shakespeare's naked words or radio's vocal air paint pictures and determine the speed of thought. In spite of a few ambitious attempts, an unreality of atmosphere, whether of fantasy and dream, or of fairy-story and farce, even of the boisterous spirit of music-hall and revue, escapes it.

The preliminary conclusion is that television is more aural, verbal and naturalistic than visual, pictorial and imaginative in its effectiveness for drama. It has been well said that the author is the *sine qua non* in a television production, as is the director in the visual medium of the film. Peter Black has declared that television is 'a pyramid of which the base is the writer'.[1] The strong emphasis on what is said allows of little visual complexity and no verbal padding, while every effect of timing and tempo is rigidly subject to the actor's speech. The producer can make little contribution, except that of technical efficiency: the appalling conditions of live production, or the need for economy in pre-recording, mean that the producer must devote himself to the

[1] In *Armchair Theatre*, p. 57.

control of the camera on the set, more or less editing the shots once for all as the performance proceeds.

★   ★   ★

Although it is pre-eminently a writer's medium, this has been a harsh summary of its limitations. What qualities, then, might encourage a playwright to work for it? It has two assets, which have nothing to do with vast audience figures. It shares with radio its qualities of *intimacy* and *immediacy*. Its actors speak, not to millions, but to the family group and the solitary viewer, and in the spirit of being in the room with them at the very time of presentation.

In incompetent hands intimacy can shrink the dramatic experience to that of a cheap curiosity about the way the other half lives, or a nosy ogle at a psychological case-history, or a morbidity about activities in hospital or court-room; the world can dwindle to the size of the living-room and yet leave the viewer cosy in his armchair. In the right hands, however, intimacy can probe the recesses of the mind and enlarge the spirit, inviting the viewer to share an experience which goads him into full imaginative activity. It offers a rich resource for drama, its subjects, form and technique.

Immediacy is an ambiguous term for dramatic criticism, in that all good drama induces some involvement in the action at the actual time of performance; on television it is the dramatist's natural ally. Complete immediacy, in the sense of something improvised there and then, could turn production into a nightmare: J. B. Priestley's B.B.C. series of experimental charades in 1955 under the title *You Know What People Are*, in which the same four actors enacted a number of life-like situations, proved how difficult it is to catch this quality. Television immediacy implies the touch of *the documentary*, which John Grierson has neatly described as 'the creative treatment of actuality'. The documentary 'feel' lends a matter-of-factness and an urgency to viewing, which many playwrights have not ignored. For this reason, documentary has slipped into place on television more smoothly than in the cinema, its progenitor, and the American C.B.S. *Reports* and N.B.S. *White Papers*, as well as Denis Mitchell's B.B.C. documentary studies, have had a justifiable success. So, too, the slice-of-life drama is never better received than when it is written and presented in the mood of topicality, when we are aware of the camera following the actors a little raggedly, when the actor is spotted groping for a word, and when there is a *commedia dell'arte* spirit of improvisation in the studio.

★ ★ ★

What is the simple grammar of 'natural' television at the present stage of its development? It cannot put weight on setting, and spectacle is out of the question. Visual attempts to evoke a sense of place tend to be clumsy. Where Clive Exton, for example, conjures a deserted cathedral or a convincing doss-house, he has done so by characterisation and not camera-work. Generally, broad cliché settings close to immediate domestic experience have become the stock-in-trade: kitchen, court-room, office, police-station, pub.

Television drama leans hard on characterisation in the naturalistic vein: the age of Freud and the Method is ripe for this medium. Characterisation of the individual, but not of people: it cannot manage a crowd-study. Its investigation must be limited to the one or two who can be convincingly developed in a short time, and the mob is a noise-off. The natural television character is at the centre of the play, on set throughout, his texture observable in every detail of speech and behaviour. His play is a monolithic piece, for a play dealing in a mixed bag of contrasting characters, like Jacques Gillies' *The Diamond Run*, is unwieldy and unsatisfying.

Television places its accent upon a dialogue of vocal, though non-poetic, subtlety. It seems casual, yet, like that of Ibsen or Chekhov, is calculated for every implication. Harold Pinter's vernacular of idiomatic rhythms, yet pregnant with ambiguity and delicately veiled threat, is true television dialogue. It must be trenchant and to the point, precipitating the viewer rapidly into the heart of the matter, revealing character at a stroke. Such dialogue will suffer by projection from a stage: it will be too feather-weight.

Natural television is small and anecdotal. In his introduction to *Marty*, Paddy Chayefsky makes the point succinctly. He posits the tiny situation where a married man of latent homosexuality throws a pass at some girl to prove his virility to himself; yet, says Chayefsky,

> deep within the framework of that gesture lies a wonderful area of drama and insight. . . . If this story were done on the stage you would find that the simple throwing of a pass barely makes your first-act curtain. You would have to invent much more incisive scenes and incidents. I cannot imagine a stage play on this subject

which wouldn't require a scene showing the man ending up with a rank homosexual, so that the dramatic point is made. Or else you would have to write pages of pseudopsychoanalysis in order to get the point across. . . . In the end, you would have a play that would interest the audience a good deal, but not to the point where they would say, 'My God, that's just like me'.[2]

Anecdotal, that is, but not necessarily narrow: if the writer can persuade his audience that latent homosexuality is a common enough property he may have touched a general sore.

In turn, the riveting of an audience's attention on some intensely particular aspect of life demands a simple Aristotelian unity of action. For Ted Willis, 'plots that are too strong and complicated can often get in the way of the people and destroy character'.[3] There is no room for 'a thick, fully woven fabric of drama', according to Chayefsky; 'it can only handle simple lines of movement and consequently smaller moments of crisis'. The crisis revolves round the central figure, and the central figure is identified by the crisis. The play may have little truck with a 'beginning', and reject an 'end' as irrelevant; but the 'middle' has truly come into its own. One character and one story, caught at its moment of maturity—this seems to be the basic formula for television drama.

If its structure is still dimly perceived, its kind of subject and style is clear: every commentator agrees that these should be close to life. According to Arthur Swinson, plots should even be snatched from the daily newspaper. The majority of serious writers seem to have followed Chayefsky's notes to *The Big Deal* unquestioningly: 'Television drama cannot expand in breadth, so it must expand in depth. In the last year or so, television writers have learned that they can write intimate dramas—"intimate" meaning minutely detailed studies of small moments of life . . . the digging under the surface of life for the more profound truths of human relationships.' The cry has gone up, in effect, to put back the clock to the beginning of the century when Chekhov perfected such techniques.

Since about 1955, intense naturalism has been the order of the day: 'the main characters are typical, rather than exceptional; the situations are easily identifiable by the audience; and the relationships are com-

---

[2] *Television Plays*, pp. 175–6.
[3] In *Armchair Theatre*, p. 23.

mon as people'. When their subjects assume a documentary flavour, it is frequently difficult to distinguish between fact and fiction in efficient plays which touch on the fallibility of the legal system, the inequality of British education, moral and social welfare, the treatment of prisoners, the effects of the colour-bar and juvenile delinquency. Such subjects must gain by being brought into focus by a fine, domestic lens.

⋆   ⋆   ⋆

It is possible to test these general assumptions about the new medium in three ways: by seeing how far existing stage plays have adapted for television; by recognising where the new medium has satisfied the mass public taste for drama; and by attempting an early assessment of the work of some of those writing directly for American and British companies.

In the beginning, all the companies relied upon existing plays, as radio did in the 1920s, and it was in adapting these that the first discoveries were made about the nature of the medium. The companies have since kept writers on contract to maintain a flow of new material. In Britain this flow remains unimpaired, but is augmented by large quantities of canned film from the rejuvenated industry in Hollywood. Yet the best quality dramatic fare on television still derives from established plays adapted for the medium.

Some types of play go better on television than others which depend upon essentially theatrical qualities. With farce and related kinds of stylised comedy like that of Molière and Sheridan, an immediate audience response is important for good performance; a studio audience has to be supplied for the B.B.C.'s Whitehall farces. When *The School for Scandal* was presented cold, all life dropped from the asides which are the spur to the situations, and Sir Peter Teazle emerged as a shallow figure of pathos.

The photographic medium tends to inhibit qualities of imaginative grandeur, much as the proscenium arch inhibits Greek tragedy: *The Trojan Women* on television was a contradiction—Hecuba grew tiny and her rhetoric hollow. Any fantasy runs the risk of failing to plant its imaginative roots in the domestic hearth: *The Skin of Our Teeth*, *The Alchemist*, even Alun Owen's smart fable of Beauty and the Beast, *The Rose Affair*, written with the medium in mind, limped where they should have taken wings, lacking the necessary sense of theatrical occasion. Television's *Waiting for Godot* offered the viewer a close-up study of life as a tramp, and killed the clown and circus movement and the symbolic content of the characterisation outright.

Shakespeare on television is an interesting case. The B.B.C.'s most remarkable dramatic achievement to date, the history plays transmitted in series under the title *An Age of Kings*, held an audience of five millions in spite of all the evident barriers to dramatic experience: the loss of a direct relationship with the audience, the absence of space for the movement of large casts, and an awkward rhetorical poetry with its constant verbal contradiction of the naturalistic acting which the medium expects. Yet television was able to benefit those peculiarly Shakespearian moments of common human insight, in the tavern scenes with Falstaff and in descents among the soldiery: here the brilliant contrasts between the public, political world and the private and humble were asserted. Above all, flexible settings, without irrelevant business and decoration, enabled the plays to build up a pace which stressed the parallelism and contrast of the scene structure. Only Alun Owen seems to have anticipated the lessons to be learned from this.

The interpretation of Ibsen and Chekhov on television has proved especially informative. Ibsen's social plays, with their extreme verbal economy, his crucial scenes often based upon duologue, and the unspoken implication and reaction, make perfect television. On the other hand, Chekhov, writing in an idiom apparently most suited to the medium, rich with detail of behaviour and his characteristic silences, has suffered mortally. For Chekhov's plays are essentially of group mood, to be assimilated as a whole, each character reacting individually to a central situation, until the total experience is re-created in the spectator's mind. In *Uncle Vanya*, the television camera was obliged to focus on the Professor as he made his unwelcome announcement in Act III, and then hurriedly survey, one by one, the responses of his listeners.

Occasionally a convention like *Richard III*'s direct address to the audience, or the asides in *Strange Interlude*, slips comfortably into place on television. But every adaptation must try to capture the style by which the original play creates its meaning and theatrical experience. As for a novel adapted for the cinema, so for a play adapted for television: the original's means of thinking and reaching out to the audience, the tone and attitude which informs it, are the qualities which present the artistic challenge, and which are full of dangers for the unwary.

★   ★   ★

We should briefly swing face about and see how television has catered for the giant and insatiable audience which, according to T.A.M. ratings, chooses a dramatic diet in preference to all other. In obvious ways this vast audience has been a curse upon all channels, but it indicates what makes for digestible television.

Intimacy invites a despicable key-hole curiosity for much of the programme content. The repetition of parlour games and quizzes is but one sign of television's cult of personality. Intimacy also fosters the habit-viewing we associate with the family serials and comedy series that remain popular. Mary Crozier argues that this mass hypnosis is possible on radio where the imagination flows freely, but not on television; but much of this kind of dramatising, not least Granada's successful *Coronation Street*, indicates that recurring faces and conventional patterns of presentation satisfy a need on the part of general audiences.

The popular need for a ritual of mass dramatic indulgence is met by the vicarious violence of the Westerns with their fixed formulae for the good and the bad, and by crime and detective plays like America's prototype *Dragnet* and Britain's more homely derivatives *No Hiding Place* on I.T.V. and the more subtle *Maigret* on B.B.C. In these, crime, investigation and solution follow a conventional form that is propped up by subordinate conventions of police interrogation and the swift passage of police cars. Matter and manner obey rules designed to give the viewer confidence in a stable order of things.

A distorting repetitive pattern also paradoxically marks the documentary trend of popular television fiction. Life as it is lived, but only so far as it obeys the rules of the romantic novel. This is non-creative actuality, and our final lack of personal involvement in the issues is important. In *Emergency—Ward 10* (hospitals), *Family Solicitor* (the law), *Deadline Midnight* (the press), *Harpers West One* (personnel problems) and especially *Probation Officer* (the courts), fiction is built up by documentary and flattery. It should be added that *Probation Officer* has the approval of the British Pakenham-Thompson Committee set up to examine social and industrial problems affecting the rehabilitation of prisoners; it has actually been used to support a legislative issue before members of both Houses of Parliament.

N

Fictionalising for the masses contradicts the matter-of-fact appearance of naturalism in most of the popular drama. Television's neo-realism does not share the non-evasive honesty of much of De Sica's work for the Italian cinema. It can inhabit the work of better writers, as well as science fiction thrillers like *Quatermass*. For a slice of life must be a meaty slice, and dangers for the television dramatist are ever-present in his invitation to create a romantic anti-romanticism which must seek out the seedy and the sordid in order to make a dramatic point at all. For us to enjoy a righteous amorality, he may strike the desperate patronising attitude which Iain MacCormick has rightly condemned. It is the case of the romantic fiction writer who in *The Writers' and Artists' Year Book* is told in a breath that 'a happy, romantic ending is essential; sincerity must be the keynote to contributions'.

The pursuit of the particular merely to flatter a mass audience and to meet the technical requirements of the medium must narrow the field of vision. Naturalistic minutiae of thought and action can unload a mess of triviality on a gullible public, and in so doing deny those symbolic values towards which good drama strains in its attempt to portray particular humanity in a universal light.

★   ★   ★

Against these opportunities and snares, it may be possible to measure the achievement of one or two leading dramatists in exploiting the medium yet avoiding its complacencies. It is sad that so few good plays have emerged from so much material; never in the history of drama has there been such encouragement for new writers, and yet there has been no sensation of a movement under way, even one to compare with that of the Royal Court in 1956. A.B.C.'s 'Armchair Theatre' has gained a reputation for violent realism in a working-class world, without covering new ground.

When television flourished in New York after the war, there was an immediate stimulus for new writers like Paddy Chayefsky, Reginald Rose, Tad Mosel, Rod Serling and Robert Dozier, among others. The first two of these, some of whose work was filmed and sent on the cinema circuits, set the pace for much that was done in Britain in the mid-fifties. Now 80 per cent of American television is on film, with its standards those of the cheap second feature and its techniques those of Hollywood at its hastiest; at present the 'packaged show' dominates world markets. At least the writer in Britain today is in a happier position than his fellow in the U.S.A. When the B.B.C. resurrected its television service in 1946, it tended to use stage plays, of which there were plenty to hand; but with the passing of the Television Act in 1954, the need to build up a corps of full-time writers on contract hit the companies old and new. The numbers of these writers now bewilder the viewer.[4]

Chayefsky's pioneer work in America is worth attention in that it holds within itself the germs of growth and of decay. His avowed intention was to create raw naturalism and his statement about *Marty* and *The Mother* has become something of a *locus classicus* for authors: 'I tried to write the dialogue as if it had been wire-tapped. I tried to envision the scenes as if a camera had been focused upon the unsuspecting characters and had caught them in an untouched moment of life.' There is, in fact, nothing wire-tapped and involuntary about his exposition of Marty, the Italian-American butcher, a 'stout, short, balding young man of 36'. He is placed in his social *milieu* and in his shop in New York's Bronx with a Chekhovian delicacy of touch, and his personal predicament is firmly, yet gently, suggested:

ITALIAN WOMAN: Your kid brother got married last Sunday, eh, Marty?

MARTY (*absorbed in his work*): That's right, Missus Fusari. It was a very nice affair.

ITALIAN WOMAN: That's the big tall one, the fellow with the mustache.

MARTY (*sawing away*): No, that's my brother Freddie. My other brother Freddie, he's been married four years already. He lives down on Quincy Street. The one who got married Sunday, that was my little brother Nickie.

The dramatic statement is nicely restrained, the ironies neatly

---

[4] For those who choose their dramatic fare by the author's name, these are a fair sample of those who have written creditable plays: Rhys Adrian, Alexander Baron, William Bast, Phillip Callon, Giles Cooper, Richard Cottrell, Peter Draper, John Elliot, Clive Exton, Jacques Gillies, Willis Hall, Ronald Harwood, Ken Hughes, Patrick Hughes, Edward Hyams, Paul Jones, Graeme Kent, Nigel Kneale, Leo Lehman, Henry Livings, Iain MacCormick, T. K. Martin, David Mercer, James Mitchell, Elaine Morgan, Colin Morris, Bill Naughton, Peter Newman, Peter Nichols, John O'Toole, Alun Owen, David Perry, Jack Pulman, Simon Raven, Steven Vinaver, Mike Watts, Ted Willis, Donald Wilson.

planted. In case we have missed the point, the genial irritation of his mood is emphasised by another customer a moment later:

> YOUNG MOTHER: Marty, I want a nice big fat pullet, about four
>   pounds. I hear your kid brother got married last Sunday.
> MARTY: Yeah, it was a very nice affair, Missus Canduso.

Every intonation is carefully calculated.

The initial comment on Arnold's prospective marriage in *The Bachelor Party* is made with fine economy by opening the play in a young married couple's bedroom, dimly lit by early morning light; a grim alarm clock wakens Helen, the wife of Charlie, the office-clerk. Charlie sits slumped distastefully on the edge of the bed, the camera focused on his expressionless face, as we hear Helen phoning mother:

> Listen, Ma, I got something to tell you. I'm pregnant . . . Yeah,
> pregnant . . . Of course I'm sure . . . Yeah, Doctor Sloan . . . Yeah,
> he said I was pregnant. Third month. He says I can expect the baby
> next February . . . Well, Grandma, act a little excited, will you? . . .
> You bet I'm excited.

Charlie sighs profoundly. Compared with the way Alun Owen carefully circles round his points, this is rather slick and direct.

Marty is the story of a lonely bachelor who goes dancing in the vague hope of finding a girl-friend. On one occasion he accidentally meets a plain girl in as sad a case as his own, and the loneliness of the two 'dogs' is a mutual comfort. In the face of objections from a possessive mother and the scathing sarcasm of his friends, he decides to telephone her again. That is all.

Chayefsky precisely marks out the social and cultural boundaries within which his characters are confined. Thus Marty and his friend Angie sit reading the sports pages, and speak without looking at each other:

> ANGIE: Well, what do you feel like doing tonight?
> MARTY: I don't know, Angie. What do you feel like doing?
> ANGIE: Well, we oughtta do something. It's Saturday night. I
>   don't wanna go bowling like last Saturday. How about calling
>   up that big girl we picked up inna movies about a month ago in
>   the RKO Chester?

When this scene in the neighbourhood bar is ironically repeated at the end of the play, it is prefaced by a snatch of conversation about Mickey Spillane:

> . . . So the whole book winds up, Mike Hammer, he's inna room there with this doll. So he says: 'You rat, you are the murderer'. So she begins to con him, you know? She tells him how she loves him. And then Bam! He shoots her in the stomach . . .

It is in this environment that Marty slowly recognises where the true values lie, while we look on sympathetically.

Each of his plays makes a gesture towards defining some simple and acceptable human principle. In *The Bachelor Party* a brash, confirmed bachelor in a circle of harassed married men arranges a party after his own taste on the evening before Arnold's wedding. It consists of an effort to recapture their bachelor days: roaming from restaurant to bar, from bar to night club and from night club to bar, while they discuss baseball and women, and Arnold wonders whether he should marry at all. Again we observe the sly social comment. The anxieties of urban living, the need to meet one's human commitments, the fear of not belonging: these give the subject its wider reference.

Chayefsky does not avoid the sentimentality that attends such intimate material. Marty the ordinary guy, Arnold the fearful bridegroom, the proud independence of the old lady in *The Mother*, the Irishwoman of *Wedding Breakfast* obsessed by the idea of a white wedding for her daughter: all sink under the emotion which accompanies naturalistic understatement, and pity blunts the satirical edge. His work suffers, too, from a shrewd evasion: the punches are not thrown at the audience, for his ironic method provides that we know better. And time and again comfortable consolation arrives before the end. When the comic uncle marries the widow in *Wedding Breakfast*, a dead convention is dragged in by the feet. An embarrassing uplift is falsely lent to *The Mother* by its dénouement. Vague comforts attend the fifty-two-year-old failure Joe Manx of *The Big Deal*:

JOE (*brokenly*): What did I ever give you?
DAUGHTER: Pa, look at me. Am I an unhappy girl? I'm happy. I love George. I love you. I love Mama. I got a responsible job. The boss is satisfied with me. That's what you gave me.

Even his best play *Marty* rests on the falsehood that a fat little butcher would be likely to meet a plain girl like Clara, teaching history at High School.

Yet Chayefsky has rendered the medium a service in guiding it along a more adult path. 'In television, you can dig into the most humble, ordinary relationships: the relationships of bourgeois children to their mother, or middle-class husband to wife, of white-collar father to his secretary—in short, the relationships of the people. . . . We relate to each other in an incredibly complicated manner. Every fibre of relationship is worth a dramatic study. There is far more exciting drama in the reasons why a man gets married than in why he murders someone.'

Of the Americans, Reginald Rose shares Chayefsky's deft touch and emphatic sensibility, although the subject is no longer the misguided vacuity of much human behaviour. Rose writes a modern morality whose characters tend to drop into stereotyped patterns serving his didactic ends. *Twelve Angry Men* is notable for the single-minded development of its plot, and for the claustrophobic pressures on a jury preparing their verdict. Such compulsive writing makes us forget that the trial itself must have been a travesty of justice, and only as an afterthought do we realise that the author's pedagogy should have been directed at the judge and his counsellors.

*   *   *

Echoes of the American pioneers are heard faintly through the work of those British writers who have largely devoted themselves to the medium. Television drama in Britain broke on the wave which carried with it the school of Free Cinema, assorted angry young men and the revolution at the Royal Court. But there is still much of the glossy documentary impersonality which unquestioningly accepts the values it reports, however acutely observed.

Ted Willis works strongly through character. What he and many British writers lack is more of that tension between the character and his background without which a writer betrays his complacency in the face of his evolving society. For *Woman in a Dressing Gown* he chose a shabby flat in a London suburb and placed in it a slattern of a housewife. Round her he built the triangle of a city-worker despising his wife and pursuing an infelicitous affair with his secretary. The sequences suffer from theatricality—a term of abuse in the medium—as when the unhappy wife takes too much to drink; but the sensitivity of the writing and observation is often true, and, with an astringency characteristic of good British script writing, the husband is denied his romantic escape from domestic torture when he finds he must return to her. Yet we miss in Willis that creative centre which truly exploits the background of the life he chooses to inspect.

Clive Exton, too, eschews the blur of American sentiment. He will be remembered for his warm and acute recording of human responses to a lonely old man in *No Fixed Abode*, a play set among those who spend a night in a doss-house, and for his introspective study of fear and the relationships between men under the stress of war in *Hold My Hand, Soldier*. In the final cathedral scene of this play, he introduces a sardonic poetry reminiscent of that in the bitterly ironic scenes in O'Casey's *The Silver Tassie*: the chastening of man's spirit is marked by Exton's fallen crucifix, and the scene is suddenly illuminated by an emphatic visual statement. By a metaphorical extension, he is trying to break down the barriers of a realistic medium.

The British dramatist who has done much to establish an individual, even lyrical, style is Alun Owen. He holds the sentiment in check and introduces a spiky, comic balance into his dialogue. Owen reports that his play *No Trams to Lime Street* was rejected by the B.B.C. because it called for a love-scene in a Liverpool accent, and for the reader who does not know him that may sum up his early qualities. He conveys an authentic sense of place and people, with all their particularity, yet imperceptibly makes us aware of the wider world for which they stand. He can take a dangerously pathetic subject and imbue it with the sharpness of modern tragic comedy. He can look microscopically at his material, yet see it coolly and objectively.

Owen writes modestly of his intentions as an impressionist: 'Little incidents and moments for me were full of poetry, the poetry of everyday speech, caught and isolated. . . . But for television I was going to have to shape these moments and give them a continuity that would illuminate people's behaviour.'[5] The unacknowledged reference is again to Chekhov. He goes on, 'The things I wanted to say were about the way people behave to each other, and I have tried to strike chords in the mind of the viewer. I am constantly trying to say, "It was like this when it happened. Not factually like this, but this was the climate, the feel of the situation. Surely you remember something like it?" ' Owen is trying to do for British audiences what Chayefsky did for American.

He consciously recognises a correspondence between the aims and

[5] Introduction to *Three Television Plays*.

methods of the short television play and those of the short story and the poem. Thus he makes no attempt to construct a plot on the pattern of the well-made play, but he tries to create a 'mood' which is tied loosely to an incident, one which is not necessarily concluded. All-important for him are the ingredients that go to make up that mood, mixed ingredients of tragicomic reality, defined by the variety of ways in which his characters react to the incident: the mood and situation form themselves in the viewer's mind because the people are what they are. His meaning is communicated by a pattern of contrasts, character against character, scene against scene. In short, Owen has the essence of a creative stage dramatist in him, but is content to let the drama live within the narrow frame and not force it into emphatic stage patterns.

Of his television plays to date, *After the Funeral*, a play contrasting the feelings of two brothers towards their ageing grandfather, *The Ruffians*, examining the nature of violence, and *The Rose Affair*, the desperate interpretation of Beauty and the Beast, were the least satisfactory because the governing impulse was a melodramatic one; especially in the last named, the heightening required by symbolic fantasy strained the fragility of the medium. Yet Owen's gift of delicacy of speech sometimes carried even these plays. When in *After the Funeral* one of the grandsons is obliquely trying to persuade his grandfather to live with him a vital relationship leaps alive in the old man's automatic response, even in the midst of his grief for his dead daughter-in-law:

DAVE: Vera and I are starting this shop——
CAPTAIN JOHN ROBERTS: You're not getting a penny out of me!

The relations between Cass and his father and Taff and his in *No Trams to Lime Street* are different again, yet equally precise and completely felt. Owen's dialogue is a shorthand that often makes Chayefsky's look forced.

No Trams to Lime Street diffuses its own aura through an accumulation of tiny insights. The theme is slender, yet strong like a fine mesh enfolding the play as a whole. Three sailors are trying simply to get their personal bearings in relation to those closest to them, as most people are trying to do most of the time. The point is sometimes insinuated by external detail, like the pub renovated in their absence at sea. Or more implicitly, the past is gently urged upon the present, as when Billy Mack the 2nd Engineer unspokenly rejects the offer of happiness a chance meeting with his dead friend's wife holds out. The sailors return to their ship a shade more mature than when they left a few hours before; little has happened, and yet we have seen an epitome of those small encounters that shape a man's life.

The absence of sentimentality in dramatising sentiment is one of his strengths, and a special delight. *Lena, Oh My Lena* is a love-story with a cold wind blowing through it. Tom is a university student with an inverted romanticism who is seeking a firmer place in a working-class *milieu*. He is drawn to Lena, a young factory girl; but while she can romance as well as he, she remains a realist. Commenting upon the scene of their love-making, she remarks, 'That down there's a reservoir, it's not a lake.' And after she has kissed him, their dialogue retains its chilly edge:

TOM: That was the most wonderful thing that's ever happened to me.
LENA: Was it now.
TOM (*imitating her*): Aye, I shouldn't wonder!

(*They both laugh*)

TOM: You've nice teeth.
LENA: Well, I've got good teeth and they're my own.

When she finally forsakes him for the lorry-driver who treats her with confident crudity, she tells Tom simply, 'Stop talking about love. He's my fella.' Yet Lena is not permitted to be callous: with the central love-scene is juxtaposed a brief episode to suggest how her friend Peggy might have treated him, and this ensures that Lena keeps her reality and her dignity.

We have only one problem as viewers: how to judge such gossamer material. With the best of Owen we are in the presence of a strictly honest sensibility, and the significant contrasting of people in their precise environments and attitudes releases an energy that illuminates positively some small part of life. Perhaps we should not ask much more of the medium in its everyday clothes.

★   ★   ★

Established stage dramatists have not been attracted to a medium they consider as ephemeral as the daily newspaper. The few plays written for television by John Mortimer, John Arden, Harold Pinter and John

Osborne, about whom others will have written in this book, suggest that it has more to offer than has been recounted. For these have retained their individuality, and only secondarily tried to bow before the exigencies of the medium. Where a success was scored, as in Arden's *Soldier, Soldier* or Pinter's *A Night Out*, it has been because the style of the writer accidentally suited television, and the dramatic momentum carried the play through all obstacles.

Osborne's *A Subject of Scandal and Concern*, in everything except its structure, is theatrical and two-fisted; but it is fierce with a sensational subject, blasphemy, and with the strength of another of Osborne's ambivalent heroes, an outspoken Victorian schoolmaster, George Holyoake. It held the screen because of a vigour borrowed from another arena, as did Priestley's polemic for nuclear disarmament, *Doomsday for Dyson*.

Arden's comedy, *Soldier, Soldier*, like his tragedy for the stage, *Serjeant Musgrave's Dance*, whose style it otherwise resembles, is set among the dull circumspect citizens of a mid-Victorian Northern town, and is rich with period atmosphere. In a style bordering upon ballad and allegory, the author barely surrenders himself to the small screen; but the energy of this style, the simple opposition of the play's attitudes, and the spirit in which its hero, a virile but theatrical creature of arrogant nonchalance, was conceived, hypnotised the viewer. These are characteristics not readily repeated outside a limited range of subjects. Mortimer's manner of caricature in *Call Me a Liar* and *David and Broccoli* lacks Arden's poetic element, while equally straining the resources of the medium. Yet television must be grateful for test-pieces of this kind, exploring its frontiers.

Pinter has the initial advantage, other than his complete confidence in his stage and audience, of a televisual authenticity of speech. Its sense of improvisation and inconsequence barely holds the stage, but grips the screen, and the very accuracy of this speech furnishes it with those kinaesthetic qualities which are the actor's working material. Moreover, his audiences quickly accept such language, and thereby lay themselves open to the shocks which are Pinter's stock-in-trade. The commonplaces of behaviour and situation, an office party, a telephone call, a welcome home, both suit the scale of television and provide springboards for his imagination. For Pinter's is a Kafkaesque world in which the known merges with the ludicrous unknown, and the familiar takes on distorted, grotesque aspects. This process of moving from well-made logical reality into a horror of inscrutable coincidence, one which need be less explicit about the motives of persons and the reasons for events, may again open windows for television drama.

One critic declared that *A Night Out* on the Third Programme was pure radio; another who watched it on television felt it was essentially visual; this contradiction indicates its urgent dramatic quality common to both media. A simple story of a young office-clerk and his possessive mother, it conveys Albert's humility before his equals and his revenge upon an inoffensive prostitute whom he in turn humiliates. The little world of this comic-pathetic hero assumes nightmarish proportions as the play probes a universal weakness, that of loneliness in the crowd, the torment of isolation felt at moments of true crisis. *Night School* is a lighter play about Wally, who was recently sentenced for forging Post Office books. He returns home to the two old dears who love him, only to find that his room has been let to a young teacher in his absence. Again the imagination is freed by the tragicomedy of sharing and judging a helpless self-torture. Pinter creates these small moments of reverberating life effortlessly; although in this piece the ending by which the girl's night school turns out to be a night club is gratuitous. *The Collection*, on the other hand, uses two finely worked sets of tyrannical relationships, between a smart, grimly married couple and a jealous homosexual and his friend. Behind a screen of casual appearances these characters weave their hate around an incident in a Leeds hotel like insects looking for an opening for attack. The viewer aches to strip off their masks, but, like Pirandello, Pinter politely refuses the false relief of the truth.

Pinter is compulsive viewing for the mass audience as well as fodder for the intellectual, and it is a sign of his major talent that we may share the dramatic experience he offers at the level of our choice. *A Night Out* obtained the top rating of all programmes of all kinds transmitted during the week of its production. Popularity of this order for such oblique drama is hard to credit in an age of divided culture.

*   *   *

This chapter is written with television in its infancy, and is but an interim report. Although there is little to justify the statement of Howard Thomas, A.B.C.'s managing director, that 'television drama has become the mainspring of dramatic art',[6] one admires Owen and

[6] In *Armchair Theatre*, p. 15.

Pinter for hinting at the way it may move in the future. For if television intimacy is to avoid triviality, the writer must give it a personal
stamp. Virginia Woolf's atoms may forever be recorded as they fall,
but we still expect a dramatist to trace the individual pattern they
score on his consciousness. The question is: under such rigid conditions
of production, with such mass audiences and so strong a naturalistic
tradition, can a writer develop a truly personal style? Television's spirit
of adventure must be the writer's or no one's, in spite of so strict a
discipline.

The attitude of the companies to the drama they promote, and their
sense of responsibility to the public and the arts, is obviously important.
It must be more than expedience that impels them to set up script
departments and place writers on contract. We should applaud the
B.B.C. for giving its Langham Group the chance to experiment and
discover what content and method best suits the medium. They have
had a fair success with *Mario* and *Torrents of Spring*, which lent television more of the quality of the film than of the stage: the eye of the
camera, this unit argues, should not stand on the floor of a stage set
at about the height of a man. Flexibility of vision may suggest the new
form that television drama seeks.

Yet what assets there are, it must be repeated, remain to be exploited
by the writer. How often is the actor used in a truly intimate role as
half character, half narrator? The virtues of Elizabethan direct address
wait to be harnessed to the power of the modern novelist to think
aloud. Again, an impressionism of many minute scenes could induce
that different dramatic structure and rhythm which will finally fling
off the three-act strait-jacket, and be dictated entirely by the content
of the drama. The dramatist is asked to see with a film director's eye
and hear with an actor's ear; to understand the medium and manipulate
a greater audience than has ever been. But primarily he is asked to
retain his individuality as a creative artist in the face of overwhelming
pressures. Only then may television create its own kind of poetry.

Index